BUILDING
CITIES

BUILDING
CITIES

Neighbourhood Upgrading and Urban Quality of Life

Eduardo Rojas

Editor

Inter-American Development Bank

Cities Alliance

David Rockefeller Center for Latin American Studies
Harvard University

**Cataloging-in-Publication data provided by the
Inter-American Development Bank
Felipe Herrera Library**

Building cities : neighbourhood upgrading and urban quality of life/ Eduardo Rojas, editor.
     p. cm.
     Includes bibliographical references.
     ISBN: 978-1-59782-108-7

1. Community development, Urban—Latin America. 2. Neighbourhood upgrading programmes—Latin America. 3. Housing—Latin America. 4. Urbanisation—Latin America. 5. Urban Policy—Latin America. II. Rojas, Eduardo. III. Inter-American Development Bank.

HT178.L3 C667 2010
307.3416 C755--dc22   LCCN: 2010921150

Produced by the IDB Office of External Relations.
Publisher a.i.: Gerardo Giannoni
Publications Coordinator: Elisabeth Schmitt
Translation from Spanish: Sarah Schineller
Editor: Steven B. Kennedy
Proofreader: Sheila Mahoney
Indexer: Andrea Battiston, Colborne Communications
Editorial Assistant: Cathy Conkling-Shaker
Cover Design: Dolores Subiza
Typesetting: The Word Express
The photos are from the IDB Photo Library except for those that have the name of the photographer. Cover photo: Willie Heinz.

Original edition: *Construir ciudades: mejoramiento de barrios y calidad de vida urbana.* Copublished by Fondo de Cultura Económica and the Inter-American Development Bank, 2009.

To order this book, contact:
Pórtico Bookstore
1350 New York Ave., N.W.
Washington, D.C. 20005
Tel.: (202) 312-4186
Fax: (202) 312-4188
Email: portico.sales@fceusa.com

Mixed Sources
Product group from well-managed forests and other controlled sources
www.fsc.org Cert no. BV-COC-070702
© 1996 Forest Stewardship Council
FSC

CONTENTS

LIST OF BOXES

LIST OF FIGURES

LIST OF MAPS

LIST OF TABLES

ACKNOWLEDGEMENTS

The contents of this book were discussed in the workshop "Settlement Upgrading Programmes: Comparative Analysis of Lessons Learned and New Approaches", held in October 2008 in Montevideo, Uruguay. The workshop was financed by the Knowledge and Learning Sector (KNL) of the Inter-American Development Bank (IDB) and hosted by the Irregular Settlements Integration Programme of the Ministry of Territorial Development, Housing, and Environment of the Government of the Uruguay. The editor is thankful for the valuable support of Verónica Adler, Cecilia Bernedo, Kirsten Funes, Federica Gómez, and Sarah Schineller as well as the detailed comments made on the manuscript by Dr. Margarita Greene, of the Catholic University of Chile, and Professor Jorge Fiori, of the Development Planning Unit at University College London.

PREFACE

In an effort to improve the quality of life for inhabitants of informal settlements and their surrounding neighbourhoods, governments and international development aid agencies have expressed a growing interest in settlement upgrading programmes. The Millennium Development Goal to significantly improve the lives of at least 100 million slum dwellers by 2020 offers an added incentive to take action. As investment levels have increased, so too have the number and diversity of programmes targeting the problems confronted by the populations living in informal settlements. The persistence of some of the problems and the emergence of new challenges—the result of the deepening of recent trends and new social and economic situations—have led designers and implementers to create a wide range of innovative programmes. The analysis and exchange of information on the principles, design methodologies, and implementation and evaluation methods for new interventions assist in this process.

Lessons drawn from past experiences can serve as a trustworthy guide to confronting emerging problems. Among these new challenges are the persistent difficulties encountered by the inhabitants of informal settlements to join in the formal economy of the cities, the increase in violence and other antisocial behaviours in the informal settlements, and the physical decay and social deterioration occurring in neighbourhoods where there is a concentration of government-built housing—the result of the physical, economic, and social marginalisation of their inhabitants.

The Inter-American Development Bank (IDB) has more than 20 years of experience supporting national, state, and local governments in these types of programmes. Bank specialists and their technical and executive counterparts in the executing agencies constitute one of world's most experienced communities of practice in this area. The chapters herein describe and synthesise some of the knowledge accumulated by this community of practice.

The volume is intended for social and urban development specialists who are devoted to improving the quality of life of the urban population; those working in public administration, in development aid agencies, or as consultants should all find its contents useful. The volume analyses the main problems of settlement upgrading programmes and presents ways of solving them. It is based on the practical experience of designing, implementing, and evaluating such programmes in the Latin American and Caribbean (LAC) region. This is the book's strength and also defines

Informal settlements provide a solution to the housing problem of low-income households, but they offer a low quality of life for residents and create problems for the rest of the city.
Informal settlement in the Ilha do Governador, Rio de Janeiro, Brazil

its limits. The volume does not provide an exhaustive analysis of the literature on settlement upgrading programmes (although there are references to these sources); rather, it provides a broad look at one of the most complex problems that the cities of the LAC region face and shows—with examples of projects under execution—that it is possible to solve it.

This volume documents the evolution of settlement upgrading programmes both in theory and practice and describes the most critical challenges in improving the quality of life of the settlements' inhabitants. Seven chapters each address a theme, presenting current knowledge on the theme, challenges, and successful experiences in confronting these challenges. Among the volume's overarching recommendations is a call for the expansion of the scale of the interventions so that the more than 100 million poor people living in LAC cities may see marked improvements in their quality of life within a reasonable time span.

The Institutional Capacity and Finance Sector of the IDB and the Cities Alliance publish this material as a contribution to the policy dialogue and to the debate about the design and implementation of settlement upgrading programmes taking place in all countries of the LAC region. It is expected that the analysis of the rich operational experiences will be of interest to specialists and elected officials of other developing regions that are confronting similar problems.

Mario Marcel
Manager
Institutional Development
and Finance Sector
Inter-American Development Bank

William Cobbett
Manager
Cities Alliance

INTRODUCTION

Throughout the Latin American and Caribbean (LAC) region, public resources are commonly used to solve the physical and social integration problems of illegal city neighbourhoods. These settlement upgrading programmes, as they are known, are integrated interventions financed with resources from central, state, and local governments but mostly executed by local governments. The concepts, working methodologies, and implementation mechanisms of these programmes have evolved since they were first introduced in the early 1980s.

Guiding this evolution are the lessons learned over the past three decades by agencies working to eliminate the problems of irregular settlements in the LAC region. Although they were drawn from local experience, these lessons have global significance. Among the most important lessons is that to be effective, settlement upgrading interventions need to be integrated—covering the physical, social, and economic problems of neighbourhoods—and designed and implemented with the full involvement of the community. The many contributions of these programmes to the development of the cities can be summarised in three words: *they build citizenship*. As neighbourhoods integrate physically and socially into the formal city, their inhabitants gain rights and obligations. They are able to access potable water and sanitation and must pay tariffs. With improved access to roads and public transportation, they become more likely to fully integrate into the formal labour markets and to obtain public goods offered by other neighbourhoods in the city. Inhabitants benefit from better access to health, education, and recreation services, which allow them to maintain and increase their human capital. The development and strengthening of the community organisations further builds social capital in the neighbourhoods. Land tenure regularisation, in addition to providing beneficiaries with a formal address, provides them with legal protection of their property rights and increases the market value and liquidity of their real estate assets.

Despite the proven success of such initiatives, there is still much work to be done in turning all informal settlers into full citizens. The main challenge faced in settlement upgrading programmes is that of scale. Only a small part of the population has benefited from the investments in infrastructure, urban services, and tenure regularisation: directly, the inhabitants of the settlements where the interventions are implemented, and indirectly, the inhabitants of the surrounding neighbourhoods. Nonetheless,

Upper picture

Living conditions in irregular settlements are very precarious. **Shaky houses in Tegucigalpa, Honduras**

Lower picture

Investments in settlement upgrading greatly improve the living conditions of the population. In this case the upgrading also improved access to the houses. **Informal settlement in the hills of La Paz, Bolivia** in the majority of cities, the number of households living in informal settlements is on the rise, and in certain cities some formal neighbourhoods are beginning to exhibit problems similar to those of the informal neighbourhoods.

Thus, the scope and scale of the interventions must be expanded to extend the benefits of citizenship to all inhabitants of informal settlements and to prevent others from gradually losing these benefits. How can this objective be accomplished? First and foremost, more affordable housing must be built to prevent the proliferation of informal settlements. The experiences reviewed in this volume indicate that in order to increase the availability of low-cost housing for households living in overcrowded conditions or sharing houses with others—the most likely to move to informal settlements—it is necessary to provide land for residential use at prices affordable to these households and support their efforts to incrementally build their houses. Other citywide interventions are also needed to improve the provision of public transportation and health and education services to these households to improve their living conditions and access to city employment and services. Clearly, such interventions require a change in the scale at which the problems are analysed and solved; thus policymakers need to look beyond the neighbourhoods to the city or metropolitan level.

The same is true for interventions that seek to provide inhabitants of informal settlements with the basic conditions they need to access and fully exercise their citizenship rights. Two conditions are paramount: earn sufficient income to sustain a minimum quality of life and enjoy a safe, harmonious existence in a community. It is not enough to give households access to serviced plots of land if they do not have enough resources for food and clothing. As the informal neighbourhoods are more fully integrated into the formal city, the beneficiaries acquire new financial obligations, including fees for potable water, sewerage, and electricity services; land taxes; and contributions to community organisations. Interventions therefore must promote, facilitate, and expand beneficiaries' ability to cover these expenses and integrate into the city economy. Programmes have ranged from the development of the human capital through education and vocational training to the improvement of public transportation so that inhabitants can access more jobs within reasonable travel times. Improving the productivity and stability of the informal economic activities that provide employment to this population also contributes to this objective. To be effective, these interventions must be designed and executed at the city or metropolitan level rather than simply at the neighbourhood level.

Safety is another basic condition for exercising citizenship. The freedom to congregate in and otherwise use a city's public spaces and services is an essential right. Relinquishing public spaces to gangs and antisocial groups—as when citizens withdraw into their houses or gated communities—constitutes a partial renouncement of citizenship. Interventions are needed in the neighbourhoods and throughout the cities to ensure safe

The formal and informal cities coexist in the same territory.
Formal and informal settlements in Rio de Janeiro, Brazil

environments on the streets and in the parks. Some of the interventions are the responsibility of the government, while others must be agreed upon and executed by the community.

The physical and social deterioration seen in housing built by the state for low-income households impacts the entire city. These neighbourhoods, built on the periphery of cities to save on land costs, had from their inception poor access to the cities—the result of their distance to the city centres and limited public transportation—and lacked adequate services. These factors, combined with the almost complete absence of nearby employment opportunities, have resulted in a partial and fragmented form of urban citizenship for residents of these neighbourhoods. They physically live in the city, but they have only limited access to urban employment and services. Because most housing complexes were designed for households of only one income level, residents are socially isolated as well. In short, the neighbourhoods have gradually turned into ghettos. Apartment buildings of social housing are particularly susceptible to decay, as most lack an organisation to manage the property's common areas.

Solving these problems is a huge task, both financially and organisationally. International experience indicates that fully integrating these neighbourhoods into the life of the city requires no less than rebuilding

the deteriorated social relations, the public spaces, and the neighbour-hoods' connectivity with the city. To prevent the emergence of these problems in the first place, it is necessary to build fully serviced neigh-bourhoods in more centrally located areas, which have multiple func-tions (housing, commerce, services, light manufacturing) and satisfy the needs and preferences of households with different income levels; in sum, these neighbourhoods should offer the benefits of urban citizen-ship near their homes.

The poor living conditions of the population of informal settlements creates a moral imperative and a social priority for upgrading.
Informal settlement in Recife, Brazil

The rapid horizontal expansion of cities surpassed the capacity of local governments to provide adequate infrastructure and services (as required by urban development plans and regulations) to newly developed out-lying areas. Outside the high- and middle-high-income neighbourhoods that can afford to pay for these services, large sections of formally sub-divided lands lack standard infrastructure and urban services. The inhab-itants of these areas also face diminished urban citizenship rights and usually have more obligations than rights. Settlement upgrading pro-grammes have made these problems more glaring by providing inhabit-ants of informal settlements with better urban services than inhabitants of nearby formal, yet substandard, areas, who own their houses and pay taxes for public services they do not receive. The full integration of these substandard areas is crucial for the development of the whole city.

The lessons learned from the execution of settlement upgrading programmes are very useful in the quest to improve the lives of informal settlers; however, they also pose a clear challenge to governments to increase the scale of their interventions in accordance with the size and dynamics of the problem. Attaining this scale depends not only on devoting sufficient resources to settlement upgrades and using them efficiently, but also on diagnosing the problems and implementing the solutions at the most appropriate territorial scale: the metropolitan region for the integration of the population into the urban economy; the city for providing access to serviced land for housing and improved citizen coexistence and safety; and the neighbourhoods for the building of harmonious communities in the newly urbanised areas. Accomplishing this objective ultimately depends on facing these issues as an integrated urban development problem that involves all spheres of public management. There are indications that this approach is gaining traction in the LAC region and that progress is being made to solve the problems discussed in this volume—that is, government officials, community leaders, and specialists are beginning to acknowledge that, although the problems of the informal settlements affect mainly low-income households, they are essentially problems of the whole city.

EDUARDO ROJAS and
VICENTE FRETES
CIBILS

1

BUILDING CITIZENSHIP FOR A BETTER QUALITY OF LIFE

A Fragmented City

The Forces Behind Urban Informality

The Latin American and Caribbean (LAC) region is the most urbanised developing region in the world. At the beginning of the twenty-first century, three out of every four inhabitants were living in settlements of more than 2,000 inhabitants and more than half of the population was living in settlements with more than 5,000 inhabitants. Recent projections indicate that in the year 2030, more than 600 million of the 725 million inhabitants of the region will be living in urban areas (see Table 1.1). To date, approximately 80 percent of gross domestic product (GDP) growth is generated in urban areas, and there is a positive correlation between urbanisation and per capita income (see Figure 1.1). These trends, observable in the majority of regions of the world (World Bank, 2009), are the result of market forces that generate economies of agglomeration and favour specialisation, raising the productivity of urban enterprises and workers.

In the past three decades, despite high levels of urbanisation, the economic growth of the LAC region has been slow and unstable (see Table 1.2). With few exceptions, the average growth rate of the economies of many countries has barely doubled the growth rate of the population. Frequent economic crises have further inhibited economic growth and have negatively affected the low-income population. This situation is made worse by broad disparities of income and opportunities across the population. There is a growing duality: (i) the concentration of income in entrepreneurs and workers linked to the modern and global segments of the urban economy, which demand highly qualified labour, and (ii) a simultaneous expansion of the informal economy, which provides temporary informal employment linked to services and the manufacturing of simple products that are not tradable in international markets. In the past decade, two out of three urban jobs were generated by the informal sector of the economy.

Upper picture

The informal settlements occupy public lands or lands without commercial value, often in central areas of the cities.
Favela in Rio de Janeiro, Brazil

Lower picture

Informal commerce is an important source of income for urban, low-income people.
Informal market in San Salvador, El Salvador

Table 1.1 Urbanisation Trends in the LAC Region, 1950–2030: Census Data and Projections (population in millions)

	1950	1950–75	1975	1975–2000	2000	2000–30	2030
Total population	179		320		523		722
Total population growth		141		203		199	
Urban population	71		196		392		606
Urban population growth		125		196		214	
Urban population as percent of total	41		61		75		84

Source: UN-HABITAT (2007a) and author calculations.

Figure 1.1 Urbanisation and Economic Development in the LAC Region, 1980–2010

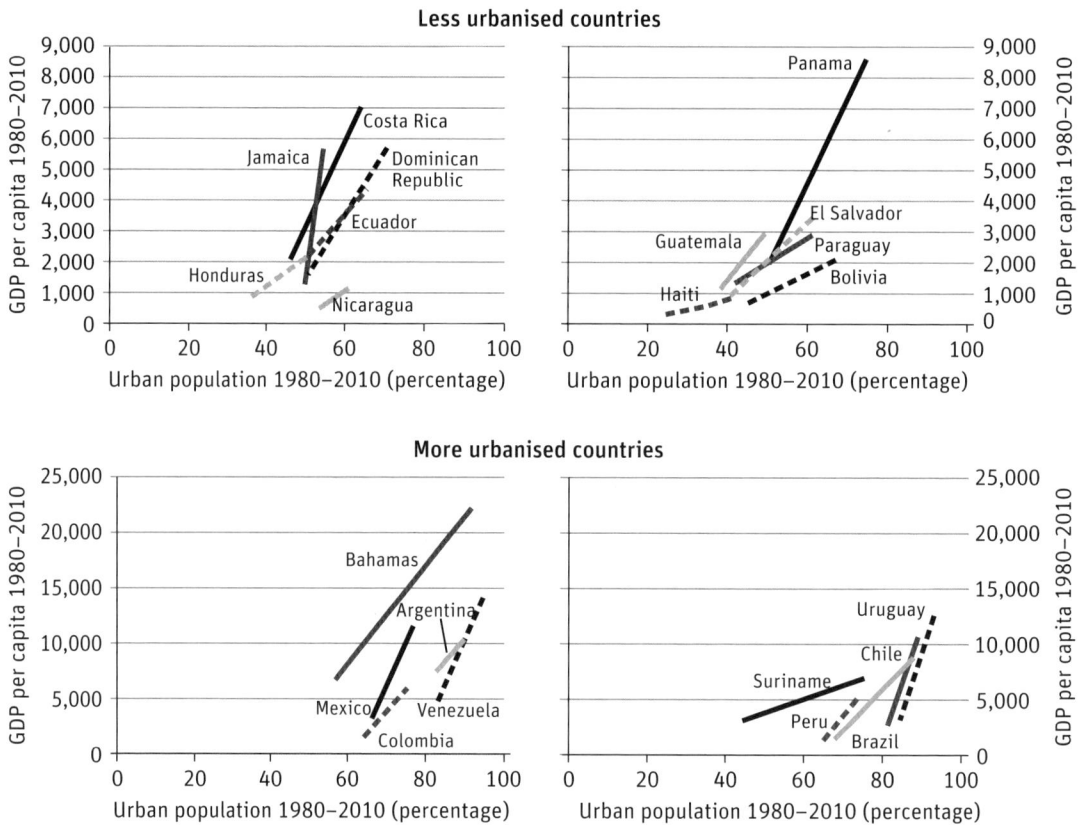

Source: UN-HABITAT (2007) and IMF (2008).

Table 1.2 GDP Growth Rates in the LAC Region, 1999–2009

Year	Percent
1999	1.62
2000	2.92
2001	0.74
2002	1.50
2003	3.69
2004	4.89
2005	4.98
2006	6.41
2007	5.39
2008	3.56
2009	3.73

Source: IMF (2009).

Economic, Social, and Territorial Exclusion

In the cities of the LAC region, citizens do not have equal access to the benefits of living in an urban area. On one hand, the residents linked to the formal sector of the economy have jobs with relatively high levels of income, stability, and benefits (health insurance, retirement plans, paid vacations) and have good access to public goods and services. On the other hand, some citizens have access to only the informal sector of the economy, with low productivity and income, greater instability, fewer or no benefits, and limited access to public goods and services. As a result of this duality, in 2006 almost 130 million of the more than 400 million urban dwellers of the LAC region lived in poverty and 35 million of them were destitute (ECLAC, 2007).[1]

Informality—which in economic terms involves low income, underemployment, and high vulnerability to economic downturns—also keeps the low-income population from reaping all the benefits of living in cities. Along with limited consumption, this population often has less access than the rest of the urban population to health and education services (Fay, 2005). This situation not only hinders the development of their human capital but also contributes significantly to intergenerational reproduction of poverty. Furthermore, the urban poor are more vulnerable than the average citizen to the negative effects of antisocial behaviours and are frequently stigmatised by the rest of society, making it difficult for them to integrate into the economic and social life of the city.

In LAC cities, poor households tend to concentrate in areas far from urban centres and poorly served by public transportation systems (Sabatini, 2005). Such isolation limits inhabitants' access to urban jobs and services (see also the next section on the urban land markets). These areas also concentrate social problems that acutely affect the most vulnerable segments of the population (single mothers, female heads of households, the handicapped, and children and adolescents) by stunting their social and human development. The precarious habitat in which these segments live and their socioeconomic and family vulnerabilities multiply

---

[1] In the design and implementation of policies and programmes aimed at reducing poverty, it is customary to distinguish among three types of poverty: (i) *food*, which comprises the population that is incapable of acquiring a basic basket of food even using all the household income; (ii) *capacities*, which is made up of the population whose total housing income does not allow them to purchase food and cover health and education expenses; and (iii) *patrimony*, which comprises those whose income does not cover the cost of food, health, education, clothing, housing, and transportation.

the risks they face. The poor sanitary conditions, lack of economic opportunities, high incidences of school desertion, and domestic violence, gangs, drug trafficking, and teenage pregnancy are consequences—and in turn causes—of the deficient urban, social, and economic conditions affecting these areas.

In territorial terms the urban poor have only limited access to the goods and services offered by the city, including housing. In LAC cities, low-income households generally settle on less demanded land, usually located on the outer fringes of cities and lacking basic services such as potable water and sewerage. Table 1.3 illustrates that, although a high proportion of the general population receives public services, the lowest two-income quintiles still lack adequate coverage (IDB, 2008b). The sanitation deficits are compounded by the shortage of public transportation services connecting these areas to the rest of the city and the lack of urban facilities (schools, health centres, parks) in the neighbourhoods.

Other manifestations of the informality in cities are the informal vendors and retail markets that occupy the streets and public spaces in central areas. The informality is also present in cities in the multitude of unregistered economic activities and personal services provided by a vast number of self-employed labourers. The gap between those that have and those that do not have access to basic urban services affecting mostly the low-income population is also evident in lack of access of these households to fully serviced houses produced by the formal sector that forces them to resort to informal solutions. At the beginning of the twenty-first century, 25 percent of the LAC urban population, or approximately 130 million people, were living in tenements and informal settlements. The United Nations Human Settlement Programme (UN-HABITAT, 2003b) estimates that almost 1 billion people live in slums around the globe—mostly in the developing world where slum-dwellers account for 40 percent of the urban population—and this number could climb to 2 billion by 2020. The contribution of the LAC region to the world population in these settlements is greater than its percentage contribution to the world population, although with significant variation among countries and cities.

The informal city is intertwined with all the dimensions of the formal city, impacting labour, markets for goods and services, social relations, and the territory. Accordingly, the problems of the informal settlements affect not only their inhabitants but also those of the surrounding neighbourhoods and the city as a whole.

The Reproduction of Informal Urbanisation

Informal urbanisation can be understood in part as a market response to the insufficient supply of formal housing services. When low-income consumers cannot find formal housing solutions (serviced land or houses) at prices they can afford, they acquire land through informal means and build their houses incrementally. This solution provides them with shelter, although not always with adequate living conditions. The short supply

Table 1.3 Public Service Coverage Gap for the Urban Poor in the LAC Region

	Year	Sanitation		Water		Electricity		Telephone		Telephone/ Cellphone	
		Coverage	Gap	Coverage	Gap	Coverage	Gap	Coverage	Gap	Coverage	Gap
Argentina	2003	60.4	39.2	98.4	4.0	99.5	1.2	64.8	39.5	93.0	11.1
Bahamas	2001	12.8	−0.1	86.7	12.4	96.1	5.7	n.d.	n.d.	n.d.	n.d.
Belize	1999	n.d.	n.d.	n.d.	n.d.	n.d.	n.d.	62.7	38.9	93.3	n.d.
Bolivia	2003–04	61.2	−3.2	90.2	9.7	92.5	6.1	45.5	27.0	86.6	11.0
Brazil	2005	65.5	30.2	95.6	9.9	99.6	0.9	95.7	7.0	98.0	4.0
Chile	2003	91.8	11.2	99.3	1.3	99.7	0.6	69.8	24.9	93.1	13.0
Colombia	2004	87.6	10.4	89.9	5.2	90.4	4.6	76.2	13.7	94.9	4.8
Costa Rica	2005	43.4	5.8	98.9	0.6	99.9	0.2	74.1	15.0	87.8	14.2
Dominican Republic	2006	32.3	14.6	80.6	18.9	94.4	4.7	40.6	43.8	84.9	20.1
Ecuador	2003	67.4	28.7	91.1	9.7	99.3	1.2	49.3	39.2	77.9	31.5
El Salvador	2004	50.6	30.7	73.7	23.8	90.7	14.4	59.0	19.2	87.2	8.9
Guatemala	2004	66.7	23.9	77.9	0.8	96.0	11.0	42.9	25.1	84.3	14.0
Guyana	1992–93	1.6	−3.3	88.7	7.3	91.0	14.6	83.3	1.6	95.2	0.4
Haiti	2001	n.d.	n.d.	23.2	11.1	61.9	28.7	n.d.	n.d.	n.d.	n.d.
Honduras	2006	63.8	31.1	n.d.	n.d.	97.0	10.1	51.3	5.8	70.5	6.7
Jamaica	2002	32.9	1.3	65.3	12.0	92.3	6.3	n.d.	n.d.	n.d.	n.d.
Mexico	2005	69.5	37.1	94.9	8.9	99.6	1.0	68.4	20.3	81.4	23.3
Nicaragua	2005	36.4	23.8	89.5	13.4	95.5	12.8	37.1	32.4	79.5	18.8
Paraguay	2005	15.0	14.7	89.7	20.1	98.4	3.8	40.1	48.0	82.6	28.9
Peru	2006	77.6	34.3	83.4	23.8	96.3	12.6	58.2	50.5	82.2	29.1
Suriname	1999	97.8	0.1	87.3	7.4	99.3	0.2	n.d.	n.d.	n.d.	n.d.
Uruguay	2005	66.2	38.3	98.8	1.5	99.3	1.9	71.9	42.1	90.1	21.4
Venezuela	2002	95.1	5.7	93.9	6.7	99.1	0.9	69.2	24.5	89.8	12.6
Average		56.9	17.8	85.6	9.9	94.9	6.5	61.1	27.3	87.0	15.2

Source: IDB (2008b).
Note: n.d. = no data available.

of affordable housing in the formal housing market is the result of several factors, including the peculiarities of the urban land market and misguided policies that reduce the profitability of real estate investments in this segment of the sector.

Economic theory recognises that urban land markets are imperfect because goods that are transacted are not homogeneous, the market lacks transparency, there is asymmetry of information, barriers to entry are high, and such markets are affected by numerous regulations. Land subdivision regulations imposed by urban land use codes have prompted the rise in the cost of serviced land and the expansion of the informal market (Souza, 2009).[2] In this market, price formation depends largely on exogenous factors, and the land transactions outside the urban codes are but just a market response to the lack of supply of legally subdivided residential land. The agents operating in the informal land market fulfil similar functions to those operating in the formal market, although the subdivided land they supply does not have the infrastructure and services of formally subdivided land and their transactions are not legally registered. The lack of transparency typical of land markets is worse in the informal sector than in the formal sector.

Households that cannot obtain a house or a lot in the formal market resort to either buying land in illegal subdivisions or invading public land or other lands lacking demand in the market. These facts lead Brueckner and Selod (2008) to argue that the formal and informal segments of the land markets are not independent, although they have ill-defined boundaries. The prices of land in illegal subdivisions are lower than those in legal subdivisions given the lack of infrastructure, the low environmental quality, the reduced access to the rest of the city, and, above all, the lack of secure tenure. The illegality of these transactions and the dubious property rights of the sellers do not deter the low-income households looking to acquire a place to live. Such ways of accessing residential land generate negative externalities, however, particularly in terms of environmental impacts. Illegal settlers reduce their risk of expulsion either by invading public lands or by choosing lots with little commercial value. As a consequence, a considerable portion of settlers invade land that is not suitable for residential use because it is located on a steep grade; in a creek bed or riverbed, old quarry, or flooded area; on contaminated soil; or in or near a garbage dump. Some settlers also invade land reserved for public works or ecological reserves.[3] Land invasions are less frequent in cities

---

[2] Land subdivision regulations usually stipulate a minimum lot size, define the width and quality of paving of public roads, specify land extractions for public spaces, and dictate the minimum infrastructure to be supplied as a condition for approving the subdivision. Building codes and rules dictating the maximum usage of lots and the types of land uses allowed are generally strict and inflexible: they impose high costs on the legal subdivision of land and additional costs on and barriers to the regularisation of informal lots.

[3] Examples of these strategies can be found in the land invasions taking place in the alluvial plains of the Parana and Paraguay rivers in Argentina, where periodic

Purchasing lots in subdivisions that do not comply with planning regulations is a solution for low-income households excluded from formal housing markets.
Illegal subdivision in Mexico City, Mexico

where they are not tolerated and the state takes action against them. But in places where the state fails to take action and thus tacitly condones the practice, invasions account for a good portion of urbanised land

Insecurity of tenure diminishes settlers' willingness to maintain or improve their houses, for without a minimum of security, they risk losing their investment. In fact, settlers do invest in their houses in countries or cities where evictions are not the rule or where the public sector is lenient with the illegal occupants. By contrast, settlers are much less likely to invest in their houses in places where governments act to protect private property and suppress land invasions.

The characteristics of the invasions—in terms of the density of land use, urban structure of the settlements, and typology of shelters—usually

---

flooding forces the evacuation of the settlers every other year. Also, in Quito nearly 80,000 inhabitants occupy the slopes of the Pichincha volcano that is currently exposed to land slides and volcanic and seismic risk.

PHOTO: GERMAN BARRETO

exacerbates the original problems of the occupied land. The material precariousness of the houses, the high density of occupation, and the lack of infrastructure are compounded by environmental hazards on the land itself and difficulties in accessing the city. For instance, the unplanned and high-density use of the land complicates the flow of traffic within the settlements—which makes it difficult for service and emergency vehicles to operate, and rarely makes allowance for parks or public recreation space. These characteristics make it difficult to upgrade the informal settlements—for example, by constructing new roads and public spaces—because doing so would often require moving a portion of the households. Illegal subdivisions are usually more orderly, since developers create regular lot patterns to maximise the number of available plots. But as with informal settlements, the developers do not reserve sufficient space for roads, public facilities, and parks or provide adequate sanitation or drainage infrastructure.

Invading environmentally protected areas is a common way of establishing informal settlements. **Nueva Esperanza neighbourhood, Bogota, Colombia**

Responses to Urban Informality

From Resettlement to Upgrading

The attitude of public officers towards illegal settlements has changed over the years. Initially government officials denied their existence or treated them as transient phenomena that could be solved by resettling the occupants in public housing built on the periphery of the cities (Brakarz, Greene, and Rojas, 2002).[4] But this strategy did not eliminate the informal settlements and they continued to grow. This reality forced the authorities to change their strategy; they opted to upgrade the illegal settlements and integrate them into the formal city, settling the population on the occupied or illegally subdivided lands. This change in the intervention paradigm prompted the emergence of settlement upgrading programmes that, as discussed in the present volume, gradually incorporated more objectives and components.

The first generation of programmes focused on the physical integration of the informal settlements into the formal city. They provided roads and connections to the potable water and sewerage networks and solved the drainage problems. Although these programmes—that started early in the 1980s—improved the health of the settlers and the overall quality of the settlements, they proved insufficient in providing the inhabitants with adequate living conditions, as the benefits of the infrastructural improvements were offset by the social problems facing the settlers. Chief among these problems were social disintegration and, above all, the lack of health and education services. As a result, a second generation of programmes—which began in the early 1990s—had a more integrated approach, adding interventions to improve the social integration of the settlers to those improving the physical integration to the city.

Current settlement upgrading programmes—of which there are several outstanding examples in this book—seek to integrate the settlers with the formal city both physically and socially. They seek to organise the community; encourage their involvement in the decisions concerning investments; take full advantage of the investments made by households in their homes and their settlements; ensure their cooperation in the execution, operation, and maintenance of the works; and provide the most urgent social services. The integral improvement of the settlements is to date the preferred strategy used by local, state, and central governments to solve the complex issues posed by informal housing.

This evolution of settlement upgrading programmes has led to the design and execution of increasingly more comprehensive interventions in informal settlements. Projects currently under execution include a wider variety of components than the projects implemented in the

---

[4] Until recently the official maps of the city of Rio de Janeiro showed the invaded areas near the centre of the city as green areas for environmental protection despite the fact that they have been occupied by illegal settlers for many years.

1980s. They include investments to physically integrate the settlements by completing the existing infrastructure (access roads, potable water and sewerage networks, drainage systems) and to mitigate environmental problems. The objective is for the informal settlements to attain the physical characteristics of the formal settlements in the city. All projects set as a priority the provision of secure tenure on the lots, which—as discussed earlier—provides stability to the households and induces them to invest in their houses. A third group of interventions included in the projects seek to improve the social integration of the informal communities to the city. They bolster social development, encouraging members of the community to take part in decisions and work as partners of the state in the operation and maintenance of the facilities. The programmes also provide much-needed health and education infrastructure and coordinate the provision of these services with the appropriate institutions. Many programmes continue supporting community activities after the works are completed to ensure the continuity of the community organisations and the stable supply of the services entrusted to them (for instance the operation of nurseries in Rio de Janeiro).

Programmes under way still do not promote sustained economic development or the effective integration of the beneficiaries into the formal economy. Some programmes have offered sporadic training in marketable skills for the urban service industry, while others have encouraged participation in employment promotion activities executed by municipal or state governments. No programmes, however, have promoted the economic development of the communities through private sector involvement, thus improving inhabitants' access to more stable and productive work opportunities. As will be discussed later, attainment of the economic integration objective would only be possible in a context in which the definition of the problem and its solutions transcends the needs of each specific neighbourhood.

Growing Challenges in Execution and Financing

As these programmes have evolved, both their execution and the measurement of their accomplishments have grown more complex. New programmes often have numerous components administered by different levels of government. Fortunately, many programmes have been executed in a coordinated fashion. LAC countries have a strong track record in upgrading settlements via concerted interventions that significantly contribute to improving settlers' quality of life. Moreover, the experiences show that it is possible, efficient, and equitable to invest in the integrated improvement of the habitat of the low-income population.

The more integrated approach to improve the quality of life of the residents in informal settlements presents a financial challenge, however. Not only are these interventions costly, but also residents, due to their low-income level, are often unable to afford them or to pay real estate taxes once land tenure is regularised. These programmes are therefore usually financed on a grant basis and, in many countries, with contributions from different levels of government, involving a transfer of wealth to the settlers. The coordination of these contributions has been achieved through ad hoc institutional structures (see Chapter 5 of this volume) via a wide spectrum of institutional arrangements. In one scenario, national governments provide non-reimbursable grants to state governments or municipalities to cover the intervention costs, while in another, municipalities, regional and national governments, and the beneficiaries all contribute funds towards the improvements. LAC countries have been particularly successful in defining how much money to spend per household and how to spend it. Most programmes use economic cost-benefit analysis to establish the amount of spending (see Chapter 7) and rely on the involvement of the community to assign these resources to the areas that need them most (see Chapter 6).

Beyond the Neighbourhood

Settlement upgrading programmes improve the quality of life of the residents through a variety of means. They provide infrastructure and public spaces and physically integrate the neighbourhood with the rest of city. They increase the physical assets of the settlers and enhance their market value through the regularisation of tenure. They contribute to the development of the human capital of the beneficiaries by giving them access to better health, education, and recreation services. They enlarge the social capital of the inhabitants by creating community organisations and promoting settlers' involvement in investment decisions and in the operation and maintenance of urban facilities and services. Yet these programmes still have significant shortcomings both in scope and scale.

The programmes' scope is always limited to a set of neighbourhoods and does not include an integrated view of the habitat problems faced by all the areas in the city or metropolitan area that have physical social and economic integration problems. As a result, the interventions often end up generating an island of good urban services and secure tenure amid formally urbanised areas that face shortages similar to those of the settlements included in the programmes. Because many programmes are allowed to operate only in settlements where at least 80 percent of the population is poor, they are banned from devoting resources to areas housing a mix of poor and middle- to low-income families (see Box 1.1). To increase the impact of the interventions, it is necessary to expand their scope and make them more compatible with an integrated approach to improving the quality of life in cities.

The settlement upgrading programmes in Latin America and the Caribbean also face problems of scale in relation to the size of the challenge posed to cities by the informal settlements. Conceived as a sector intervention by the local governments—with or without support from upper tiers of government—these programmes are usually narrow in their objectives, addressing specific problems within well-defined territorial

BOX 1.1 THE HABITAT OF LOW-MIDDLE-INCOME HOUSEHOLDS

CARLOS A. PISONI

Upgrading settlements has done away with ineffective and unequal urban policies, such as the eradication of illegal settlements and their removal to the periphery of cities. This approach complements new and more effective programmes that seek to produce new homes for low-income households and thus reduce the need to illegally occupy land. The approach is grounded on the principles of territorial targeting, decentralised implementation, beneficiary involvement, shared financing across different levels of government, an emphasis on measuring impacts, and the universal satisfaction of the needs of the low-income population—in other words "to differentially care for those that are socially different". The beneficiary population receives not only material goods and secure tenure, but also assistance in ensuring the desired, although little achieved, sustainability of social policies.

Approximately 40 percent of the total population in Latin America and the Caribbean live below the poverty line. Settlement upgrades address one of the most basic needs of this substantial, underserved population. The level of development attained by such programmes in the LAC region merit their widespread implementation—perhaps in varying forms—across the middle-income and low-middle-income segments of the population. Too many of these households lack sufficient urban services and infrastructure in the legal settlements they occupy and are watching their homes and neighbourhoods deteriorate. One important target population is the owners of self-built homes—often along the time span of two generations—located on the periphery of the cities, where they have only partial access to services and infrastructure and poor accessibility to the rest of the city. True, at least these homeowners have a roof over their heads. But their homes are undergoing a progressive deterioration that cannot be mitigated by the owners alone. As governments support low-income households and upper-middle-income households to find housing solutions in the markets, housing-related policies and programmes forget the lower-middle-income segment of the population. It is necessary to expand urban programmes to solve the problems of the middle and lower-middle-income segments of the population. This will expand the government support to cover nearly 70 percent of the qualitative housing deficit (ECLAC, 2007). To face these challenges, all actors must act in concert: the national, state, and local governments, as well as beneficiary households, which—in spite of their limited incomes—can contribute towards improving their houses and neighbourhoods.

Extracted from the inaugural speech of the technical workshop "Settlement Upgrading Programmes: Comparative Analysis and Lessons Learned and New Approaches", Montevideo, Uruguay, October 14, 2008.

units—the informal settlements understood as neighbourhoods. As such, the programmes must compete for financing and institutional resources with all the other sector investments and territorial development programmes of the local government (or the regional and national governments, depending on the case). Budget constraints and the multiple demands on the limited budget force authorities to limit the amount they invest in settlement upgrading. As a consequence, settlement upgrading programmes often end up benefiting only a portion of the informal settlements. Moreover, as they are conceived as remedial interventions, most do not tackle the structural problems that bring about the establishment of informal settlements in the first place. Therefore, even as a city is busy solving the problems of the existing settlements, more informal settlements emerge.[5] In other words, the programmes do not have a large enough scale, to solve the problems of informal settlements, even in the long term.

Unfortunately, the allocation of more resources to settlement upgrading programmes does not solve the problem. The very nature of informality extends its effects to all components of the city structure, all sectors of the local economy, and all spheres of social interaction. This is why interventions territorially focused on the settlements—although they improve the quality of life of the beneficiaries—do not solve the problems posed by the informal construction of the habitat in cities. The elimination of these problems requires more than only expanding settlement improvement activities (more of the same), but new approaches that diagnose the problem and seek solutions at the adequate territorial scales: that of the country or region for the economic dimensions of the problem, of the city or metropolitan area for the social dimensions, and of the neighbourhood or city for the spatial dimensions. In other words, to gain scale and eliminate the informal settlements, it is necessary to change the scale of analysis and action.

This is easier said than done. But several measures can help. First, it is important to reinforce the role of local governments in the diagnosis and design of solutions. Municipalities are in the best position to coordinate programmes for improving the habitat and the social and economic integration of the affected population. This is true even if another level of government provides the resources or coordinates the sector interventions. Second, the diagnosis of problems and implementation of solutions must go beyond the scale of the neighbourhoods and take into account all the substandard areas of the city. This would ensure that actions are coordinated, sufficient in scale, and executed in the appropriate sequence to

---

[5] The case of Chile is mentioned later in this volume. For more than 30 years, Chile has been implementing a housing policy that has succeeded in significantly reducing the housing shortage by building new homes. This accomplishment, together with the results of a sustained and successful settlement improvement programme, has enabled the Chilean government to set a goal of eliminating all informal settlements by 2010 (MINVU, 2004).

attain their objectives and take advantage of the synergies that may exist among them.

Accordingly, the settlement upgrading interventions should become the responsibility of the whole municipal administration, not just the sector unit in charge of housing. This will require breaking down the silo culture that is common in the management of most local authorities, in which interventions by one unit are not revealed to the others. As occurs in large urban projects that are coordinated from the office of the mayor or state governor, settlement upgrading interventions demand a high level of coordination in order to change the silo culture of the institutions. The experiences of some integrated urban rehabilitation projects in the LAC region have demonstrated that a high level of coordination among sectors is indeed a viable objective (Rojas, 2004). Municipalities should begin implementing this approach now in their attempts to solve the problem posed by the large number of neighbourhoods with multiple shortages of urban services.

The city of Medellin in Colombia is implementing an urban development policy along the lines described. Since 2004 the municipality has allocated a significant proportion of its capital investment programme to neighbourhoods with lower levels of human development and lower standards of quality of life. Investments in the expansion of public utilities, transportation, roads, education, health, and social development are targeted to these neighbourhoods, moving sequentially from the most in need to the better-off. The city also pioneered the use of land management and urban development financing instruments, contemplated in the legislation, that give priority to the production of social housing in Colombia (García, 2009). The coordinated investments have contributed to significant improvements in the physical, social, and economic integration of the neighbourhoods and the concerted effort to expand the supply of low-cost housing has reduced the expansion of informal settlements.

Scale Is Key

Notwithstanding the successes of the LAC experiences in settlement upgrading, the region has not been able to transcend its concentration on individual settlements or neighbourhoods when trying to diagnose and solve the problems of the informal habitats. This narrow focus stands in sharp contrast with the reality of the informal economy, society, and habitat or the cities, which are intimately connected with the formal economy, society, and habitat of the cities in a symbiotic relationship that not only provides benefits to both sides but also generates big problems. The thesis of this volume is that, in order to expand the scope and scale of the interventions, and attain more stable and effective solutions to the problems posed by the informal habitat, it is necessary to change the way the problems are defined and the solutions are designed and implemented. This new approach must be carried out at the territorial scale where the problems and their underlying causes exist. In most cases, this scale is not the neighbourhood.

To eradicate informal settlements and improve the quality of life of the settlers it is necessary to adopt an integrated approach to urban policy, one capable of designing and implementing multi-sector policies and programmes at the territorial scales where the problems emerge and where solutions are viable and effective. This approach changes the relevance and scope of several issues tackled by the settlement upgrading programmes and also adds new challenges and concerns. First, it prioritises actions that improve the quality of life of the settlers: for example, integrating them into the urban economy so they may earn a higher income and ensuring their legal security and safety. Second, it gives precedence to interventions that help prevent the emergence of new illegal settlements and that keep the formal settlements from deteriorating socially or physically to the point where they begin to resemble the informal settlements. Guided by these new priorities, the approach encourages the expansion of the interventions beyond the informal settlements into all the substandard urban areas that provide only precarious living conditions to their populations.

These changes in priorities will require changes in the execution and financing of interventions. In short, all agencies that bear responsibility for improving or maintaining the quality of life in cities—those that are sector-based and territorially based as well as local, regional, and national—must be involved and must coordinate their budgets and institutional resources accordingly. This level of coordination represents a serious organisational and institutional challenge, but it would significantly expand the amount of resources devoted to the problems of informal settlements, which have to date been addressed only piecemeal due to the narrow mandates and limited funding of individual agencies. The following is a discussion of the conceptual and operational implications of this proposal, which is further developed in the succeeding chapters with the support of analysis and case studies.

The Economic Dimension: Income Generation and the Improvement of Employment Conditions

A necessary condition to improve informal settlers' quality of life is that they must have higher and stable incomes. But even in the few instances in which settlement upgrading programmes have explicitly sought to improve the income and employment conditions of the beneficiary households, they have not had significant success. Why? In part because the strategies used have been limited in scope. But more important, the territorial targeting of the programmes has been too narrow. One such strategy has been programmes that promote the use of local labour, particularly unskilled labour, in the execution of upgrading projects. These boost the workers' incomes temporarily but do not have a long-lasting effect. Programmes like the *Favela Bairro* (Urban

Upgrading) programme in Rio de Janeiro—which promotes the hiring of workers from the neighbourhoods for the operation and maintenance of some services, such as garbage collection and the operation of day care centres—provide more permanent employment but in insufficient quantities to satisfy the needs of all the inhabitants. Other programmes include training female workers in skills such as hairdressing, nail care, and sewing to enable them to earn income working from their homes, but because there is little follow-up, it is unclear whether the training actually leads to increased incomes. To date, the strategies used so far have achieved temporary and localised results, fundamentally during the execution phase of the interventions. To significantly improve the quality of employment and the income of the target population, it is necessary to implement interventions that go beyond the confines of the neighbourhoods and are linked to city- or region-wide economic development policies or programmes.

One thing is certain: programmes that seek to raise settlers' income in a sustained way must involve the private sector, for it is the only sector capable of generating employment in sufficient quantities to have a significant effect. But on what territorial scale should the problem be tackled? While a sector-based approach has its advantages, including the possibility of addressing the issues related to the productivity of the informal economy, it might be difficult to implement. The proposals included in many of the strategic plans drawn up by local LAC governments are a case in point (CIDEU, 2008). They include solving the social and urban problems posed by informal street vendors, training workers in skills that are demanded in the city, updating the technology of small informal enterprises, extending access to credit and technical assistance to informal manufacturers, and organising purchase and sales cooperatives. Designing and financing these types of interventions demands cooperation among a variety of institutions at the national, state, and local level, as well as coordination in the territory. Few local governments can achieve this, since the programmes' objectives lie outside the mandates of the sector institutions in charge of housing and urban development that traditionally manage settlement upgrading programmes.

Solving the economic integration and income generation problems that households in informal settlements confront requires combining the territorial targeting of the settlement upgrading programmes with the strategic focus of the sector-based approach, focusing in particular on interventions that make it possible for the population to enter the formal economy of the city and on improving the productivity of informal activities. For example, a sector-based intervention might offer inhabitants of informal settlements technical training to improve their employment options, while a territory-based programme might work to eliminate the stigma that reduces the chances of exercising those options. The multitude of programmes requiring such coordination highlights the scope of the challenges faced in this area. As discussed previously, many interventions require a territorial approach that goes beyond the neighbourhoods to operate at the scale of the city or even the region in the case of metropolitan areas. Moreover, the programmes must be conceived and executed in close coordination with other related urban policies, in particular those related to housing, which define the areas of the city where the working population lives, and public transportation, which determine to a great extent these workers' ability to access the employment opportunities available in a city (Prud'homme and Lee, 1999).

Citizen Security and Harmonious Coexistence

A second necessary condition to improving citizens' quality of life is ensuring that their neighbourhoods are secure and the social relations within them are conducive to harmonious coexistence. As discussed in Chapter 2 of this volume, violence is the result of profound social, political, and economic issues, of which social exclusion, inequality, and discrimination are the most prominent. Citizen security affects the entire city—and both the formal and informal sectors—but has the greatest impact on the most vulnerable population. People who earn their living from informal economic activities are disorganised and have fewer resources to protect themselves, either physically or in terms of their jobs and assets. Violence is more prevalent in areas of the city where the government is less present, such as in informal settlements and deteriorated areas. The traditional paradigm for confronting the problem—to enforce public order using the police and other authoritarian state interventions—has not been successful, as shown by the persistent conflicts and crime in cities. The traditional approach is being gradually replaced by a wider set of interventions undertaken by the society as a whole (public and private sectors and civil society organisations) to promote the full exercise of citizens' rights and fundamental liberties, justice, and the peaceful solution of conflicts. Citizen security is conceived as a public good that derives from the coordinated efforts of society as a whole and in which respect for laws and norms balances with freedom to exercise rights and liberties. This approach presents a significant implementation challenge to city governments since it requires the coordinated action of a variety of agencies across different levels of government. But it is possible, as shown by several LAC experiences. For example, the integrated citizen safety programme in Chile, *Plan Cuadrante*, coordinates the action of entities across national, regional, and local governments with those of community organisations.[6]

It is also possible to improve citizen safety and promote harmonious coexistence at the neighbourhood level by supplementing investments in infrastructure, social services, and community development with preventive interventions. For example, "crime prevention through environmental design" focuses on controlling the risk factors that favour

---

[6] http://www.carabineros.cl/sitioweb/web/verSeccion.do?cod=74.

crime and promoting preventive, as opposed to defensive, behaviours. These local interventions (improved street lighting, greater connectivity between neighbourhoods, rehabilitation of derelict public spaces, and the like) are, however, ineffective in an urban context marred by violence and deteriorating citizen relationships, thus requiring the effective implementation of policies and programmes that reach the entire city or metropolitan region.

Preventing Further Development of Informal Settlements

Settlement upgrading programmes have proven to be effective in reducing the infrastructure shortages and community development problems in informal settlements; however, public housing and urban development policies do not always prevent the formation of new informal settlements. Across the LAC region, the proportion of households living in informal settlements continues to rise even as national and local governments allocate resources for their improvement. The most effective and lasting way to prevent informal settlements is to provide low-income households with access to formal housing solutions. This requires changes in how the housing sector operates, including a revision of the self-owned, rental, and government-subsidised housing policies at the local and national levels. The objective would be to create conditions in which new households from all income levels have access to formal housing. It has been found that an efficient approach to achieve this goal is for the state to use its financial and institutional resources to enable key housing markets to work better, including the markets for urbanised land, mortgage financing, real estate development, and the production of construction materials. This approach has been found to be more effective than one in which the state itself constructs and finances housing (IDB, 2006a). A possible road to expand the reach of government interventions is to set up programmes to improve the effectiveness of the savings and investment capacity of households (savings in construction materials, self or community help, family contributions) and to avoid over-subsidising middle-income households—a common outcome in countries where the state directly builds and finances social housing with subsidised interest rates. Effective programmes "build with the households", supporting them in acquiring urbanised land and in building their homes incrementally. The first step in transforming this informal housing strategy into an efficient activity for both the households and the cities is to provide access to serviced land ready for residential use. The second step is to support the incremental construction of housing with technical assistance and micro credit (Greene and Rojas, 2008).

It is not easy to supply serviced residential land to low-income households. The creation of public land banks for social housing with land acquired in the markets is a costly strategy that is unsustainable for most governments. A widely used mechanism in Europe is to extract land from private developers and designate it for public use. These extractions may

The quality of houses built through self or community help improves when the builders receive technical assistance and the help of skilled labour to complete the most complex building operations.
Home built with community help in Belem, Brazil

affect up to 50 percent of the land available in government-sponsored pro-grammes (for instance in the final phases of recycling abandoned indus-trial lands in Bilbao, Spain). More frequently, it is requested that between 15 and 25 percent of the serviced land be transferred to the public sec-tor for different community uses, including social housing. As expected, this policy is widely resisted by real estate developers and is financially viable only in buoyant real estate markets. The capture of part of the value gained by the urbanised land as a result of government invest-ments (roads, extension of the water, sewerage mains) is another poten-tial source of financing the purchase of land for social uses. In Chapter 3, the authors argue that the rural-to-urban land conversion process gener-ates sufficient increase in the value of the land to finance all investments in infrastructure and services for the land and still generates a surplus that can be designated for public use. The implementation of this strat-egy requires sophisticated legislation and institutions that are not avail-able in many countries, and is certain to encounter the strong resistance of landowners. The implementation of land readjustment projects—in which the public sector captures part of the price increment resulting from the urbanisation of privately owned land—is another strategy that can put serviced land under the control of the public sector. But this strategy makes it difficult to set up operations at a scale commensurate with the size of the problem.

Some advocate for the creation of more flexible land subdivision regulations as a way of making land more affordable to low-income households. In El Salvador, the market for low-cost land subdivisions and financing produces lots with few if any services in lands usually outside the urban area that are sold under lease purchase agreements. As discussed in Chapter 3, this widespread practice, which has allowed one-third of the population in El Salvador to access housing, has largely taken place outside the legal framework. Lots are often on agricultural land not designated for urban use, the settlements generate environmental problems, purchasers may not have security of tenure even after fully complying with all the conditions of the lease purchase agreement, and many lots lack basic services, which negatively impacts the quality of life of inhabitants and forces them to wait a long time for the government to provide them. This is, in fact, one of the variants of the strategy used in illegal land subdivisions (and land invasions) in most countries of the region. By not complying with land subdivision regulations, the illegal land subdivisions de facto incorporate a subsidy from the community to the illegal settlers in the form of the public resources used later to regularise the settlements. The experience of Porto Alegre in Brazil, also discussed in Chapter 3, is an attempt to formalise such activities, and it has succeeded in making the process more transparent and efficient. Despite such achievements, however, the majority of LAC countries have made little progress in reforming the housing sector to the point where it caters for the needs of all newly forming households and of those currently sharing their dwellings with other households.

Avoiding New Informality

Many LAC cities confront what can be considered a second-generation problem: the deterioration of the physical fabric and social relations in government-built public housing neighbourhoods. These neighbourhoods are starting to have problems similar to those of informal settlements, which include decreasing service levels of infrastructure, deteriorating houses, deteriorating community relations, and a high incidence of citizen safety and coexistence problems. As discussed in Chapter 4, the massive construction of social housing on the periphery of many LAC cities has created vast areas of affordable houses occupied by low-income households. These neighbourhoods are far from the employment and service centres of the cities and are poorly served by public transportation. They also have few urban facilities. Most inhabitants lack resources to properly maintain their homes and, with time, social relations in the communities have deteriorated. Entire populations become increasingly marginalised

Many houses built by the state for low-income families are rapidly deteriorating because of poor maintenance of public spaces and community property. **Schwager neighbourhood, Coronel, Chile**

PHOTO: MINISTERIO DE LA VIVIENDA Y URBANISMO DE CHILE

as their homes and community facilities deteriorate and their neighbourhoods become crime-ridden.

The social and urban consequences of this process range from a loss of real estate value to the stigmatisation of residents, which, as mentioned in the preceding section, reduces their chances of getting formal and better paid employment in the urban economy. Solutions, however, are complex and costly, as proven by experiences in developed countries and recent efforts in Chile. One common feature of these solutions is the need for intense social work in the community to re-establish social relations among neighbours and rebuild community organisations. In apartment buildings, this social work must expand to set up condominium organisations to manage the common property in the buildings (roof, stairs, facades, structural components). The Chilean programme focuses on the refurbishing, operation, and maintenance of public spaces. The international experience, however, indicates that social work and improvement of the public spaces is not enough to solve the urban and housing problem posed by these neighbourhoods. It is also necessary to invest in the rehabilitation and improvement of homes (including baths, kitchens, roofs, and windows) to make them attractive in the real estate market. This will achieve a double objective: it will recuperate, for society at large, the flow of housing services that the state is seeking for its beneficiaries, and it will generate more liquidity from the accumulated value of the homes. These objectives favour residential mobility, which not only improves quality of life but also promotes labour mobility.

Preventing the emergence of the urban housing problems described in the preceding paragraph is a challenge, particularly for countries or cities that make large investments in social housing produced by the state or by the private sector. To this end, urban and housing policies must prevent the construction of large homogeneous neighbourhoods that are poorly connected to the city. The objective is to promote good urbanism in new residential neighbourhoods so that they become dense urban areas, well connected to the city, complete—that is containing houses, commerce, services, employment, and recreation opportunities—and integrated, with houses that are attractive and affordable for households of different incomes. Attaining this objective requires changes in the system of incentives under which the public housing institutions and private suppliers of affordable houses operate. Existing incentives encourage institutions and suppliers to maximise the number of houses built within a given budget; this forces them to save on the cost of the land by building outside urban centres and on the cost of construction by using low-quality materials and small house designs. For public institutions, it is necessary to raise standards and allocate more resources to the construction of urban facilities. The objective must be to build sustainable neighbourhoods and communities—and not only just the maximum possible number of houses within a given budget. For private builders to build houses in better located and serviced lands, it is necessary to create a virtuous association among municipalities and real estate developers to cooperate in the provision of the services required by integrated and sustainable neighbourhoods. The need for transfers from the national or regional government to finance these investments can be justified on the basis of the avoided expenses and the present and future benefits of better connected and serviced neighbourhoods. This is the most effective way to prevent the deterioration of existing formal neighbourhoods.

In order to prevent the emergence of new informality in cities, programmes must address the problems produced by the formal sector when it offers only precarious living conditions to its inhabitants. They can do this through the approach advocated in this volume. The problems described mainly impact the rapidly growing urban peripheries, where it is common for informal settlements to be established amid formal land subdivisions, which, for different reasons, have significant urban shortages. In the majority of cases, these formal subdivisions have low-quality infrastructure: unpaved roads, insufficient drainage, low-quality public lighting, and a lack of public facilities and parks. This situation may be because the subdivisions were created before more strict norms were put into place, because of concessions made by authorities to cope with emergencies or yield to community pressure, or simply because of a lack of supervised compliance with urban regulations. Commonly, the inhabitants of these areas are middle- and low-middle-income households, have title to their properties, and pay taxes and rates for public utilities. Such conditions are not fulfilled by the informal settlements that emerge in close proximity. The implementation of the investments commonly contemplated in the settlement upgrading programmes discussed in this volume often leaves the informal settlements with better infrastructure, public spaces, parks, and urban facilities than the surrounding neighbourhoods. The paradox is that after the public interventions are implemented to improve informal settlements, the households that have purchased their land and have paid their tax and utility bills are left in worse conditions than settlers of occupied lands or illegal subdivisions.

Many local governments, aware of this inequity, are designing and implementing urban improvement interventions that benefit wide areas with shortages of infrastructure and urban services. Contrary to upgrading interventions that focus on specific settlements, these programmes expand the spatial scale of the interventions by looking at the needs of these substandard formal areas from the perspective of the whole city. Priority is given to investments that are not usually included in settlement upgrading programmes, for instance, main links to existing infrastructure networks (main sewers, drainage discharge mains); the completion of urban facilities (health clinics, schools, labour training centres); and the construction of parks, sports fields, and recreation areas benefiting several neighbourhoods. The urban benefits of these interventions are unquestionable and, in the majority of cases, the cost-benefit analysis of the investment yields positive results. But this approach poses complex design, financing, and execution challenges. In terms of design, it is difficult to delimit the intervention areas and avoid taking on improvements across the entire city or urban area under the jurisdiction of the municipality—efforts usually outside the financial and implementation capacity of the local governments. The use of multiple-criteria methods of spatial analysis alongside a focus on the key issues impacting the quality of life of the population (sanitation, drainage, accessibility, health, education, and recreation services) makes it possible to identify areas whose service levels are below the city average. Concerning the financing of these investments, the challenges arise from the need to ensure contributions from different stakeholders. The difficulties arise from the fact that the infrastructures under the responsibility of public utilities controlled by private concessionaires or national or regional entities whose priorities do not necessarily align with those of urban planners. Meanwhile, in terms of implementation, the challenge originates in the need to coordinate the interventions of different stakeholders so they are implemented in the territory at the same time. The movement from a focus on specific informal settlements to that of entire areas facing a shortage of services requires new methods of analysis, financing, and implementation that, as a whole, compose a new form of urban intervention.

A Work Agenda

The preceding review of the implementation experience of settlement upgrading programmes and of the new challenges confronted in cities leads to a complex public action agenda. Among the topics mentioned in this and other chapters of this volume, three are worth highlighting: the targeting of public housing programmes; the incorporation of economic development and employment generation in the urban agenda; and preventing the degradation of formal urban areas. This is, essentially, an urban development agenda, although it has significant sector components focused on reducing the incidence of poverty and crime. It involves all levels of government, with a leading role for local governments, and must be developed on different territorial scales with an emphasis on cities and metropolitan areas.

Targeting housing programmes. As stated in the preceding sections, preventing the emergence of informal settlements requires expanding low-income households' access to formal housing solutions. This requires the implementation of new public housing programmes, complementary to those promoted by the enabling approach to housing markets centred in direct demand subsidies under the *Ahorro, Bono, Crédito* scheme (ABC, "savings, voucher, loan"). One of the scheme's key components is the production of serviced residential lots at prices that correspond with the investment capacities of the households in need of housing and the government's ability to assist them. A first step in implementing these programmes is to put regulatory mechanisms into place to make land available for social uses through, for example, forced land extractions from developers, land readjustment procedures, and value and betterment capture for land purchases. This requires a strong political commitment as it directly impacts the interests of landowners and real estate developers. Another important step is to ensure household access to microcredit and the technical assistance needed to incrementally expand and improve housing.

Economic development and job creation. The full integration of informal settlers into the urban economy is a third-generation challenge for settlement upgrading programmes (the first- and second-generation challenges were physical and social integration, respectively). Education and skills training programmes should continue to be central to this effort, as should the expansion of informal settlers' involvement in the most dynamic sectors of the urban economy. In addition, there is a need to promote local small- and medium-sized enterprises catering to local demand by expanding the markets for their products, improving their efficiency, and enhancing the benefits they provide to their employees.

Maintaining social housing neighbourhoods. An emerging challenge is the deterioration of low-income, state-funded social housing neighbourhoods and the disintegration of their communities. The cost of postponing action is too great and could lead to multiple losses in terms of, for example, inhabitants' quality of life, real estate value, effective use of public space, and impact on surrounding neighbourhoods and entire cities. Effective interventions promise to be costly and difficult to finance in an equitable and sustainable manner. The best preventive action is to promote the construction of mixed-use neighbourhoods that are well connected to the cities and attractive to households of different incomes. These neighbourhoods provide a better quality of life to the population and maintain their real estate values.

2

INCOME AND SECURITY: PREREQUISITES FOR CITIZENSHIP

EDUARDO ROJAS

Building Citizenship through Neighbourhood Upgrading Programmes

Informal settlement dwellers are marginalised from many of the economic benefits that their cities offer and are too often the victims of violence. Both phenomena conspire against their integration into city life and prevent them from fully exercising their citizenship. A high proportion of the urban poor, unable to obtain stable and well-paid employment in the most dynamic sectors of the city's formal economy, subsist on the informal market. Even when formal employment is obtained, it is usually in low-skill jobs, which are unstable and poorly paid. Low, irregular income is a primary cause of the vulnerability that afflicts the urban poor. The other factor undermining their citizenship is the deteriorating security found in many cities throughout the Latin American and Caribbean (LAC) region. Increasing levels of violence and the rise of organised crime in some informal settlements and social housing neighbourhoods are common phenomena seen across LAC cities today. Added to the material losses and psychological harm suffered by the victims of such violence is their stigmatisation by the rest of the society, which perceives the informal settlements as dens of violence—without drawing a distinction between the victim and the victimiser. Solving such issues goes beyond what might be achieved solely within the framework of a neighbourhood upgrading programme. This chapter makes the case for programmes and policies that benefit the city as a whole.

The integration of the residents of informal settlements into the urban economy is hampered by the fact that most have low levels of education and few of the skills demanded by the high-income and high-productivity labour market. The majority of these residents are self-employed, work in small informal businesses, provide petty services, or subsist by trading or selling in the street. The informal sector has grown throughout the years of rapid urbanisation in the LAC region. One study estimates

Upper picture

Informal family production is a significant source of income for the poor. **Home manufacturing in San Salvador, El Salvador**

Lower picture

Security is an essential right and necessary for the development of neighbourhoods. **Security consultation with residents, Bogota, Colombia** that the informal sector has generated two out of every three jobs added to the urban economy in the last two decades of the past century (Arriagada, 2000).

Marginalisation from the formal economy has many consequences for informal settlement residents, the most significant being extreme poverty. Families often lack income sufficient to acquire the basic basket of goods necessary to satisfy their biological and emotional needs or even to maintain minimal food consumption. Residents' marginalisation from the formal economy has other negative effects: (i) they are not covered by social security or unemployment benefits; (ii) their instable, scant incomes, coupled with the insecure tenure of their dwellings, marginalises them from credit and microfinance systems for both production and consumption, limiting their ability to invest in and improve the productivity of their activities; (iii) they are frequently stigmatised by the rest of society, making it more difficult for them to find employment outside of the settlements; and (iv) their marginalisation from the formal economy is passed on to the next generation, driving the intergenerational transmission of poverty. In spite of these drawbacks, the informal economy of the LAC cities is very dynamic, sustaining large populations and providing goods and services to many enterprises and to a large part of the population. The very resilience and persistence of the informal urban economy leads to the conclusion that it is a structural and not a transitory feature of these economies, in which case it can be neither ignored nor eliminated. One promising new approach seeks to maximise the income-generating potential of these informal activities by improving their productivity and the working conditions for those involved.

Neighbourhood upgrading programmes have not tackled these problems systematically. Chapter 1 of this volume suggests that the majority of such programmes have prioritised the physical integration of the settlements into the formal city by favouring investments in infrastructure such as roads, sanitation, and drainage. Some programmes have also focused on the social integration of the beneficiaries into the city through activities such as the promotion of community organisations; the construction of public spaces designed for leisure or coexistence; and the provision of social services such as health, education, and public safety. Little has been done to identify effective measures that promote the integration of the residents of informal settlements into the formal economy, and any such efforts undertaken have been insufficient.

Although some programmes have trained beneficiaries in skills demanded by the formal economy, effective mechanisms for placing them into well-paid jobs have not been developed. Other programmes have attempted to promote job creation through public projects (garbage collection, the maintenance of public spaces, nursery school management, and so on). But a common characteristic of such programmes is their limited scope and low replicability.

These failings are, in part, due to the goals and design of neighbourhood upgrading programmes and can therefore be partially resolved within

Informal commerce
is another source
of income for the
dispossessed.
**Public market in Deluge,
Haiti**

the programmes themselves. But a comprehensive solution requires a more integrated approach and policies implemented beyond the neighbourhood; that is, at the metropolitan and regional scale. In the section "Urban Upgrading and Job Creation", Michael Cohen tackles this theme in his examination of the most effective scale at which solutions can be conceived and their success measured. The author points to the questions that emerge while searching for the best way to integrate programme beneficiaries into the urban economy: Should these mechanisms be territorial or sectoral? Should investments be made direct or funneled through an incentive-based system aimed at motivating interested stakeholders? Cohen assesses various projects whose design and execution showcase these and other issues. The achievements attained by several programmes implemented in African countries (see Box 2.1) are promising but indicate the need for further research and experimentation.

The second part of this chapter deals with the challenges of reducing violence and improving coexistence in informal settlements. An increase in acts of violence can be found across LAC neighbourhoods and cities, and its causes are to be found further afield than in the specific problems faced by informal settlements. In fact, violence is also on the rise in government-constructed housing for low-income households (an issue that is further discussed in Chapter 4). Residents of informal settlements—and, increasingly, those of social housing neighbourhoods—are particularly vulnerable to the rise in violence and other antisocial behaviours, owing to the state's limited presence in their communities, inadequate social capital, and a general lack of resources to protect themselves. In their assessment of the problem, Alvarado and Abizanda suggest that social exclusion and poverty do not in themselves cause crime in a given territory. Instead, they create vulnerabilities that, when combined with other factors, make it more likely that individuals in certain circumstances will be inclined to either commit or be victim to crimes. Alvarado and Abizanda examine the individual, family, and community factors affecting individual violent behaviour. These factors include a history of family violence, a lack of education and opportunities, a breakdown in social relationships linked to the presence of facilitating factors such as easy access to drugs and weapons, the presence of organised crime, and the sense of impunity that holds sway in certain countries. In short, violence is a phenomenon with mutiple causes closely linked to the social and physical marginalisation of informal settlement dwellers. As their cultural and emotional links with urban society are degraded, antisocial behaviour that goes beyond the mere need for survival is induced. The scant empirical evidence on this problem indicates that it is driven more by a lack of hope and opportunity than by poverty itself. The high proportion of poorly educated and chronically unemployed young people involved in violent acts seems to validate this conclusion. Together, these many factors explain the differing incidence of violence and coexistence problems across cities and even across neighbourhoods in the same city.

The possible solutions are as complex as the problem. The need for multi-sector action, sustained over time and supported wholeheartedly by the very communities it seeks to benefit, is stressed in this chapter. Efforts to improve education, work skills, and employment opportunities among residents of informal settlements—which, as the first part of this chapter shows, have not been given priority until now—need to be complemented by other actions. These include the strengthening of social relationships within the communities; an increased state presence inside informal settlements (not as a repressive force, but rather as a promoter of good social relations and citizens' control of the territory); the improvement of public spaces in order to reduce the incidence of so-called facilitating factors (dark or abandoned areas that are difficult for citizens to control); the improvement of relations between the police and the community to encourage cooperation in crime prevention (mere repression does not yield positive results); and the integration of young people (who are most at risk) into the community through cultural and sports programmes.

Putting into practice this integral approach to the problems of security and coexistence poses numerous challenges, the most obvious of which is coordinating activities across various institutions within a given territory. In the case of neighbourhood upgrading programmes, it is possible

Abandoned public spaces become unsafe. **Padre Hurtado neighbourhood, Santiago, Chile**

PHOTO: MINISTERIO DE LA VIVIENDA Y URBANISMO DE CHILE

to take advantage of the mechanisms already in place for implementing traditional interventions (such as improvements in infrastructure, public spaces, and social services), which improve the safety, security, and coexistence of the citizens. In some countries, progress has been made in the implementation of security programmes based on inter-institutional and community cooperation. In Bogota, for example, public intervention has been directed towards those areas with the highest incidence of security and coexistence problems, thereby making the most effective use of limited resources (see Box 2.2). This chapter also presents the Barcelona model for tackling problems raised by the antisocial behaviour of young immigrants. In those neighbourhoods where the problems of social and physical degradation were most pronounced, the Barcelona City Council developed a youth integration programme that promotes the transformation of gangs into cultural societies with access to funds and support to organise the activities that most interest them (see Box 2.3).

These experiences, together with those described by Alvarado and Abizanda, bear witness to a wide-ranging and creative movement aimed at finding effective solutions that encompass the city as a whole. While there is still a long way to go, several issues are clear: it is more effective to seek reintegration into the community for those individuals involved in antisocial behaviour than to merely repress them, violence can be prevented by improving community coexistence and cooperation between the state and community, and special attention must be paid to implementing situational crime-prevention measures that improve the safety

BOX 2.1 ECONOMIC INTEGRATION IN AFRICA

PAMELA HERSHEY

Job creation, or the promotion of beneficiaries' capacity to obtain better-paid and more-stable employment, is rarely a priority of neighbourhood upgrading programmes. A review of completed projects financed by the World Bank in Africa indicates that although these projects did have some impact on employment, only in exceptional cases did they include investments that improved employment conditions for some of the beneficiaries.

A Rehabilitation Programme of the District of Accra, Ghana

Between 1985 and 1986, the government of Ghana implemented the Priority Public Works Project and the Urban Project II with support from the World Bank. These projects included investments in upgrading infrastructure and basic services in low-income residential areas in four cities— Accra, Tema, Tamale, and Kumasi—and in improving working conditions for 160,000 beneficiaries. Neighbourhood upgrading works were completed in the Suame Magazine, an informal commercial area of Kumasi well known for its high concentration of informal employment in the automobile mechanical sector. The projects sought to create employment giving priority to labour-intensive works that, due to their small scale, could be accomplished by local builders and contractors.

Improvements in street paving and sanitation, along with the construction of more reliable electrical supply systems, in the Suame Magazine were considered to be beneficial for local economic development by the majority of residents. The area even became the preferred destination of those seeking to learn skills in the automobile mechanic sector. Similarly, the projects generated direct local employment based on small-scale contracts that prioritise the intensive use of local labour and employ local contractors (World Bank, 2002).

A Small Enterprise Project in the Periurban Zones of Lusaka, Zambia

CARE International, a non-governmental organisation (NGO) was invited by the government of Zambia in 1992 to lend emergency assistance during the serious drought that afflicted the country at the beginning of the 1990s. In 1994 CARE Zambia initiated the project known as Periurban Lusaka Small Enterprise, or PULSE. The aim of this project was to give loans for working capital to microentrepreneurs, mostly women, in the periurban zones of Lusaka to help increase the earnings, economic security, and employment generation opportunities of the poor.

Musona and Mbozi (1998) indicate that the loans did generate positive effects for the recipients. They found that employment was generated and businesses were strengthened, and that providing credit was therefore a sustainable way of reducing poverty. The assessment points out that although the project was directed towards women who were the sole bread-winners in their households, it also encouraged participation by men and young people. It mentions that commerce was the participants' preferred economic activity, not only because it did not require large capital investment, but also due to the relative ease with which a business can be started. The success of the project can be attributed to the utilisation of existing structures, client participation in the decision-making process and in the concession of loans, the existence of a transparent information management system, and the setting up of a loan guarantee fund.

of public spaces by strengthening the social control over them. Adopting these approaches poses a complex institutional challenge that goes beyond the narrow territorial focus of neighbourhood upgrading programmes (even though, as has been stated, incorporating these concepts into such programmes represents an important step forward). Local governments must make a sustained effort to put these reforms into practice, implement preventative programmes, reduce impunity, and improve peaceful coexistence among all sectors of the community. Solid cooperation between governments at the local, national, and state levels is needed to implement a national crime prevention and citizen coexistence policy that facilitates the implementation of neighbourhood upgrading programmes.

MICHAEL COHEN   Urban Upgrading and Job Creation

Few existing studies assess how urban development programmes in general, and neighbourhood upgrading projects in particular, affect job creation (Miller and Cohen, 2007). Any such assessment should be framed within the context of the urban development policy within which programmes are deployed, a policy that is usually determined by the developmental pressures faced by the city in question. The urban policy framework, within which the impact of neighbourhood upgrading programmes should be studied, is dominated by three main operational challenges:

- Dealing with cities' sustained demographic growth
- Designing low-cost solutions to meet the growing demand for urban services and to provide these services on a wide scale
- Leveraging the economic impact of urban investments

None of these problems has been satisfactorily solved and each continues to be controversial both within the cities in question and among international development organisations. As the number of people and informal settlements in cities grow every year, the public funding available to meet their demands remains out of scale with the size of the problem.

A critical challenge facing the new generation of urban improvement programmes is facilitating the integration of beneficiaries into the greater urban economy. What is such programmes' productive potential? Can they seek to generate economic benefits for residents of both the informal settlements and the adjacent neighbourhoods? Before answering these and other questions, we must identify the ways in which residents of informal settlements are constrained from integrating into the formal economy. Constraints vary by place, but most frequently include:

- Insecure tenure of assets
- Deficiencies in infrastructure (for example, water and electricity)

- Regulatory costs (including of licences to undertake productive economic activities)
- Restricted access to credit
- Lack of access to intermediate goods (depending on the industry or service)
- Lack of market information and limited horizontal and vertical links with similar or complementary industries
- High transportation costs

Each of these constraints calls for a different solution, ranging from changes in policy and regulations to institutional changes, information exchange, and organisation.

Urban Investments and Economic Growth

There has been a wide consensus from the beginning of the 1990s that urban economic activities account for, at the very least, 50 percent of the gross domestic product (GDP) of developing countries (World Bank, 1991) and even higher percentages in the most urbanised of them. Nonetheless, there is little research on how policies such as public investment in housing, infrastructure, or urban development programmes contribute to macro-economic development or to municipal and neighbourhood economies. This gap is both theoretical and methodological; measuring the benefits and their impact across territorial levels (national, regional, or local) is complicated and potentially inconclusive.

A key factor in this analytical problem is the *definition of scale.* What is the most adequate unit of analysis: the neighbourhood, the city, or the metropolitan area? Where, and on what scale, can the "economic benefits footprint" of an individual urban improvement project be traced? The notion of the "economic footprint" is an adaptation of the concept of the "ecological footprint" developed by William Rees in the 1970s (Rees, 1988). From this point of view, the following questions become relevant: Will the benefits be most visible near the investment site—that is, within the improved neighbourhood—or will there be observable benefits in other areas, for example, the places where the bricks and cement for the project have been manufactured? Will only the income and wealth flows of households in the upgraded areas improve, or will outside enterprises and households also benefit from the higher investment and consumption power enjoyed by beneficiaries in the upgraded neighbourhood?

There are at least two kinds of scale that should be included in any analysis of the possible impacts of neighbourhood upgrading programmes on productivity and the overall economy. One is the *scale of the programme itself,* meaning the number of settlements, households, and individual beneficiaries covered and, therefore, the amount of capital, manpower, and materials used. The other is *the geographical scale,* in which primary, secondary, and tertiary effects can be observed through

Microenterprises—often informal—generate much of the urban employment in Latin America.
Microenterprise in San Salvador, El Salvador

the economic multipliers effects. Regarding the programme scale, it should be possible to estimate the number of jobs created and the volume of income generated by specific investments. Furthermore, there are also *direct and indirect effects* that should be considered—for example, the extent to which the demand for more manpower increases the number of days worked in the construction sector, and how this might be transformed into higher consumer spending that, in turn, creates employment.

Neighbourhood Improvement Programmes' Economic Impact

Since the very first neighbourhood improvement programmes were undertaken with international funding at the beginning of the 1970s, investments in infrastructure and housing have indeed been linked to job creation and improvements in productivity. It is important to recognise, however, that these effects are rarely considered the primary objectives of individual projects. Rather, they are considered secondary to the key components of infrastructure upgrading, and thus fall outside the projects' operative logic and design.

An analysis of neighbourhood upgrading programmes indicates that some do include components linked to job creation.[7] Examples include:

- The inclusion of specific components, such as microcredit, to help set up small businesses, train people in special skills, build markets to increase product sales, assist in product marketing, and link up with value chains
- The use of contract management modes that promote the participation of small enterprises in the process of project implementation
- The favouring of labour-intensive projects and appropriate technology for infrastructure building and the provision of services
- The use of agency-style enterprises (AGETYPES) to privatise specific urban and municipal functions, such as infrastructure management and waste disposal, in order to obtain greater efficiency in the level of services offered or to generate new employment
- Improving the business climate for both direct foreign and local investment in select cities by implementing reforms (usually including deregulation), providing tax breaks to stimulate investment, and offering exemptions from various forms of code requirements

Land consolidation and zoning, such as the development of free enterprise zones, are used to generate economies of agglomeration and proximity. In the majority of cases, these measures have been designed without the extensive analysis of factors such as the predominant economic conditions and infrastructure in the city, the location of complementary economic activities, and the magnitude of private sector investment. There has also been a tendency to ignore both the sources of improved productivity and economic value creation within the local economy (that is, the sources of wealth and income) and the specific local constraints on productivity and wealth creation. As previously mentioned, these components were not considered central to the projects. For example, a 2007 study of the development strategies of cities supported by Cities Alliance concluded that although they paid attention to economic factors such as productivity, they offered no specific guidelines for the design of individual projects (Miller and Cohen, 2007).

A large proportion of projects in the portfolios of international development institutions do not include detailed analysis of the local economic conditions and the constraints faced by the residents of informal settlements. The studies carried out during the preparation of these projects contain uneven empirical data gathered from household or business

---

[7] For more information about these projects, see, for example, Kessides (1997), UN-HABITAT (2003b), and Viloria-Williams (2006)—studies commissioned by the Cities Alliance and the World Bank's assessment reports.

The use of simple technologies to improve the neighbourhoods opens the opportunity to hire unemployed residents during construction.
Street improvements in Bogota, Colombia

surveys and are usually highly influenced by the disciplinary approach favoured by the functionaries of international organisations.[8] The lack of systematic attention paid to local economic development was reflected for many years in the World Bank's publications dealing with urban upgrading (Kessides, 1997; Viloria-Williams, 2006). In many urban development programmes, the operational diagnosis of local economic conditions tends to be superficial, premature, and without a solid and systematic analytic base.

Furthermore, numerous projects seem to have been designed without taking into account the scale of the urban area in which they are to be implemented. Whenever implicit hypotheses on urban multiplier effects exist, they are usually formulated without regard for possible interrelationships or their magnitude. The economic hypotheses of the majority of urban aid projects are therefore superficial, highly speculative, and generally lacking in analytic foundations or quantitative specifications.

Taking the above-mentioned practices into account, and with the objective of improving the productive links of informal neighbourhood upgrading programmes, it is first necessary to define the differing possible scales of operation before specifying the scope of the objectives. Table 2.1 shows a matrix in which different types of economic effects can be observed.

---

[8] For example, architects rarely take an interest in topics relating to economic development, while economists are often unaware of the consequences of the choice of technologies or their environmental effect.

Table 2.1 Project Scale and Spatial Scale

Project scale	Spatial scale of economic impact		
	Neighbourhood	City	Metropolitan region
1 neighbourhood	X		
2–5 neighbourhoods	X	X	
5–10 neighbourhoods	X	X	X

Source: Author's elaboration.

Another aspect of this matrix is the *time dimension*. Most projects seek and expect physical and economic results to appear within the same time frame—and frequently during the project's implementation period. This begs the question as to whether the physical and economic time periods should necessarily overlap. It could be argued that the economic consequences of physical investment can only appear later, given that workers employed in projects or in the production of materials will spend their wages on other goods and services only when the construction is complete and their wages paid. The multiplier effect of salaries cannot come into effect at the very same moment that the employees receive their payment. It is therefore necessary to determine the possible points at which the economic impact of the investment will first become apparent. Obviously, the longer the time period, the greater the impact will be. The existence of this temporal imbalance is something that must be addressed when assessing the economic effects of neighbourhood upgrading programmes.

Another important dimension of any relevant assessment is determining whether or not the new funds (investments and salaries) injected into the local economy will be translated into increased consumer spending, investment, or savings. The study of remittances, for example, seems to suggest that remittance receivers tend to use them in a variety of ways, depending on diverse prior conditions. It is therefore important to analyse whether consumption, investment, and savings directly turn into (either by themselves or in combination with other economic actions) a higher level of employment, and whether these resources will make their presence felt in local value chains of goods and services. Both the assessment and expectations of productive effects depend, to a large extent, on the analytical framework adopted.

These assessments indicate that the achievement of radical and long-lasting results can best be obtained if measures to promote job creation are given priority over initial improvements in infrastructure. This means turning the accepted logic and operative design of most projects on their head: instead of being a primary intervention, infrastructure should support a longer-lasting and wider-based programme of economic development.

NATHALIE ALVARADO
and BEATRIZ
ABIZANDA

An Integrated Approach to Safety, Security, and Citizens' Coexistence [9]

Levels of violent crime in the LAC region are among the highest in the world: in 2005 the region's homicide rate was 25.6 homicides per 100,000 inhabitants—almost triple the world average. But there is significant variation among countries of the region. For example, the 55.3 homicides per 100,000 inhabitants in El Salvador in 2005 contrasts sharply with that measured in Chile in the same year: 1.9 homicides per 100,000 inhabitants. Variation can be found within countries as well; for example, the 2006 violent crime rates in Cali, Colombia, and São Paulo, Brazil (63 and 39 homicides per 100,000 inhabitants, respectively) were higher than the general levels in those countries (37 and 25.7, respectively) for the same year. In other cases, the crime rate in big cities is similar to the national average, as in the case with the rate in Santiago compared with that of Chile and Montevideo compared with that of Uruguay (Dammert, Alda, and Ruz, 2008). The increase in violent crime is reflected by the increasing concern that it causes among Latin Americans. The 2005 *Latinobarometro* survey indicated that security was an important worry for the region's population, second only to unemployment.

High crime rates come at a high cost, eroding regional competitiveness, discouraging private investment (both foreign and domestic), and raising corporate operating costs by increasing the amount spent on private security and insurance premiums, among other things. The Global Competitiveness Report for 2008–09 (WEF, 2008) uses its Global Competitiveness Index (GCI) to assess countries' ability to compete. Among the factors used to calculate the GCI are the costs of crime and violence, which negatively affect the GCI average.[10] For example, 2007–08 GCI ranks were 74 for Colombia, 60 for Mexico, and 64 for Brazil out of 134 countries. These scores contrast with these countries' rankings in the crime and violence parameters used to calculate the GCI, which were 118, 125, and 123, respectively, for the same year. High crime rates also put countries' future economic health in jeopardy, by forcing the state to devote resources to law enforcement that might otherwise have been directed towards public spending programmes in infrastructure or education.

The Characteristics of Violence

The most prominent characteristics of violence in the region can be summed up in the following points:

---

[9] The first two sections of this chapter are based on an internal document of the Inter-American Development Bank (IDB, 2008a).

[10] See http://www.weforum.org/documents/gcr0809/index.html.

- *Violence disproportionately affects young people.* Nearly 40 percent of registered homicides in Brazil are people under the age of 29, and in Colombia, 30 percent of homicide victims are under the age of 25.
- *There is a high incidence of violence within the family.* According to the United Nations Development Programme (UNDP), between 30 and 45 percent of the region's women have been victims of some form of violence (domestic violence or physical or verbal abuse). An estimated 80,000 boys and girls die each year as a direct result of family violence in the region (Buvinic, Morrison, and Orlando, 2005).
- *The majority of violent crimes are related to the use of firearms.* These often occur during or immediately after times of civil conflict or in conjunction with organised crime activities.
- *Violent crime takes place predominantly in urban areas,* particularly within the megacities of Latin America. According to the United Nations Centre for Human Settlements (UNCHS), more than half of the violent crimes perpetrated in Brazil, Mexico, and Venezuela were carried out in the metropolitan areas of Rio de Janeiro (48 homicides per 100,000 inhabitants in 2005), São Paulo (39 homicides per 100,000 inhabitants in 2006), Mexico City (27 per 100,000 inhabitants in 2005), and Caracas (88 homicides per 100,000 inhabitants in 2005) (UN-HABITAT, 2007b). In Brazil, nearly 20 percent of all homicides were concentrated within less than 2 percent of the urban geographical area (Beato, 2006).
- *Expressions of violence within the region differ,* owing to the differing social, historical, and cultural characteristics of each country. For example, violence in Central America with its high rate of gang participation takes place against the backdrop of an internal post-conflict situation, which is characterised, among other features by the deterioration of social capital (crucial for violence prevention), the availability of weapons, a history of daily coexistence with brutality, and the presence of youth whose education and job opportunities have been curtailed by conflict.

The following factors are influencing the rise in levels of violence in the region:

Urbanisation and the urban incidence of violence. The faster a population becomes urbanised—the faster the size and population density of a given city grow—the greater the increase in conflict, violence, and crime.

Informality—fertile ground for illicit activities. In informal settlements, the state usually lacks a strong institutional presence and has difficulty fulfilling its role as a provider of basic services (drinking water, drainage, roads, street lighting, electricity), social services (education; help for vulnerable groups such as young people, women, and the elderly; employment opportunities), or security (both judicial and physical). Accordingly, surveys carried out by the *Latinobarometro* have shown that residents of these settlements express less confidence in institutions such as the Congress, police force, political parties, and legal system than do the rest of the country's population. This weakness or absence of official institutions, in turn, creates a power vacuum that is readily filled by criminals engaging in everything from commercial piracy and the sale of stolen automobile parts to organised crime. Furthermore, as has been previously mentioned, the sense of institutional abandonment perpetuates a vicious cycle of poverty and exclusion (Vanderschueren, 2007). Residents find it impossible to work outside of the settlement due to the stigma attached to living there, they have little recourse in the face of rising crime, and they share widespread feelings of fear and insecurity, making the informal settlements even less attractive for outside parties involved in productive investment and employment generation.

The roots of violence in the region and the identification of risk factors. Violence is the expression of the region's traditional social, political, and economic problems, particularly its long-standing struggles with social exclusion, inequality, discrimination, and informality. The most vulnerable sectors of the population—those living in insecure housing and working in the informal economy—are the most intensely affected by violence, as they have the least means with which to protect themselves and their possessions. Violence is, in fact, a phenomenon with multiple causes that is exacerbated by the presence of other risk factors. Identifying these risk factors is therefore an essential input for designing and implementing measures to counteract violence. Three main categories of risk factors have been identified:

- *Factors that influence the individual.* Among the important factors are early exposure to violence, inequality, and unemployment due to social exclusion, discrimination, the presence of other facilitating factors (drugs, alcohol, firearms), and phenomena such as illiteracy and academic failure.
- *Factors at work in the home.* These include dysfunctional families or domestic violence.
- *Factors at work in the community.* These include the acceptance of the culture of violence, environmental degradation, the breakdown of family and social ties, inefficiency of social control institutions, a history of social violence, civil wars, the trafficking of illegal drugs and weapons, and massive social inequalities.

Institutional failures of the state in its fight against violence. Public policies to prevent and control violence, from the national institutions down to the local level, have been inadequate in much of the region. In particular, the population's lack of confidence in the judicial and police institutions—the very institutions charged with providing security—underscores their lack of confidence in democratic institutions in general. When the justice system does not act to resolve minor urban conflicts, is too slow, or passes sentence on only 10 percent of the crimes that are committed, criminals go about their business with a sense of impunity (particularly in areas such as organised crime, corruption, human rights abuses, and money laundering) (Vanderschueren, 2007). On the other hand, punishments and prison sentences do not favour the social reintegration of those who commit crimes; frequently, prisons serve as a training ground for inmates to organise and learn about criminal networks rather than as a first step towards social reintegration (Vanderschueren, 2007).

Conceptual Framework

Public order: The traditional paradigm. In the past, the paradigm used to resolve the question of citizen insecurity was based entirely on actions aimed at maintaining or restoring public order. The state usually proposed such actions from an authoritarian perspective and the police force backed them. However, a new paradigm that emphasises security and citizens' coexistence is slowly evolving. In this new paradigm, society as a whole (the public sector, the private sector, and civil society) is adopting actions to guarantee fundamental rights and liberties, impart justice, and watch over the peaceful unfolding of individual and collective social life. This paradigm shift has led to a shift away from the centralist and single-minded vision of controlling crime levels through the police, judicial system, and prison system, and towards crime-prevention strategies with a high degree of citizen participation. These new measures aim to reduce the risk factors of violence, promote social development, and diminish the opportunities to commit crime.

Faced with growing delinquency levels and increased insecurity and fear among the wider population, authorities are again being pressed to adopt repressive policies characterised by greater numbers of police on the streets, tougher sentences, and a lowering of the age of penal responsibility. While such policies might improve conditions in the short term, they are unlikely to have a long-term impact on crime levels due to the absence or reduction of crime-prevention policies that deal with the risk factors, along with the lack of sufficient investment in the police force, the judicial services, and the prison system. In fact, such repressive policies may even create situations similar, or even sometimes worse, than those existing prior to the intervention. A broad-based and sustained approach to security and coexistence is likely to be much more effective.

The new paradigm: An integrated approach to security and coexistence. Citizens' security is a public asset to which the state, the private sector, and civil society all contribute. It allows for the development of a peaceful daily coexistence in which the mechanisms of law and order are respected and the full exercise of rights and liberties is guaranteed. The focus of security and citizens' coexistence can be described as integral in the sense that it draws in society as a whole. It does not hand over responsibility for enforcing the law to the state repression-and-control apparatus (the police-justice-prison paradigm) or to a private-sector substitute. It seeks not only to address the manifestations of violence but also to attack the root causes of violence. To this end, this approach employs crime-prevention strategies to complement control strategies, emphasises participation and community solidarity, and includes urban design interventions aimed at reducing the opportunities to commit crime (see Box 2.2). Contrary to popular opinion, well-focused strategies of crime prevention can yield results in the short term and can also be more cost effective than those based only on control and repression.[11]

Essential elements in any policy of security and citizens' coexistence include the following:

- *Shared responsibility and the integrated approach.* To be effective and efficient, citizens' security measures must include a wide range of crime prevention and control measures. Control—with due respect for human rights and within the proper legal framework—is here considered as one of the dissuasive factors that contributes to the fight against impunity, and thereby constitutes a prevention mechanism. The measures must be comprehensive and based on the shared responsibility of society as a whole, uniting the efforts of the state, private sector, and civil society and placing an emphasis on community participation (see Box 2.3).
- *Multi-sectorality.* As the nature of violence has multiple causes, multisector interventions are required. Risk factors can be counteracted with specific actions in the areas of education, health, recreation, public infrastructure (such as street lighting and street furniture), culture, sports, and social services, among others.
- *Priority given to the local level.* Because the origins and manifestations of violence vary among and within regions and countries, the policies of security and citizens' coexistence must be implemented with local-level participation. Local government is closest to those affected by the violence, and management of these policies on a local level allows for a greater degree of community cooperation and the strengthening of their social capital. Moreover, working with the community is key to understanding the root causes of violence and thereby finding solutions to it. A locally based approach also facilitates coordination among the state sector institutions and among the public sector, private sector, and civil society organisations. It favours monitoring policy results and helps consolidate decentralisation processes, thus augmenting the local government's capacity to intervene.

---

[11] Some studies show that approaches emphasising prevention are up to six times as cost-effective as those emphasising repression (Vanderschueren, 2007).

BOX 2.2 INTEGRATION OF YOUNG PEOPLE AT RISK IN BARCELONA

JULI PONCE SOLÉ

Integrating into society is difficult for some young Latin Americans who have recently immigrated to Spain. Various crises superimpose themselves: adolescence itself; the challenges facing the transcontinental family, broken and remade by family regrouping; youth unemployment; and a complicated urban and educational context. Many youth live in areas with social problems, in overcrowded or poor-quality housing, and attend segregated schools, given that Spanish policy links schools with the neighbourhoods in which they are situated (Ponce Solé, 2007). This situation goes some way towards explaining the recent rise of so-called Latin gangs. In 2007, 1,529 gang members were counted in Spain. Women were in the minority, with 219 members. Ecuadorians, with 723 members, made up the gangs' predominant nationality.

Two gangs dominate the Spanish scene. On the one hand are the Latin Kings and on the other the Ñetas. Smaller gangs, or groups, include the Dominicans Don't Play, the Black Panthers, the *Trinitarios*, and the *Salvatrucha mara*. According to the Spanish Ministry of the Interior, the police arrested 152 youths in 2006 belonging to the Latin Kings, whereas in 2005, 182 youths belonging to Latin gangs in general were arrested. In mid-2006, 66 inmates in state prisons reported links to these groups; 44 of these inmates claimed membership in the Latin Kings.

The 2003 murder of a young Colombian student in front of the gates of a Barcelona high school stirred up media interest and a measure of social alarm. Faced with this situation, the municipal security manage-

ment section of the Barcelona City Council led a collective effort, involving both the private and public sectors, in collaboration with the university. The campaign was based on the idea of the social recuperation of the conflict, rather than just police repression. Contacts were established with gangs with the hope that, by getting some measure of "official recognition", they might be convinced to adapt their structures and behaviour to the legal framework of Catalonia, and thereby take advantage of available grants and subsidies. The result was the formal institution of two associations, one for the Latin Kings (*Associació Cultural de Reis i Reines Llatins de Catalunya* [Cultural Association of Latin Kings and Queens of Catalonia]) and another for the *Ñetas* (*Asociación Ñeta Pro Derechos del Confinado* [*Ñetas* Association for Prisoners' Rights]) in 2006 and 2007, respectively. This method of tackling the conflict has since become known as the "Barcelona Approach", in stark contrast to those of other cities, such as Madrid (although comparisons are admittedly hard to draw due to the differing circumstances).[a] It must be borne in mind, however, that legalising these organisations has had only a limited impact. Only 200 of the estimated 800 Latin Kings members living in Catalonia have decided to join the new association.

---

[a] In Madrid's case the levels of conflict between gangs has been steadily increasing in recent years, and according to various reports by the police, gang activity has been particularly violent. This might go some way to explaining Madrid's inclination to use the "stick" rather than the "carrot".

The Experience of the Inter-American Development Bank

The Inter-American Development Bank (IDB) was the first multilateral development institution to provide countries in the region with technical assistance and project financing for violence prevention and citizens' security.[12] IDB involvement came about in response to growing concerns about increasing levels of crime and violence and demands for active policies against it. This clamour challenged the IDB to become involved in a more efficient, in-depth, strategic, and innovative fashion. It also required the Bank to clearly demarcate the limits of its involvement and to put in place safeguards to reduce the risks associated with its involvement.[13]

Based on lessons learned by the IDB in its operating experience and analytical work, and on other research and studies carried out on the same subject, an internal document, the "Operational Guidelines for Programme Design and Execution in the Area of Coexistence and Public Safety", was drawn up and validated by international experts in the field. The document defines the Bank's scope of action in the sector, which is aimed at improving countries' capacity to tackle violence. The document groups together actions in strategic areas and maintains a practical focus, addressing how to deliver more effective, efficient, and sustainable policies for security and citizens' coexistence while maintaining respect for human and civil rights and promoting transparency. The areas can be summarised thus:

- *Public policy planning.* Based on coordination between the national and local levels, this component includes (i) comprehensive analysis of citizens' security (sector diagnosis including surveys of victimisation and attitudes, technical assessment, and exchanges of experiences, among other gauges); (ii) institutional strengthening of the entities involved with this sector; (iii) laboratories of good governance for security (information structures that gather and consolidate data on crime and violence and facilitate the formulation and management of sector policies); and (iv) monitoring and assessment mechanisms.
- *Crime-prevention activities.* Complementing the penal justice system, these measures are aimed at counteracting the factors that increase the risk of crime and victimisation. Interventions take into

---

[12] In the past 10 years, the IDB has approved financing totalling US$227 million, over and above technical cooperation, for projects in this area.

[13] IDB programmes are characterised by their support of (i) institution strengthening (design of institutional policies and information systems about violence and criminality); (ii) prevention projects (targeting of risk factors, prevention of interfamily social violence, and crime prevention through environmental design); (iii) selected control activities (occasional support of the civil police force and the penitentiary system, as well as performance assessment and accountability to civil society); and (iv) working with the mass media (development of press and publicity campaigns).

BOX 2.3 BOGOTA: CRITICAL ZONES AND THE CITIZENS' SECURITY APPROACH

CLARA LÓPEZ OBREGÓN

In recent years, security enforcement in Bogota has undertaken a more social and participatory approach. Security is understood to be a public asset that provides the structural conditions for a dignified life and the full enjoyment of human rights and democratic coexistence. This new approach seeks cultural changes among those social groups that see violence as a way of resolving conflicts, or who have a propensity towards instrumental or professional criminality. Consequently, the participation of directly affected communities is sought during the process of planning and implementing public policies aimed at improving citizens' security and coexistence. These communities know the dynamics of the problem first hand and can offer viable solutions and help assess the immediate consequences of the implementation of government programmes and projects.

In the city of Bogota, a programme based on this philosophy has been launched with the aim of reclaiming public spaces and reducing the levels of conflict, violence, and crime in 31 critical areas of the capital. The Plan for the Prevention of Urban Conflict, Violence, and Crime is the product of a territory-focused methodology. Other factors taken into consideration include the urban structure of a given area and the territorial perceptions and opinions of the people who live in or pass by that area.

According to this approach, a critical zone is one that displays one or more of the following characteristics:

- It is clearly and repeatedly perceived to be insecure by its residents
- It is home to one or more types of persistent criminal activity
- It is an important area—at the neighbourhood, sector, zone, local, or metropolitan level—due to its dynamism, affluence, or agglomeration levels
- It is affected by a lack of control over activities with a negative social impact (prostitution, sales and consumption of alcohol and drugs) or with negative urban impacts (invasion of public spaces, illegal emplacement of industrial activities, mechanical workshops, among others)
- It could be susceptible to a reduction in criminal activity, either through the transformation of its socio-territorial dynamic, or through the direct intervention of the agents of the state

This methodology has allowed greater understanding of why the urban, historical, or socio-territorial conditions in a given zone have transformed it into a space given over to violent crime. An integrated vision of the problems that are present in a critical zone permits the definition of a public policy to tackle crime through social, situational, and commu-

Criminological approach:

- Modality
- Actors
- Temporality

Urban component:

- Functions
- Morphology
- Mobility
- Accessibility

Territorial approach to urban crime phenomenon

Territorial representations and perceptions:

- Type of spaces
- Main players
- Appropriation forms
- Perception

Public intervention policy:

- Tactical - operational
- Social - institutional

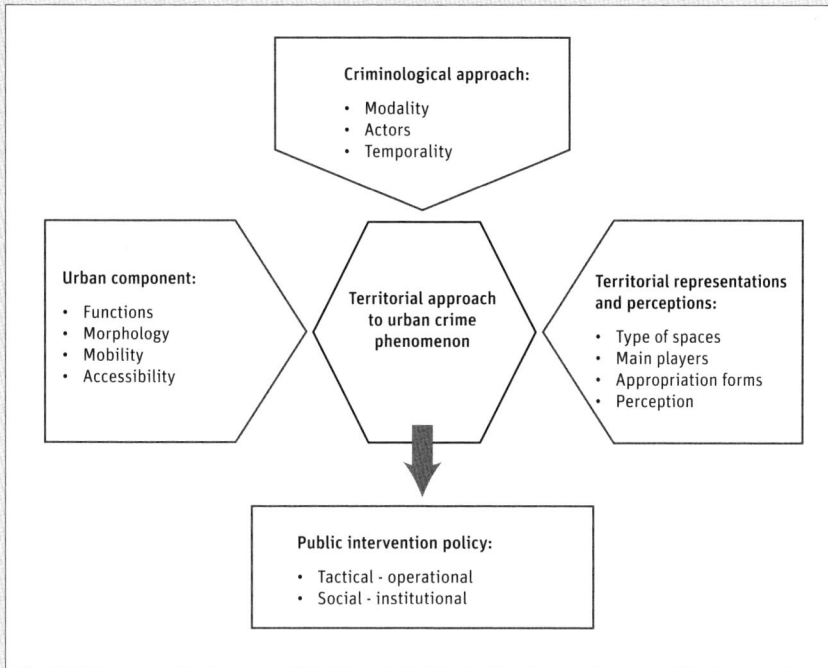

nity strategies, complemented by police control policies. The approach takes into consideration that poverty and social exclusion are not in themselves the direct cause of delinquency, but in conjunction with other factors, generate vulnerabilities that induce certain individuals, in certain circumstances, to commit a crime or become a crime victim. This integral approach, then, allows the community to become an active partner in building better living conditions. Shared responsibility and the informal social control that the community can wield in a given territory are important intermediate benefits in the process of improving security and citizens' coexistence. Through community consensus, agreements can be reached that benefit citizens and create higher levels of confidence in institutions.

account the multidimensional nature of violence and the need to implement integrated strategies that affect the distinct risk factors. These include (i) projects and activities aimed at young people; (ii) prevention of family violence; (iii) activities aimed at the community; and (iv) crime prevention through environmental design (improvement of public spaces and regulatory measures to reduce violence, such as the control of alcohol sales or firearms possession).

■ *Control activities and alternatives to penal justice.* This component includes support for institutional management of the local police force and the penitentiary system: (i) help in internal administrative institutional planning and reorganisation; (ii) improvement in the recruitment process; (iii) professional development of police officers and security guards, with an emphasis on preventative functions, human and civil rights, and attention to the public in general (paying special attention to the victims and vulnerable groups); (iv) policing programmes aimed at working with the community (community or liaison police). Financing is also available for initiatives that increase the availability of alternative services of basic justice in areas accessible to the public: police detachments, justices of the peace, houses of justice, family advice centres, and centres of mediation and reconciliation.

■ *Rehabilitation of the prison population and of young offenders (tertiary prevention).* This component includes activities oriented towards (i) integrated personal, psychological, social, and medical attention; (ii) formal education; (iii) skills and micro-enterprise management training; (iv) job placement, by fostering strategic alliances with the private sector, within the framework of corporate social responsibility; (v) development and strengthening of alternatives to imprisonment, with adequate supervision systems; and (vi) development of post-prison support and monitoring mechanisms.

Security and Citizens' Coexistence through Neighbourhood Upgrading Programmes

Previous chapters in this volume have emphasised that neighbourhood upgrading programmes help to reduce the physical and social segregation of informal settlements. In doing so, they also address the chief causes of urban violence in these areas. Actions undertaken in the fields of infrastructure, social services, and community development can thus be complemented by integrated and targeted preventive measures that are aimed specifically at tackling risk factors associated with violence.

Aims of the Interventions

Investing in infrastructure and public spaces can contribute to improved coexistence and violence prevention if these concepts are specifically incorporated into the design, planning, execution, and maintenance of the

The presence of the community in the streets improves neighbourhood safety. **Pelourinho, Salvador de Bahia, Brazil**

investments. The upgrading of public spaces, for example, can create an atmosphere that improves urban security and reduces crime. To achieve this, the public spaces and installations should enhance visual and physical connectedness, improve street lighting, and remove or avoid dead ends. Routine maintenance of this infrastructure by the community can also be of benefit by establishing a permanent presence in the areas with the highest incidence of crime; badly maintained, vandalised, and unattractive public spaces, by contrast, encourage violent conduct.

This approach has been termed "environmental prevention", or CPTED (crime prevention through environmental design). It aims to reduce opportunistic crime by reducing feelings of insecurity and enhancing community cohesion by careful management of social and environmental variables.[14] According to Rau (2007), the basic concepts of environmental prevention are the following:

- Natural control of access points: The opportunity for crime is reduced by limiting the number of access points to a public space, and to directly connecting the access points to observable areas.

[14] Several Latin American countries (Brazil, Chile, El Salvador, Honduras) have used this methodology, with variations based on their own local identity.

Spaces should be designed to give users a natural indication of the entrance and the exit.

- Natural vigilance: The appropriate design and placement of windows in surrounding houses, the lighting and design of public spaces, and the natural landscape should all enhance residents' capacity to observe activity going on in their area.
- Maintenance: This refers to management plans for the cleaning, gardening, and management of public spaces. It is related to the "broken windows" theory of crime prevention, which holds that more opportunistic crime is committed in a deteriorated area.
- Territorial reinforcement: This concept refers to the feelings of affection or attachment that residents form towards their immediate neighbourhood and that might be harnessed to inspire them to look after it.

Environmental interventions need to be grounded in the community to activate social control mechanisms. Consequently, the concepts listed above must be articulated through constant community participation in the design process and implementation.

Methodological Tools

Site-specific analysis is used to coordinate the upgrading or construction of infrastructure with the security and citizens' coexistence approach. This method helps to reveal the areas where there is a high incidence of crime or risk and to identify what environmental factors are present in these areas (deteriorated infrastructure, poor visibility, overcrowding, and deficient street lighting). Based on these observations, interventions are designed and implemented to improve visibility and protection in public areas, and thereby reduce the risk of violent acts. Other available tools are security audits and fact-finding tours. In these, vulnerable citizens from the informal settlements, generally women, walk the streets of their neighbourhood accompanied by town planners, architects, and municipal officers, identifying exactly which areas they find threatening.

The complaints that are raised during security audits or fact-finding tours are then aired publicly and specific town planning interventions are proposed to remedy the problems. This kind of activity fosters cooperation among local government officials, police, and informal settlement dwellers, and is a key part of the empowerment process for the most vulnerable groups. It is important to bear in mind, however, that environmental prevention is only one approach to the crime problem and should be employed in conjunction with a wide range of other interventions.

Preventive Social Actions

It has been previously shown that urban violence is closely linked to the inequality and marginalisation of certain groups. Accordingly, targeting social interventions to specific areas using the integrated approach to security and coexistence can usually mitigate such violence. The relationship between security policy and social policy is a key aspect of this approach. Not all social policy is security policy—to affirm the opposite would be to criminalise social policy. Social policy, however, has many points of contact with security policy, above all when aimed at protecting the most vulnerable groups in society. Violence prevention activities undertaken through social intervention have two main aims: they reduce the risk factors that encourage crime, and they instil a preventive impulse in the population, urging people to reflect on the causes of and solutions to crime rather than merely protecting themselves against it (by installing railings and burglar alarms, and so on). These interventions include (i) projects and activities aimed at young people; (ii) programmes designed to reduce interfamily violence; and (iii) activities directed towards the community as a whole.

Among the activities of a social nature that can be included in a neighbourhood upgrading programme are the following: (i) education and awareness about ethical values and peaceful coexistence; (ii) conflict-resolution programmes and alternative techniques to improve the discipline and social and cognitive abilities of young people;[15] (iii) formal education, higher education, and professional and vocational training (promotion of microenterprises and alliance building with the private sector to provide employment for the most vulnerable groups); (iv) early detection of drug and alcohol abuse, education on the risks associated with it, and programmes of detoxification and rehabilitation; (v) creation of new sport and leisure infrastructure to foster peaceful coexistence through extracurricular activities, thereby enhancing social and cultural integration; and (vi) construction and operation of health infrastructure to treat the mental health problems of the most vulnerable groups in the settlements.

To be effective, these measures must be based on a firm understanding of the causes and manifestations of violence within a given settlement. This analysis must include all forms of violence, its causes, and the actors involved (both victims and victimisers), as well as a detailed examination of the risk factors at play (academic failure levels, number of enterprises in the area, prevalence of broken homes, local perceptions about security, and environmental conditions).[16] To be fully effective, all social measures

---

[15] For example, the Open Schools Programme implemented in various states in Brazil with the help of the United Nations Education, Scientific and Cultural Organisation (UNESCO) is a positive example of an integral approach that not only includes actions aimed at preventing violence among schoolchildren, but also puts both the physical and teaching infrastructure at the community's service.

[16] Local security forums can help identify needs and call for solutions. For example, in Quito and Guayaquil, Ecuador, a programme involving security and coexistence corporations has been tested; in Buenos Aires and Montevideo, municipal and neighbourhood security forums have been encouraged; and in Chile and the Dominican Republic, the "safe neighbourhood" programmes use the same principles.

within a given settlement should be put into practice simultaneously. Furthermore, if the social programmes included in a neighbourhood upgrading project are to aid in violence prevention, they must explicitly aim to increase security within the neighbourhood, not just improve living conditions for the beneficiaries (Petrella and Vanderschueren, 2003).

One of the main motivations for including social measures in a neighbourhood upgrading programme is to reinforce the social fabric of the community. This is achieved through alliance building to strengthen forms of non-repressive control exercised by settlement residents over the common spaces in their neighbourhoods, rather than privatising security and handing control over to security firms or armed groups. Such control is based on civic values of good citizenship and well-established rules concerning the use of public spaces and shared infrastructure in the community. Encouraging residents of informal settlements to help themselves in improving security in their neighbourhoods requires a sustained effort since this population is often stigmatised by society and exhibits a high level of distrust towards the state. The needs of the community should be assessed as a first step, followed by planning, design, implementation, and monitoring of crime-prevention strategies. Furthermore, alliance building with the municipal government is a key factor in the battle to regain residents' confidence and persuade them to fill the power vacuum created by informality.

Finally, a participative approach at the local level can contribute to reforming the police forces by incorporating the concepts of community policing and problem resolution rather than repression or punishment (the example of Chile is in this sense paradigmatic). Police force transparency can also be more effectively achieved at a local level by neighbourhood organisations.

Advantages of an Integrated Security and Citizens' Coexistence Approach

Added value. Adopting the integral approach to security and citizens' coexistence adds value to urban upgrading programmes by improving both the objective conditions of the informal settlements and residents' perceptions about security levels and safety. Such an approach also improves the quality of coexistence among neighbours.

Community empowerment. One of the lessons learned from the experience of designing and implementing urban upgrading programmes is that community participation is highly beneficial. Consequently, adopting an integrated approach to security and citizens' coexistence expands the scope for community participation in matters that are of prime importance to the settlement dwellers themselves, thereby increasing their sense of empowerment. Citizen participation is vital to the diagnostic process because it helps both to identify community leaders and to design and monitor social interventions that address the community's most pressing problems.

Sustainability. Social cohesion is reinforced when the integral approach is adopted, particularly when communal efforts to appropriate, defend, and maintain public spaces are successful. This feeling of ownership in the community has a positive effect on the sustainability of the investments.

The importance of diagnosis. The most vulnerable sectors of the population must be consulted on issues of safety, security, and citizens' coexistence if the causes, forms, and perceptions of violence, all closely linked to a given territory, are to be understood. Such diagnosis is essential to formulating an effective strategy against violence. It must be emphasised, however, that there are no universal solutions, and that although best practices are useful, they are not replicable in every situation.

The capacity to build alliances and foster institutional coordination. It has been previously suggested that safety and security do not depend solely on the police, but rather are the shared responsibility of (i) the public sector, by coordinating its different levels (national, regional, and municipal) and sectors (town planning, social policy, security policy); (ii) the private sector, which is key to generating employment and microfinance opportunities, thereby alleviating persistent social exclusion; and (iii) civil society, whose participation is key to the effectiveness and sustainability of crime-prevention measures. Moreover, appropriate institutional coordination can lead to the establishment of "coexistence observatories" that facilitate monitoring of the indicators of violence, delinquency, and peaceful coexistence.

The quality and management of public space. When public spaces become degraded, criminality and insecurity increase, leading to further degradation. Consequently, it is important to include public space management and control initiatives (such as street trading, markets, parking spaces, leisure areas, and even traffic lights) in neighbourhood upgrading programmes, as these have a direct impact on safety, security, and citizens' coexistence.

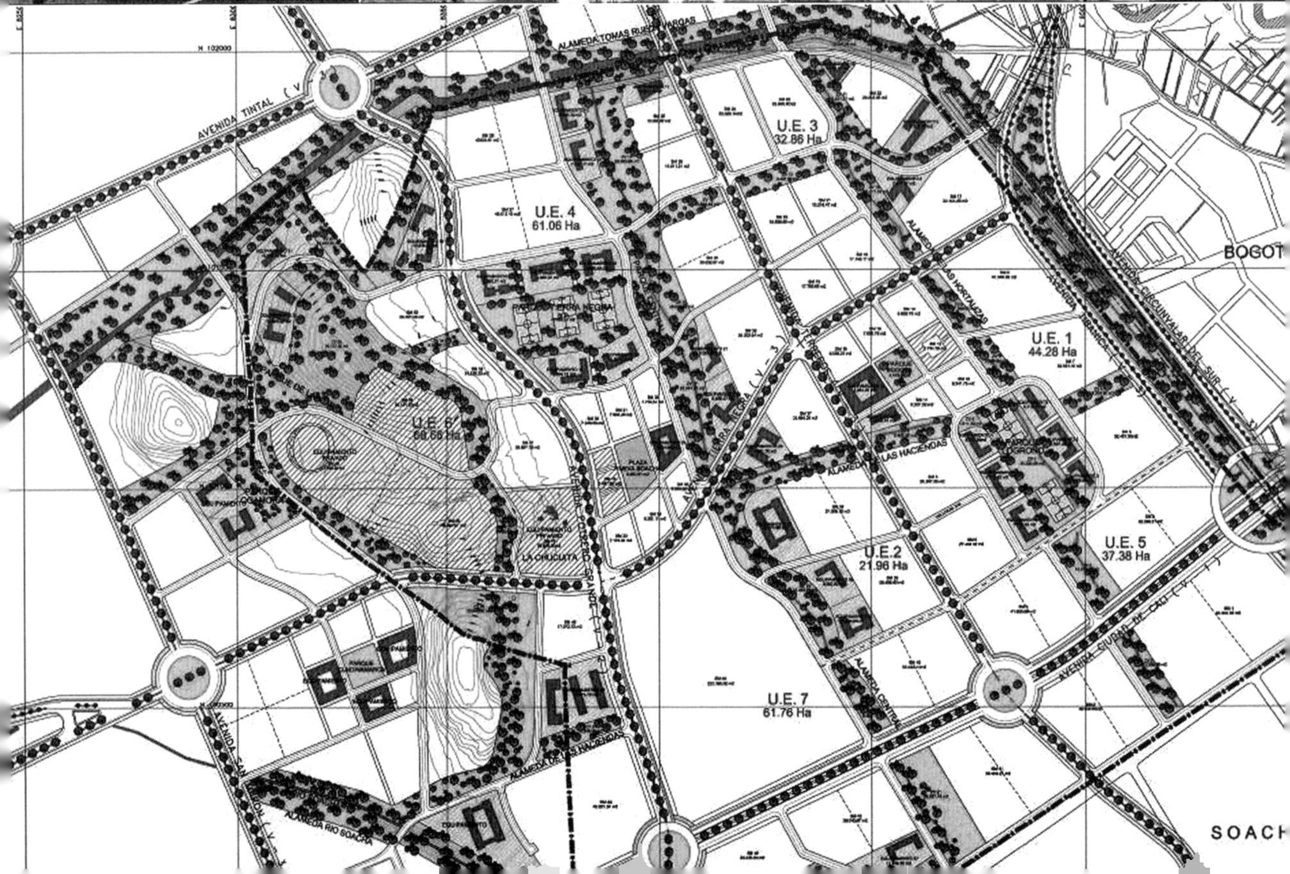
ALAMEDA TOMAS RUEDA VARGAS
AVENIDA TINTAL
U.E. 3
32.86 Ha
U.E. 4
61.06 Ha
U.E. 1
44.28 Ha
ALAMEDA LAS HACIENDAS
U.E. 5
37.38 Ha
U.E.2
21.96 Ha
U.E. 7
61.76 Ha
AVENIDA CIUDAD DE CALI
ALAMEDA RIO SOACHA

3 LAND: A SCARCE RESOURCE

EDUARDO ROJAS

Affordable Urban Land and the Prevention of Informal Settlements

It has been argued, with good reason, that neighbourhood upgrading programmes, by providing infrastructure and services and regularising tenure of illegally occupied lands, condone informal settlements. Indeed, some say the mere existence of such programmes can encourage new invasions. Integrated urban policies to improve the quality of life in informal settlements should therefore include measures to inhibit the further expansion of these settlements—that is, to prevent new families from increasing the numbers that already live in precarious conditions and without basic services.

Unfortunately, the local agencies that are in the best position to control the formation of new settlements often do not have the authority to do so. This is especially true of housing policies, which in many countries are the responsibility of a sector ministry of the central government. Chapter 1 of this volume argues that informal settlements proliferate in cities because the formal housing sector fails to provide basic dwellings for the whole population. Indeed, in the majority of countries in the Latin American and Caribbean (LAC) region, the formal economy has been able to provide housing for only a portion of the population, since fewer than 40 percent of households have sufficient income to purchase or lease a finished house produced by the formal sector. The public sector has not adequately addressed this problem, mainly because traditional solutions such as the direct construction, financing, and distribution of affordable housing are so expensive.

New approaches are clearly needed. One such approach involves improving the way the housing sector functions while expanding public support for households that cannot resolve their housing needs in the formal market. Chile, for example, has had notable success with this strategy over the past 30 years (MINVU, 2004). Since 1998 the government has built more homes than new households require, thus reducing the housing shortage and the waiting period for low-income families to obtain formal housing (Rojas, 2001); this, in turn, has essentially ended the practice of illegally occupying land for housing. Moreover, neighbourhood

Upper picture

Subdividing land in partnership with the private sector allows the state to obtain urbanised land for social housing and other public uses. **Lands included in the Ciudad Verde macroproject, Soacha, in metropolitan Bogota, Colombia**

Lower picture

The integrated planning and implementation of investments in infrastructure, parks, and urban services ensure a better quality of life for residents and promotes mixed-income neighbourhoods. **Plan for the Ciudad Verde macroproject, Soacha, in metropolitan Bogota, Colombia**

Public support for incremental construction of houses must focus on the components that residents have trouble building: baths, kitchens, and stairs.
Quinta Monroy, Iquique, Chile

upgrading programmes that have been in place since 1986 have almost completely solved the problem of informal settlements, which according to some estimates will be eradicated by 2010.

The conditions under which the housing sector operates and public housing policies do not always help the cities solve their problems. Several LAC countries have not adopted housing policies to support the development of the housing markets or modify their public housing programmes in a significant way. Consequently, many households in these countries still lack formal housing and are forced to access serviced residential land through informal means or invade lands and then build incrementally.

Until the formal housing sector succeeds in satisfying the needs of the entire population, it will be necessary to adopt measures to prevent the proliferation of informal settlements. One promising strategy is to speed up and streamline the incremental building process by which needy households—particularly those living in informal settlements—acquire housing. An analysis of incremental housing construction reveals two activities that, with sufficient support, can make the process less burden-

Public support leads to better results in incremental home building and allows the beneficiaries to expand their homes based on the components provided with the core unit.
Quinta Monroy, Iquique, Chile

some for families: providing access to serviced residential land and supporting the construction of a basic shelter. This chapter centres on the first of these two activities. For further details on the second, see Greene and Rojas (2007).

The best way to reduce the number of informal settlements is to increase the availability of serviced residential land to low-income households. This means, first and foremost, making it more affordable through public intervention, as prior experience indicates that land sold on the open market is not accessible to the poorest population (Smolka, 2005). In the first part of this chapter, Smolka and Larangeira analyse the ways in which this strategy may be carried out in the LAC region, underlining both their merits and their limitations. They highlight programmes that reduce urban planning regulations to allow for subdivisions with smaller lot sizes, fewer services, and lower costs—such as the Areas of Special Social Interest (AEIS, in its Portuguese acronym) allowed by Brazilian legislation—but conclude that these measures are not enough to solve the problem. Rather, the authors argue that a sustainable solution requires interventions in urban land markets that induce the urban landowners and real estate developers to sell low-cost serviced land. According to Smolka and Larangeira, the conversion of land for urban uses generates large capital gains, some of which should be channelled towards the production of land for social housing. To achieve this, states should use a combination of tax instruments (updated appraisals of property for tax purposes; betterment and capital gains taxes) and planning tools such as land use norms that would force those who subdivide the land to reserve part of it for public uses. Public-private partnerships should also be developed so that the state could take advantage of the capital gains derived from the changes of land uses.

Two of these approaches are described in the following sections: the first case study relates the experience of the "social urbaniser" a programme implemented in Porto Alegre, Brazil, and the second shows how low-cost subdivisions were developed by private enterprises in El Salvador. Although low-cost residential land was produced in both cases, each strategy presents specific problems.

A social urbaniser is a generic name for a private real estate developer dedicated to the subdivision of land based on standards negotiated with the public sector. The social urbaniser makes an agreement with the municipality to discontinue illegal land subdivision practices in exchange for flexible norms—agreed upon by all parties—that permit a decrease in the development costs of designated parcels of land. These flexible norms are part of Porto Alegre's Urban Development Plan and operate under the aegis of the City Statute Act. The statute permits the designation of AEIS, where the subdivision of land with reduced urban services is authorised in order to decrease the cost of producing legally serviced residential land and discourage illegal occupation. In these areas, social urbanisers and landowners may devote a significant part of their land to social housing while keeping the remainder in the formal commercial housing market. However, as subdivisions consolidate and the urbanised areas improve their connectivity to the city, social urbanisers tend to produce serviced land for higher-income households.

By contrast, the *lotificadores* (land developers) of El Salvador, taking advantage of the opportunities offered by a hole in the legislation that does not regulate the subdivision of agricultural parcels, subdivide rural, minimally serviced land close to cities. The lots are then sold to low-income households through rental-purchase contracts. While these developers satisfy the housing needs of some lower-income households in the short term, they also cause significant urban and land tenure problems. The lots are mostly located on rural land, with poor access to the cities and inadequate infrastructure. Moreover, they are delivered without full land titles, so the ownership of the subdivided land is often in dispute.

Preventing the proliferation of informal settlements through the development of low-cost, serviced residential land clearly presents significant challenges. The authors of this chapter stress the need for this activity to be carried out as part of an integrated urban development policy, one that protects the environment, ensures that residents of the new neighbourhoods have adequate access to the city, and provides the necessary infrastructure and public spaces. In other words, to ensure the quality of life for the new tenants, the small initial investment made in these low-income neighbourhoods by the developers should be supplemented by public investments in areas under the jurisdiction of the urban government. Such investments could be financed by capturing some of the capital gains generated by the urbanisation of rural land—currently, the landowners and illegal land developers are the only ones to benefit from the difference in value. As the authors of this chapter argue, the integrated implementation of this type of instrument offers an opportunity to gain scale in preventing the spread of informal settlements and regularise those that already exist.

MARTIM SMOLKA and
ADRIANA DE ARAUJO
LARANGEIRA

Gaining Ground

Informality is a growing phenomenon in the majority of LAC cities, and while urban poverty is a leading cause of it, other factors exacerbate the problem. These include the high price of serviced residential land in urban land markets, the reduced scale of public housing programmes over recent decades, and the growth of illegal urban developments due to the insufficient enforcement of land use plans. Thus, despite increased investments in infrastructure in recent years and an upsurge in neighbourhood upgrading and land tenure regularisation programmes, informality continues to spread in the LAC region. The cases in this chapter offer at least two explanations for this trend: (i) these programmes would be efficient, but not effective to cope with the magnitude of the problem; or (ii) they are not only ineffective but they deepen the informality, prompting further illegal occupations by increasing settlers' expectation that their neighbourhoods' infrastructural deficiencies will be solved by the government. In the latter interpretation, these solutions become part of the problem—that is, the upgrading of informal neighbourhoods and land tenure regularisation processes become part of the reproductive cycle of informality in cities (Smolka, 2003).

Although neighbourhood upgrading programmes have brought about tangible improvements in the living conditions in some settlements, these local improvements do not necessarily extend to the city as a whole or provide long-term solutions. They do not introduce substantive changes in the mechanisms for accessing citizenship rights, alter the operation of the real estate market, or lead to increased access to serviced urban land with adequate infrastructure and housing at a scale that covers the demand. Rather, only a small part of the qualitative housing deficit is reduced within specific areas. Indisputably, these programmes have been far more effective than previous programmes designed to eradicate informal settlements. Nevertheless, these interventions have not accomplished their objective of socially and economically integrating the neighbourhoods into the city, or benefiting cities as a whole.

In summary, the neighbourhood upgrading programmes present a paradox: on the one hand, they improve the portions of the city that benefit from the regularisation projects, but on the other hand, they lead to a deterioration of living conditions of the urban community more generally by encouraging more irregular settlements and siphoning away public resources from other precarious areas of the city. Chapter 4 analyses this latter problem by highlighting a case in Uruguay. In short, despite the range of strategies employed in the LAC countries to stop the practice, the informal use and occupation of urban land continue to impact the growth of cities in many ways. A reassessment of these strategies is therefore in order.

New Strategies

The process of reinstating democracy in the LAC region in the 1980s and 1990s and the revision of the institutional and legal frameworks of these countries allowed the emergence of urban management processes more in sync with democratic objectives to increase access to citizenship in a broad sense. In some countries, individual property rights were subordinated to the social or collective function of land, while at the same time the rights of the residents of the informal settlements to remain in the areas they had originally occupied were more widely recognised. Concurrently, urban development decision making was decentralised, and local administrations gained recognition as entities capable of managing housing and urban issues. The traditional viewpoint that the public sector had sole responsibility for social housing was also challenged, opening up possibilities for public-private cooperation and helping to put to rest the erroneous perception that low-income housing is a non-profit niche in the real estate market—as is documented later in this chapter, informal and illegal land developers operated with a virtual monopoly in this market for decades and extracted large profits.

Fiscal instruments began to be used in urban policy to correct the imperfections of land markets and ensure the sustainability of legal land development options capable of competing with informal ones. A better understanding of the impact of urban development regulations on the operation of land markets has helped to dispel false convictions, such as the supposed housing price reductions that would result from the reduction of urban development and building standards, although some of these still persist. Interventions that anticipate the spread of informality offer more positive results than those that address settlements that already exist, especially when they are proactive strategies that improve the operation of the urban land markets, help in developing new alliances, use the existing regulatory frameworks, and seek alternative sources of financing for urban development.

The False Dilemma of Urbanisation versus Land Titling

During the past decade, urban development interventions in Latin America and the Caribbean have addressed the problems of informality from two angles: (i) through programmes that emphasise the provision of infrastructure and urban services to the neighbourhoods and (ii) through programmes that focus on regularisation of land tenure or titling. These initiatives need not be mutually exclusive.

The Origin of the Dichotomy

A new (and false) dichotomy has recently arisen between urbanisation and land titling, which stems from several sources. One is the belief that "the lack of infrastructure and services and the difficulties encountered in overcoming this (shortages) are, even more than insecure tenure, the main criteria for defining irregular settlements" (Durand-Lasserve, 1996: 18). Another dichotomy is the current perception (although not demonstrated) that regularisation of land tenure is an essential condition to expand the market in cities and stimulate the urban economy, while yet another is the sense that programmes that provide significant solutions in urban development and the security of land tenure simultaneously cannot be implemented integrally. As yet, however, none of these assumptions has proved to be true.

For example, the titling programme in Peru—promoted by the *Organismo de Formalización de la Propiedad Informal* (COFROPI, a state commission to regularise informal property)—delivered more than one million titles between 1996 and 2004.[17] But an analysis of the programme by Calderon (2007) indicates that, in practice, the regularisation of land tenure has not facilitated access to creditors or more generally improved the quality of life of the low-income households that received titles. Although such results are not expected to be immediate, it is surprising that after four years of operation (when 76 percent of the titles had already been distributed), fewer than 3 percent of those holding titles had obtained bank loans using the titled real estate as a guarantee. Although the titles were legally registered, no further individual or public investments were made in the property, and so the settlements remained as physically precarious, socially excluded, and spatially segregated from the formal cities as they were before the titling took place. Thus, the programme did not achieve one of its key objectives, that of integrating the informal settlers into the formal economy of the city. The "mystery of capital", as predicted by De Soto (2000), was not revealed.

Argentina's land regularisation programme, *Programa Arraigo*, obtained similar results by granting titles to fiscal lands to de facto occu-

---

[17] This figure is remarkable when considering the modest number of titles issued by the majority of the land titling programmes in the LAC region.

piers. As in Peru, there is no proof that the regularisation of land tenure had an effect on urban development or urban and social integration. Only when a variant of the original model was adopted—one that included urban, social, and economic development components in addition to land titling—were improvements registered. In other words, the integration of the settlement into the formal city was the result of the effective investment and management of public resources, which provided infrastructure and services, not the result of the actions of the beneficiaries triggered by the regularisation of land tenure (Basualdo, 2007); again, the "mystery of capital" was not revealed. Nevertheless, it is not easy to replicate this experience, as will be demonstrated in this volume.

Just as the programmes dedicated exclusively to land titling produced scarce results when compared to their original objectives, alternative neighbourhood upgrading programmes were also ineffective in deterring the growth of informality. Thus, the objective of integrated interventions encompassing the legal, environmental, social, urban, and physical dimensions of the problem seems weakened, allowing for the emphasis to oscillate between the improvement of living conditions and the regularisation of land tenure. This creates an apparent tension, as if the two sides are irreconcilable and do not pertain to the same phenomenon.

A Precarious Sustainability

At the opposite extreme from land titling, Paraguay focused on the material aspects of the housing problem in its urban development policy.[18] But although progress was made, especially in terms of broadening participation in the decision-making process, the results were not impressive. During the 16 years that this housing policy was in effect (1991–2007), only 17,000 residential units were produced, while the need was estimated at 300,000 units. Moreover, a significant number of units were delivered to the beneficiaries without perfected titles, creating a new path to informality and urban decay (Flores, 2007). Because their land tenure status was uncertain, some residents stopped making their mortgage payments and many of the homes ended up in a condition of informality—abandoned or neglected.[19]

At the same time, officials are often consumed by the fear that the expulsion-succession (gentrification) process will have a negative effect on the beneficiaries. As a result, they expend an enormous amount of effort ensuring that the original beneficiaries remain in the homes that

---

[18] The Paraguayan housing policies include a number of initiatives, including the urbanisation of informal settlements, the delivery of finished houses, support for incremental housing construction, construction of residential units (urban and rural), cooperative housing, and direct housing subsidies.

[19] In Paraguay, revisions to the rules of legal ownership have been suggested but have not been implemented; for example, in the case of *usucaption*, 20 years of quiet possession is still required in order to recognise the rights of the possessors.

Settlement upgrading programmes often include an expandable core unit.
Settlement upgrading project in Rosario, Argentina

were financed by the regularisation programmes. Controls on the buying and selling of real estate in these areas are applied to little or no effect, as if the key question were the spatial mobility of the population rather than the difficulty (or impossibility) of accessing formal housing solutions.

Plenty for a Few or a Little for Everyone?

Those who seek to fix the problem of informal settlements with limited resources have several options to choose from. One is to universalise land titling at a low cost; this would legalise the settlements but would not solve the problems of housing quality, urban integration, social inclusion, or economic development. Another option is to devote all resources to the integral improvement of a few selected areas, but this would not have a significant impact on the entire city. A third alternative is to implement partial improvements in all informal settlements; this would narrow the vast differences in infrastructure, urban equipment, and services among urban areas, thereby narrowing the differences in real estate prices and leading to a more balanced operation of the land markets. In all three cases, however, one must overcome a serious obstacle to their implementation: the limited institutional management capacity of most LAC city governments.

As discussed previously, municipalities should not have to choose between land titling programmes and neighbourhood upgrading programmes, for when they are employed together, the two types of programmes are complementary. For example, Esquina, Argentina, a province of Corrientes, took part in the *Programa Arriago*, but in this case other components were added to land titling (Basualdo, 2007). Besides granting each family access to a serviced lot that is reasonably connected to the city, the implementing agency offered programmes to supplement income, improve skills, and develop cooperatives, along with health and education services. This collaborative effort is exemplary with respect to the management of urban regularisation and land tenure processes, as it connected the inhabitants with opportunities available in their physical and institutional milieu. It was made possible through the integration of existing programmes executed by different levels of the government—national, provincial, and local. Such integration generated positive synergies that explain, to a great extent, the project's success. But like the majority of the LAC programmes, it was implemented on a small scale, assisting only 52 households in need.

Legal Limitations and Management Potential

Urban legislation has long been an object of criticism. First, it often supports standards that do not reflect the realities of the majority of the population, thus becoming an instrument of exclusion and socio-spatial segregation (Maricato, 1996). Second, it inadequately fulfils the needs of the city and the society as a whole, thereby being bypassed by the poor (who invade the land or purchase informal subdivisions) and the rich (who build more than is allowed according to the building regulations or occupy land that is not designated for urban uses) (Bentes, 2003).

Regulatory frameworks that do not account for social needs have thus contributed to the expansion, rather than the reduction, of informality, although decades of social mobilisation for urban reform have recently brought about some improvement. Colombia and Brazil, for instance, have a wide array of new instruments included in the 1997 Land Development Law (388/97) and 2001 City Statute, respectively. Nevertheless, legislation alone cannot increase access to urban land and housing for those in need. Even in countries or cities in which the legislation has been revised, it is still taboo to recognise and negotiate with informal land developers or non-governmental organisations (NGOs) that promote the occupation of public land—in official declarations, these agents are abstractly referred to as "implementation obstacles".

In Brazil, 13 years elapsed between the promulgation of the 1988 Federal Constitution and the approval of the 2001 City Statute, which regulates the articles of the constitution dedicated to the urban development

Coordinated management of land by the private and public sectors can make a significant contribution to preventing informal settlements.
Informal settlement in Tegucigalpa, Honduras

policy. Four years later, in 2005, the instrument of collective "usucaption" (to acquire by prescription) was put into practice for the first time.[20] But even with this widely favourable legal framework in place, some Brazilian land regularisation programmes still maintain a hesitant and uncreative relationship with the new legislation, which is evident in the case of *Morar Legal* (a land titling and property regularisation programme in informal subdivisions in Rio de Janeiro) that relies mostly on traditional land titling procedures that are slow and costly (Jesús, Veríssimo, and Pereira, 2007). There are untapped opportunities available with the approved but unutilised instruments.

---

[20] On May 31, 2005, the association of the residents of Vila Mangete, Olinda, and Pernambuco obtained a favourable ruling of collective *usucaption* (process No. 2003.008384–4) under the terms established by the 2001 City Statute (Ministério das Cidades, 2005).

Some instruments implemented previous to Brazil's 2001 City Statute have been similarly underutilised. For example, the Special Areas of Social Interest (AEIS), in its preventive connotation, allows special urban planning parameters for low-cost land development.[21] But by and large, local administrations failed to take advantage of their legislative and management capabilities—for example, to define the urban fringe or to stimulate urban growth through urban planning and fiscal instruments—to solve and prevent problems generated by informal settlements. Generally, these administrations limit themselves to maintaining the status quo, going outside the plans (when plans exist) only to deal with specific demands or emergency situations. In so doing, they waste resources and make few lasting improvements

Still today, few initiatives provide serviced land for housing on terms that are compatible with the effective demand (that is, the needs and purchasing power) of low-income urban households.[22] And yet the instruments to fulfil this objective are available. The experience of Diadema in São Paulo, Brazil, demonstrates not only the potential of the AEIS but also the difficulties and limitations in its application. Baltrusis (2007) demonstrates how the same instrument could have a role in both the success and failure of a programme, and analyses the variables that determine each of these outcomes. Success factors include designating the illegally occupied area as an AEIS, using the instrument appropriately to solve problems in the area, and having an effective facilitator managing the dialogue between the interest groups and local administration. Gathered around a negotiation table, landowners, representatives of the pro-housing social movements, and representatives of the local administration were able to find solutions. Failure factors—in the same jurisdiction, but in different times and places—had less to do with the nature of the instrument than with ineffective management.

New Sources of Financing

It is important to emphasise that local administrations have latent resources at hand, including financial resources that can be mobilised to help solve the problem of informality. The social urbaniser programme in Porto Alegre, Brazil, illustrates a viable option. Instead of punishing the developers of informal subdivisions through the legal system (an initiative attempted as many times as it has failed), the programme taps their knowledge and managerial capacity. Moreover, rather than simply sus-

---

[21] This legislation also has a remedial connotation as it allows flexible subdivision standards to regularise land tenure in favelas and consolidated illegal settlements in a vast number of Brazilian municipalities. There are 755 municipalities with AEIS legislation in place (IBGE, 2001).

[22] Exceptions include the experiences of Belo Horizonte, Brazil, through the implementation of Law 8.137/00 (concerning parcelling, land use, and occupation) signed on December 21, 2000, and Santo André, Brazil, which incorporated low-cost land subdivisions in its 2005 Municipal Housing Plan.

pending the informal activity, the programme enables and formalises it, opening the way to the production of formal housing solutions.

A social urbaniser is a registered private real estate developer who has an interest in developing areas identified by the municipal administration as suitable for low-income housing. The conditions in which these developers operate are negotiated from the start of a project to guarantee that their operations lead to the supply of lots at prices that are accessible to the target population. In essence, the public sector allows private developers to provide infrastructure and services incrementally and at standards lower than those required in the rest of the city in exchange for offering land at affordable prices—that is, prices that are comparable to those for lots without adequate services and infrastructure offered in the informal market.

This is a complex operation because it requires a legal mechanism that regulates the involvement of the public sector in an essentially private undertaking, the establishment of special lines of credit for the final buyers and the financing of the infrastructures, and the introduction of community control mechanisms on the quality of the products offered. The operation is viable due to the improved efficiency brought about by the involvement of the public sector, which allows for the expansion of the scope of the interventions both horizontally (geographically) and vertically (attributes and coverage); the reduction of risks, due to the previous registration of the potential buyers; and the anticipation and redistribution of capital gains that otherwise would exclusively benefit the illegal developers.[23] Through negotiation, a "win-win" situation occurs, in which the real estate developer wins by offering a legal product and not having to operate in secrecy, the occupant wins by receiving a formal lot at the same price as or cheaper than an informal lot, and the public sector wins by orienting development towards high-priority areas that are suitable for immediate occupation, with a reduction of the investment in infrastructure and services.[24]

In a discussion of this experience, Damásio (2007) discredits the theory that simply relaxing the urban development standards would necessarily reduce the final prices of serviced lots. She demonstrates that, in fact, the final prices are not lower on account of their lower quality because the landowner, not the buyer, captures the savings in the production cost. But Damásio (2007) shows that the social urbaniser programme has had an impact by incorporating into the urban policy agenda an understanding of how the informal land market operates and an attempt to reform its structure. This experience complements con-

---

[23] Moreover, it is reasonable to expect that the simple existence of the instrument promotes changes in the behaviour of the urban agents, leading to a decrease in points of conflict that need to be solved through negotiation, among other benefits.

[24] The costs of providing the infrastructure and services ex post (in restorative character) are higher, while the expansion of the networks in more compact areas is more cost efficient.

ventional policies and highlights the need for all urban agents to work together to solve the problem of informality, as it is impossible for the public sector alone to operate at the scale required to satisfy the demand for affordable housing.

A social urbaniser programme of the type implemented in Porto Alegre requires the public sector to accelerate and facilitate the approval of projects and the issuing of construction permits for alternatives to formal housing solutions. In this way, the typical problem of segmentation of the municipal administrative structure may be avoided and the public sector's capacity to regulate and coordinate the urban development process is strengthened. The public sector should locate the projects according to sustainable urban growth principles—that is, in places where infrastructure and services can be expanded and the public-private management capacity developed. Above all, the social urbaniser is an instrument designed to introduce discipline into the land markets and the financing of urban development, gaps that the public sector has traditionally been unable to fill.

The social urbaniser programme in Porto Alegre unfortunately was aborted due to the political-partisan discontinuity in the local administration in the 2004 elections—an ever-present risk for programmes of this kind. In this case, the programme's interruption can be interpreted as a need to affirm the break with the previous administration. Nevertheless, the initiative was already sufficiently advanced to demonstrate the viability of public-private partnerships in the production of serviced lots for the poor population (Smolka and Damásio, 2005). The project was later developed in three municipalities in the same metropolitan region.

Similar to the social urbaniser programme, the mobilisation of capital gains—allowed by the Colombian legislation and applied in the cases of the *Operación Nuevo Usme* in Bogota and the *Macroproyecto de Vivienda* in Pereira—offers an opportunity to generate low-cost land in urban expansion areas where the informal land occupations are concentrated (Maldonado, 2007). In these cases, the landowners (whether they are real estate developers or not) are invited to reap a part—but not all—of the capital gains generated in a large-scale public initiative of urbanisation.[25] If a landowner rejects the offer to participate in the programme, the alternative applies, which is the compulsory acquisition of the land by the public sector at its price before the operation was initiated. The compensation to the landowners who contribute land to the project is determined by the value of their contributions and is paid back with more valuable urban land; the state keeps a part of the land as compensation for its participation in the operation.[26] The municipality can thus regulate city growth,

---

[25] The *Nuevo Usme* operation in Bogotá comprises 900 hectares of new urbanised land in a city of 7 million inhabitants, and the *Macroproyecto* programme in Pereira comprises 155 hectares in a city of 400,000 inhabitants.
[26] This operation involved the use of "land readjustment" techniques that allow the equitable distribution of contributions and benefits.

as well as the land uses and densities in the areas of expansion, tackling the root cause of informality: the lack of serviced land that is sufficiently integrated into the city to satisfy the housing needs of the growing low-income population.

These examples show that it is possible to finance all or a significant part of the urbanisation costs with the difference between the price paid for the rural land incorporated to the city and what is earned in the final sale of serviced lots, even using the competitive prices charged by the informal land developers.[27] In other words, the approach allows for the production of urbanised land at prices similar to—and in some cases even lower than—the prices of illegally urbanised lots that lack services. Moreover, this mechanism is less onerous to the public sector than neighbourhood upgrading, which regularises the land a posteriori.

As previously mentioned, the current mechanisms to produce serviced land for social uses can be characterised as ineffective. On the one hand, there is the "indispensable subsidy" model, which is based on the premise that poor households are unable to access urban services and/or a respectable home without public help. This model does not take into account the resource mobilisation and housing production capacity of the informal economy and does not consider state support in the form of technical assistance, community organisation, the promotion of efficient channels to supply building materials, and, above all, the regulation of the land market—areas in which individual households have little influence.

The experiences analysed emphasise the fact that informality is more a function of public management (or mismanagement) of urban development and the logic of real estate markets than of actual poverty. These experiences also indicate that the capital gains generated in the process of illegal land subdivision—which is practiced regularly in the peripheries of many LAC cities—could almost fully cover the costs of urbanisation ex-ante.[28] Note that there is an ample margin between the minimum price at which formal private agents can offer serviced land and the base price of land that is not serviced. In the current practice in the region, "pirate" land developers absorb this margin as compensation for the risks of operating in informal markets and for the time it takes to recover their profits, since these subdivisions are occupied gradually, "lot by lot", sometimes

---

[27] In the case of *Nuevo Usme*, non-urban land cost between US$1 and US$2 per square metre and informal lots without services cost between US$15 and US$19 per square metre; in other words, there was a mark-up of between US$14 and US$17 per square metre.

[28] The mere transformation, in the legal classification, of rural land to urban land—which does not require an investment—could inflate the price by a factor of three to six, while the transformation of residential land to commercial land leads to price increases from 50 to 110 percent (Smolka, 2005). The subdivision of large farms produces even more pronounced increases in prices per square metre, reaching valuations of around 700 percent. These amounts are not depreciable and can be channelled into investments to improve the quality of life in urban areas, provided that they are captured by the public sector.

over several years. Also, the informal developers are able to capture the amount that the occupants are able and prepared to pay for the freedom of not having to comply with land use and construction regulations.[29] *Operación Nuevo Usme*, *Macroproyecto de Vivienda*, and social urbaniser programmes transform these types of operations into ones that are far more beneficial for households with unsatisfied housing needs and for cities in general.

Cities are confronted with a dilemma: politically they must do something about the informal settlements, but it is clear that the regularisation strategies, at least as they are currently being implemented, are insufficient and unsustainable. The fact that 130 million people in the LAC region live in informal settlements—a figure that does not seem to decrease in spite of the regularisation initiatives—shows that the solution lies beyond regularisation alone. To prevent the formation of informal settlements more effectively, public officials need to take advantage of the "space" created by the distortions of the urban land market and used by the informal operators. The increase in land values associated with occupation, when adequately identified and handled, may be used to subsidise serviced lots for low-income families. In addition, leveraging this increase promotes greater discipline in the land market because it reduces the scope for the manipulation of unearned gains, facilitating negotiation among stakeholders

To be truly innovative, local administrations must overcome their preconceived ideas about both private real estate companies and low-income families. Contrary to popular belief, low-income families do have the ability to pay for developed land, as many already pay a great deal in cash for land without services even with the poor quality of life during the period before the regularisation process takes place. In addition, the administrations will have to develop the technical capability to identify and measure (or negotiate) the increase in land value that results from the urban development process, to capture the capital gains in the sale of the land, and to invest these profits for the benefit of the community. Finally, as part of the future agenda, it is necessary to highlight the role of the local administrations in promoting the use of land management instruments that foster negotiations and allow the convergence of interests in the distribution of the costs and benefits of the urban operations among landowners, the inhabitants of the informal settlements, and the real estate developers.

---

[29] The concept of "freedom not to comply with urban development norms" was coined by Abramo (2003) to explain the market value of the ability to occupy land without abiding with lot size, density, and setback restrictions.

CLÉIA BEATRIZ H.
DE OLIVEIRA and
DENISE BONAT
PEGORARO

Porto Alegre:
The Roles of the Social Urbanisers

This section analyses the characteristics and achievements of the *Projeto Integrado Desenvolvimento Sustentável da Lomba do Pinheiro* (Integrated Sustainable Development Project) of Lomba do Pinheiro, Brazil, which has been in operation since 1998 in the municipality of Porto Alegre. The project is remarkable not only as an example of successful public management but also because it supports alliances between the public and private sectors, making possible the construction of low-cost housing in areas of urban expansion that are attractive to real estate developers. Recognising the need to provide services and generate employment and income opportunities in the peripheral areas of the city—while at the same time protecting the environment—the public sector leads the incorporation of new lands into the city, and in doing so it confronts the problem of informal land occupation in an organised manner. The social urbaniser is an additional tool in such planning efforts. The application of this instrument—which seeks to promote a public-private partnership in the production of housing for the low-income population—offers a new option in constructing the habitat, one that meets both the landowners' and private developers' financial goals and the public sector's urban development objectives.[30]

The work developed through this integrated project—which was made official by the municipality's *Lei de Operação Concertada Urbana Lomba do Pinheiro* (Lomba do Pinheiro Joint Urban Operation Law)—made possible the coordinated intervention of different municipal agencies in implementing the investments required to produce land for social uses in areas suitable for urban uses. The project put into practice new procedures and instruments of urban management that made possible the construction of basic and ancillary infrastructure and urban and community facilities; and, especially, the provision of land for social housing integrating the knowledge and capacities of the private and public actors involved.

The Region of Lomba do Pinheiro

Porto Alegre is the capital of the state of Rio Grande do Sul in Brazil. It is situated in the eastern part of the state and occupies an area of 470 square kilometres (see Map 3.1). It forms part of a metropolitan region made up of 31 municipalities with a total of 3.9 million inhabitants (Municipality

---

[30] The signing of an agreement between the municipality of Porto Alegre and the Lincoln Institute of Land Policy in Cambridge, Massachusetts, in June 2003, to test the viability of the social urbaniser, stimulated this effort. The results show that the landowners and real estate developers operating in the integrated area of the project showed interest in using the special policy guidelines for the occupation and subdivision of land and for the progressive construction of the infrastructure and facilities proposed for urban feasibility.

Map 3.1 Porto Alegre Metropolitan Area, Brazil

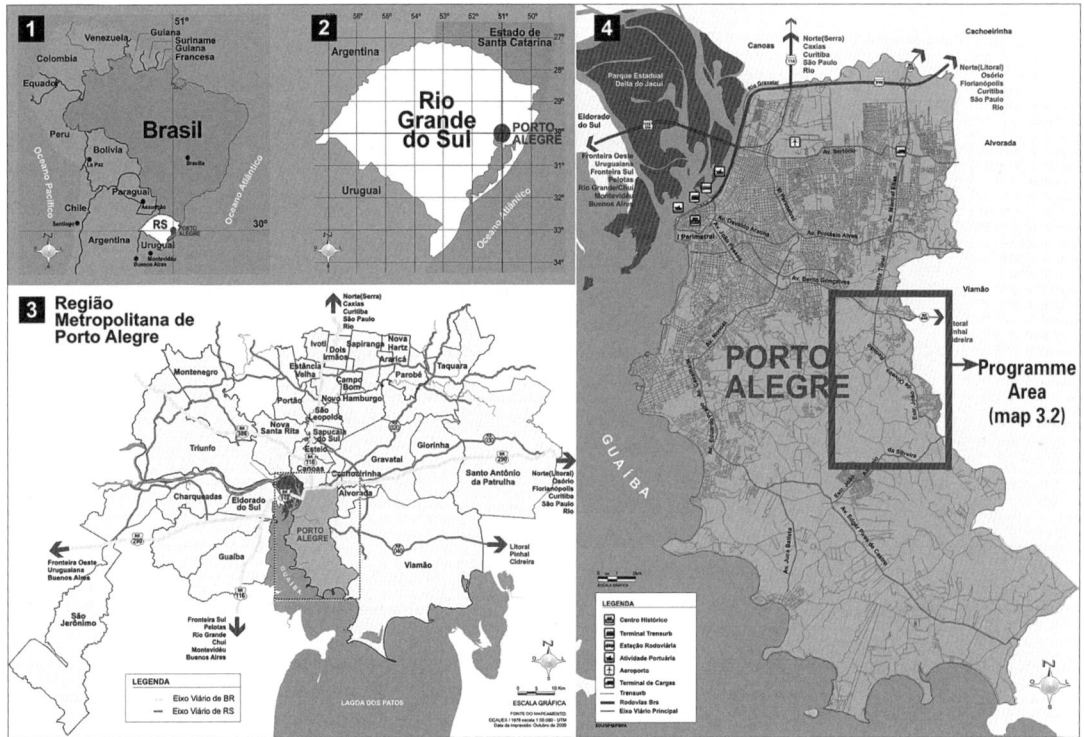

Source: Prefectura Municipal de Porto Alegre (2004).

of Porto Alegre, 2004). Porto Alegre's population is more concentrated in the northern part of the city, which contains major urban facilities such as the airport, highways, and railways. A mountain range creates a natural barrier to urban expansion in the south, and thus much of the land in this area is still in its natural state. In 2004 the city had 736 informal settlements, of which 477 were invasions and 259 were informal land divisions where the land was commercialised. The majority of these settlements are fully occupied and built, although 83 percent of the lots have informal or illegal land tenure.

Loma do Pinheiro is situated in the eastern part of Porto Alegre and borders the municipality of Viamão (see Map 3.2). Comprising approximately 32 square kilometres, this area is dissociated from the compact urban grid and contains natural resources that are important to the city and the metropolitan region. The area has long been occupied by informal residential settlements with inadequate public services (such as basic sanitation) and poor infrastructure; it suffers from environmental degradation, and the risk of natural disasters is high. In 2008 the population of the area was approximately 64,000 inhabitants, made up of low-income

Map 3.2 Location of the Lomba do Pinheiro Area in the Metropolitan Area of Porto Alegre, Brazil

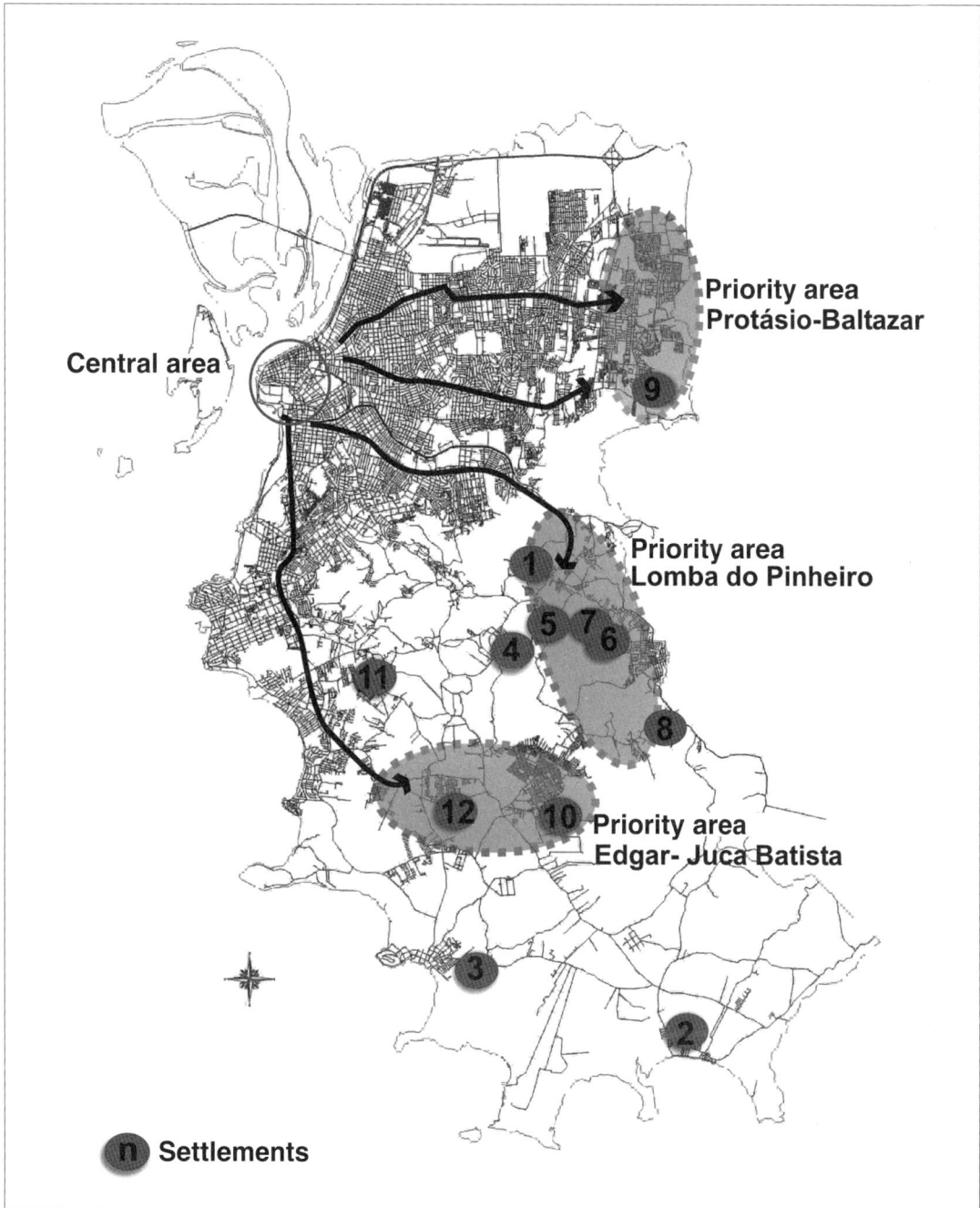

Source: Prefectura Municipal de Porto Alegre (2004).

families mostly from the interior of the state.[31] The average income for the head of household was 2.92 times the minimum wage (US$525 per month in 2009).[32] The rural origin of the population explains the urban morphology of the region, which is made of conventional urban lots with patios where trees are planted and domestic animals are cared for. The buildings are mainly single-family homes, and many are partially constructed or in the process of being upgraded. The community is organised into several neighbour associations, linked to the neighbourhoods formed as a result of the land occupation. These organisations have a long association with the social conquests achieved by the inhabitants of the region. Through community mobilisation in the participatory budgeting processes, the population was able to get the public sector to install basic service networks and make improvements within the neighbourhoods for their to physical integration to the city.[33]

The current situation in Loma do Pinheiro is the result of an occupation process that accelerated with Brazil's rapid urbanisation in the 1960s. Responding to demands for residential land by the low-income population, some landowners divided their land and sold the plots, a practice they found to be more profitable than agricultural production. Another boom in land subdivisions and informal land occupations took place during the 1970s (Municipality of Porto Alegre, 2000). The Urban Development Plan, in force between 1979 and 1999, designated the area for rural use due to its potential for agricultural production, thus outlawing the division of land for urban uses. This legal impediment led to the informal subdivision of the land without respect for urban development standards such as adequate street width; the setting aside of land for public spaces, education and health facilities; and the preservation of natural resources.

Clandestine lots and informal housing solutions proliferated during this period, as low prices for land (due to the illegality of the subdivisions) attracted eager buyers and the public sector did little to stop them. Today there are about 50 informal or illegal settlements in Lomba do Pinheiro, representing approximately 6 percent of the population of the area. But practically all the urban settlements in the area exhibit some form of irregularity. Environmental degradation has been one of its most obvious effects, as the settlements extend to the riverbeds, contaminating the water and creating risks of flooding during periods of heavy rain. The resultant deforestation has also increased the risk of mudslides. The lack of adequate infrastructure is another problem. The illegal real estate developers cut out and sell land without any commitment to providing

---

[31] These figures are drawn from 2000 census data from the Brazilian Institute of Geography and Statistics (IBGE), updated in 2006 by the Municipal Planning and Urban Development Secretariat of Porto Alegre.

[32] These figures are drawn from 2000 census data from the IBGE.

[33] For further details about the participatory budget experience in Porto Alegre and in Brazil in general, see IDB (2005).

infrastructure, such as water and sewerage systems, lighting for public spaces and streets, street paving, and basic facilities like schools, parks, and health-care centres. As the population has increased, these shortcomings have become even more dire, and the incremental provision of infrastructure and services by the public sector since the 1980s has not come close to meeting the needs of the inhabitants.

A Plan to Manage Urban Development

Lomba do Pinheiro still has a significant amount of empty land, some of which has potential for future urban development. Of all the territory considered in the integrated project, around 50 percent is empty and approximately 28 percent is considered eligible for urban uses. What form the development takes is a matter of debate. In areas that are approved by the *Plano Director de Desenvolvimento Urbano Ambiental* (PDDUA) (Environmental and Urban Development Plan) for high-density occupation, developers interested in building social housing will produce regular urban lots to supply the pent-up housing demand of the low-income population of the city. At the same time, the region is also attractive to developers who build housing for middle-income households, which seek to improve their quality of life by moving to larger homes in more peripheral zones of the city.

The Special Project

The special project seeks to strengthen the role of the municipality as a promoter of urban development. The PDDUA allows the municipality to go beyond its traditional role of devising, enacting, and enforcing urban development legislation and become an active social agent in reaching specific urban objectives: in this case, to improve the living conditions of determined urban spaces. The special project requires agreement among landowners, developers, the community, and the municipality to execute interventions based on a detailed knowledge of the territory. Depending on the complexity of the problem it aims to solve, a special project is categorised as priority, first level, or second level. A second-level special project makes possible the study of large urban areas that, because of their peculiarities, characteristics, and conflicts, require creative and integrated solutions with unique and differentiated norms. By contrast, a priority special project is mostly concerned with a limited set of issues affecting a small portion of the territory and a first-level special project mostly with the coordination of public actors.

The Integrated Sustainable Development Project of Lomba do Pinheiro is a second-level special project that implements several instruments of the PDDUA. It represents a significant advance in the management and planning practices of the municipality of Porto Alegre because it enables a detailed and in-depth weighting of the economic, social, and physical characteristics of the region; allows for the articulation of the disparate

Contributions
from private land
developers partially
pay for the cost of the
infrastructure required
to accommodate more
intense uses of the land.
**Infrastructure
construction in Lomba
do Pinheiro, Porto Alegre**

municipal organisations and respective local planning initiatives; and identifies development opportunities that take into account the potential of the territory and the local identities. It is important to emphasise that participatory budgeting has led to the development of new channels of dialogue between the planners and the community. These channels enable citizens to be effective and legitimate participants in the decisions that impact the development of the region to and of the entire city through the discussion of the budget allocation to sector or citywide investments (IDB, 2005).

A New Management Method

The Integrated Sustainable Development Project of Loma do Pinheiro was officially launched in August 1999, with the opening of offices in three municipal schools in the region. These offices served several functions. First, they encouraged local residents to participate in and contribute to the project. Second, they allowed the municipal government to gain a better perspective of the local situation. Third, they helped the municipality to educate the community about the serious conflicts between urbanisation and environmental preservation in the region. Finally, the offices enabled the municipality to help developers find ways to improve the connectivity between the region and the city, strengthen its urban structure, protect the environment, produce new homes, and mobilise necessary financial resources to execute the interventions in the region. These actions, it was hoped, would help to satisfy the repressed demand for housing and create jobs and other sources of income.

The long road travelled by this project can be divided into three main phases. The *first phase* focused on the training of the main actors in the municipality and in conducting the survey of the region. The *second phase* included the formation of the *Grupo do Planejamento Local* (Local Planning Group), which prepared a review of the natural and built environment, including a survey of the perceptions of the population involved in the area, the Rapid Participatory Diagnostics. This review sought to define the capacity of the natural environment to accommodate a variety of urban uses and the capacity of the different built areas to provide urban services. Three thematic axes were analysed:

- *Urban infrastructure*. The existence and condition of basic networks (water, electricity, sanitary, and rain sewerage system) and complementary networks (public transportation, trash collection, paved streets).
- *Urban structure*. The provision of neighbourhood facilities such as schools, nurseries, health centres, and parks.
- *Socioeconomic profile*. Population, income, education level, and residence characterised using data from the 2000 Census of the Brazilian Institute of Geography and Statistics (IBGE).

Four levels of vulnerability were obtained by crossing variables of the natural and built environment, and each level had a different capacity to absorb development and different preservation needs. The resulting environmental vulnerability map provided the basis for defining the suitability of the different areas for urban use, as well as the type and intensity of land uses best suited for each.

The *third phase* included the drafting of the Law of the Joint Urban Project, an urban development model for the region. It set out four principles to guide interventions in the territory:

- Regulate the use of land favouring the occupation of the vacant urban land with measures to discourage land speculation; include land use controls to prevent the destruction of environmental assets.
- Improve the urban planning process, focusing on local economic development and the strengthening of citizens' participation to build mechanisms for organised and coordinated joint action.
- Advance the execution of the environmental policies through strategic planning that reconciles the interests of the different stakeholders.
- Promote changes in the models of urban land production and the consumption of local environmental goods.

The Social Urbaniser[34]

According to the *Plano Diretor de Desenvolvimento Urbano Ambiental* (LC 434/99) (Porto Alegre Master Plan), the social urbaniser is the private real estate company registered in the municipality to undertake urban operations of social interest in urban development areas identified by the public sector. The objective of this instrument is to subdivide land that is suitable for urban use in order to satisfy the demand for housing among low-income households (earning up to five minimum salaries, US$900 per month in 2009). With the goal of reducing the incidence of informal urban development, the social urbaniser can also work with households of other income levels that have acquired lands in the informal land market. This instrument was established by a specific law (Law 9.257 of 2001) and later by detailed rules enacted by municipal decree (Decree 14428 of 2004). For it to reach its full potential, it should be integrated with existing urban policy instruments in the PGUA, such as the *Áreas Urbanas de Ocupação Prioritária* (AUOPS) (priority areas of developed land) and the AEIS, as well as others to be developed, such as value capture.[35]

The social urbaniser programme aims to create a third pathway between the private market and direct public intervention by bringing public and private players together in a joint effort. The Integrated Sustainable Development Project of Lomba do Pinheiro creates adequate conditions for attaining this goal because it does the following:

- Makes possible joint action by the public and private sectors
- Encourages the public sector to assume a proactive role in the management of the urban land development process
- Diversifies the formal mechanisms of private production of serviced lots, making it possible to meet the demands of the population and reduce the appeal of the informal market
- Promotes shared decision making in the approval and execution of the real estate deals

Moreover, it is worth mentioning that the social urbaniser programme promotes changes in the following areas:

- The basic urban policy strategy, which shifts from confronting informal methods of accessing land to incorporating these methods into a managed urban development process

---

[34] The information and data presented here were extracted from the studies of the Social Urbaniser Project that were completed as part of the agreement with the Lincoln Institute of Land Policy. Architect Claudia Damásio also contributed to these studies.

[35] The *Áreas Urbanas de Ocupação Prioritária* (priority occupation areas) are part of the *Áreas Urbanas de Ocupação Intensiva* (high-density development areas), which are set aside for development in the short term, with regulations for their adequate usage (PDDUA, Article 79).

- The role of the public sector, which becomes much more active in addressing irregular development in two ways:
  - In creating an incentive for the occupation of areas that are suitable for the production of housing for the low-income population
  - In offering land at prices that are compatible with the purchasing capacity of the inhabitants who presently have only two options for accessing land—occupying land illegally or acquiring illegally subdivided lots

The Urban Project Consortium of Lomba do Pinheiro

The Urban Project Consortium of Lomba do Pinheiro not only regulates the norms of the use and occupation of the land (urban regimen), but also defines the *Plano de Melhorias* (Urban Improvement Plan),[36] establishes a contract that will regulate the obligations of the investors, and puts together a development committee in Loma do Pinheiro to execute the plan.[37] The Urban Project Consortium complements other instruments, such as the sector development plans and the investment programmes funded by the municipal budget: the *Fundo de Desenvolvimento Urbano Municipal* (Urban Development Municipal Fund), with the capacity to finance housing policy;[38] the *Reserva de Solo* (Land Bank), which allocates land for social facilities and housing programmes; and others, such as the *Direito Real de Uso* (Land Occupation Rights Grant), the *Imposto sobre a Propriedade Predial e Territorial Urbana* (IPTU) (Urban Land Tax), or the *Índice de Aproveitamento* (Floor Area Ratio) and *Solo Criado* (Purchased Floor Area Ratio).

In order to attract investors, the municipality offered two different urban development regimes under the consortium: the basic land development allowance consistent with the existing conditions in a given area, and the maximum land development potential allowable if investors executed the necessary investments to sustain the more intense uses of the land. Developers' contributions are in amounts proportionate to the increase in real estate value of the land due to the change in land use. Instead of just changing the regulations to increase the development potential of the areas suitable for urban use, the project allows more intense development of the land in exchange for urban improvements paid for by the developers and calculated as a portion of the real estate value generated by the change in

---

[36] Along with the integrated diagnosis of Lomba do Pinheiro, parameters were established to promote urban structural transformations, social improvements, and the protection of the environmental assets. This diagnosis identifies the areas lacking urban and community facilities and proposes incentives for the occupation of areas that are suitable for urban use. These areas are provided with urban development regulations that are appropriate for the sustainable use and occupation of the land, as well as the facilities needed for the population density proposed.

[37] According to the Law of the Urban Project Consortium of Lomba do Pinheiro, the committee should be composed of representatives of the municipal government, members of civil society, and residents of the area.

[38] This capacity is based on the terms established in Chapter IV, Title V of the Organic Law of the Municipality of Porto Alegre.

land use. This is a mechanism to make social interest projects viable. The Urban Project Consortium is the result of a wide debate over existing problems, whether physical, social, or economic in character, and of the search for solutions that are compatible with the interests of the different parties involved. These agreements are included in a contract signed by the stakeholders. This legal structure, the first of its nature in Porto Alegre, allows the public sector to take the initiative and implement the urban transformations that are needed to promote an environmentally sustainable urban development process, opening spaces for the construction of social housing along with houses for sale in the regular market.

These social, economic, and territorial development proposals and their execution mechanisms are the culmination of years of planning, with the participation of the local community. The benefits of the Integrated Sustainable Development Project of Lomba do Pinheiro are clear. The municipality now has a stronger presence in the region and is in a closer dialogue with the civil society. Residents' self-esteem has increased (as told by their growing involvement in the yearly participatory budgeting processes), while the number of informal land subdivisions has decreased. But several unexpected effects of the Social Urbaniser Programme counterweight this positive outcome, as many of the new regular subdivisions of Loma do Pinheiro are sold to households with greater purchasing power.

This is yet more evidence that the city must strive to keep formal subdivisions open to the low-income population by using the planning and fiscal tools available to it to intervene in the land development process. It is difficult to articulate and guide opposing economic interests, which in the end always respond to forces that favour the private appropriation of public investments. In order to prevent the urban development and occupation of Lomba do Pinheiro from unfolding in a predatory and exclusive manner, it is necessary that the process adhere to rules that safeguard public interest from private interest, granting the low-income population access to lands that are developed in an environmentally sustainable way. In short, the process should seek to:

- Strengthen the role of the public sector as the manager of urban development processes
- Establish institutional mechanisms that guarantee that the public interest prevails over the private interest
- Reach consensus that the social, economic, and environmental sustainability of urban development is a responsibility to be shared by all social actors
- Promote the production of social housing as a collective commitment of all agents involved in making the city
- Differentiate the right to build from the right to own property
- Establish institutional mechanisms that ensure the fair distribution of development costs and benefits among beneficiaries
- Capture and redistribute the land value appreciation that results from public action

The Urban Improvement Plan contemplates building trunk infrastructure for the Lomba do Pinheiro Region. **Main sewer construction, Porto Alegre**

The contributions of the general guidelines set out by the *Estatuto da Cidade* (Statute of the City) (Federal Law No 10.257 de 2001) related to the Urban Project Consortium are significant. To make these principles and guidelines effective, it is necessary to deal with the process of urbanising Lomba do Pinheiro in its entirety, anticipating the increases in value generated by public investments and by changes in land use and building regulations. This would allow the community to appropriate at least part of the value generated by changes in urban land use regulations. In sum, the objective is to set off an urbanisation process in which the capital gains generated by urban development help finance the provision of infrastructure and services throughout the territory, while allowing low-income households access to developed land for residential use via the formal market.

Organisers of the Social Urbaniser Programme planned that it be implemented in discreet stages. This is important given that the programme will outlive three municipal administrations. In its first stage, the programme will make possible the construction of more than 10,000 lots for residential use through the Social Urbaniser Law. But this does not solve the problem of how to modify the system of incentives affecting the participants in the Urban Project Consortium, strongly influenced by the expected appreciation of the land, without closing off access to the city's poor. The solution lies in requiring developers to pay for changes in the land use and building regulations, as foreseen in the Statute of the City and the Urban Project Consortium. The aim is to try to recuperate for society as much of the increment in land prices generated by public investment. To achieve this goal, a detailed investigation of commercial land prices in the region was made in November 2004. These prices were considered a reference point in the calculation of the increment in value generated by changes in land use and building regulations. They were also used to create the basis for negotiations between real estate investors and landowners interested in benefiting from the maximum development potential of their land allowed by the land use regulations.[39]

Investors who want to subdivide land or build houses for higher-income households, commercial real estate, and other for-profit services must contribute to financing public works. The increased production of urbanised lots for low-income housing is one of the expected benefits of this initiative. This process does not prevent the generation of profit from private investments; but it allocates part of the real estate gains to finance collective goods. The potential social and environmental benefits, in addition to expected profits, are significant incentives to convert these undertakings into extremely successful urban development investments.

The Urban Project Consortium is quite different from most urban development models. It does not focus exclusively on the regularisation of land tenure or the compensation of at-risk populations (although such goals are integral to the project), but is a structural component in the urban development investment process. Accordingly, the consortium creates the conditions for the landowners to contribute to the urban investments contemplated in the Urban Improvements Plan based on the land valuation. The consortium also sets up a favourable environment in which to develop social housing.

The consolidation of Lomba do Pinheiro into a diversified, environmentally sustainable neighbourhood with residents from different social groups certainly has the potential to attract investors. Diversified land use, including residences for middle- and upper-middle-income households, as well as commercial land uses—which are important for the provision of services and the creation of jobs and income—is necessary for the financial viability of private investments. An urban development plan with this profile will prevent the formation of ghettos, as it will not create new areas where the poor are segregated. But for the idea to become reality, the local government must counteract the real estate market's tendency to favour the construction of houses for the middle class, thus maintaining the social objectives of the urban operation.

---

[39] The Lincoln Institute of Land Policy and the Municipality of Porto Alegre executed this study.

VERÓNICA RUIZ # El Salvador: Land Subdivision (Lotificación)

The subdivision of minimally serviced land to be sold for residential use at a low cost—a process known as *lotificación* and executed by private businesses in El Salvador—has facilitated land access for families with incomes of less than two minimum salaries (US$177 in 2009). The developers provide loans under a rental-purchase agreement for up to 15 years, with monthly payments that oscillate between US$12 and US$60. Most lots are not initially connected to urban services, with the idea that such services will be added incrementally, mostly through public investment. The supply of land at prices affordable to low-income households has been possible due to agrarian reform and the decreased price of coffee, which have reduced the earning potential of agricultural land. On the other hand, the demand for urban land has increased with the massive internal migration during and following the armed conflict that took place in El Salvador in the 1980s.

The market response to the demand for low-cost land suitable for housing took place outside urban development regulations. The responsible institutions could not control the phenomenon, resulting in the proliferation of informal settlements in periurban and rural areas with little or no access to required services. While such subdivisions allowed many people in El Salvador access to housing, they were for a long time left with poor sanitary conditions and little access to services. Such deficiencies in infrastructure and services generated environmental problems and overcrowding in adjacent neighbourhoods.

The phenomenon has created a significant challenge for the government. It is estimated that in 2008, one out of every three Salvadorians lived in lots that had been incrementally developed. Increased subdivision activity has led to the disorderly expansion of cities into areas not designated as suitable for urban development. Moreover, the indiscriminate use of incremental development has created a proliferation of informal settlements that lack social integration and adequate living conditions. Uncontrolled by enforced regulations, this phenomenon has left households with insecure tenure, a problem that has been difficult to resolve due to the complexity of the matter and relevant legal restrictions.

The next section provides a general overview of the land subdivision process, its causes, and its impact on the housing situation in El Salvador. It is based on data elaborated by the government in efforts to quantify the land subdivision market, and it describes the strategies and programmes underway to resolve the problem from both a technical and legal standpoint.

The Land Subdivision Market

Origin

PHOTO: VERÓNICA RUIZ

Cheap land for housing.
Advertising lots for sale in El Salvador

The land subdivision market has two historic sources. First, the rapid population growth of the 1950s, 1960s, and 1970s triggered an increase in overall population density, particularly in the metropolitan area of San Salvador (MASS). This was accompanied by rapid urbanisation during the period of armed conflict (1980–1992), which forced thousands of families to concentrate in the MASS. In the early 1980s, the number of illegal subdivisions began to increase and spread not only into city peripheries, but also into the areas around highways. The transfer of land in the successive phases of the agrarian reform and the resettling of populations following peace agreements contributed to the complexity of the problem. Second, after 1989 policies of economic liberalisation and reduced government intervention impacted housing policies, with the private sector taking the lead role in the provision of social housing. The peace agreements were followed by strong economic growth and a subsequent period of stagnation as better macroeconomic discipline was established, the economy was pegged to the dollar of the United States of America, and the country was rapidly integrated into the global economy.

Land subdivisions are difficult to quantify, as they occur throughout the country and have varied impacts. Among their benefits, they have resolved the problem of housing for thousands of low-income families who may not have had the opportunity to acquire houses through the formal housing market. Also, they have resolved the economic difficulties of many farmers who lacked viable options to reconvert their agricultural activities into more profitable production opportunities, and who thus sold subdivided land at higher prices. On the other hand, this phenomenon supplied land without the amenities necessary for proper housing due to a lack of infrastructure and services. The process also had negative environmental effects, leading to imbalanced urban development and the loss of good land that could have been used for agriculture, livestock, or forestry. Moreover, land subdivisions have been plagued by the inconsistent fulfilment of contractual commitments, which have affected the interests of many buyers, especially those in the low-income group. But the land subdivision market continues to be active and to contribute to a surge in the number of service enterprises managing subdivisions, many of which are profitable but carry out their business with little transparency and public control.

The problems surrounding subdivisions indicate that it is necessary to regulate the multiple commercial relations that grow up around them and to coordinate private and public sector actors. Regulations should permit subdivisions but also ensure the protection of the environment and an orderly urban development process. The new framework must establish virtuous equilibrium among the interests of the different participants in the relations derived from land subdivisions.

Actors

The actors involved in land subdivisions are in addition to the governments, landowners, land developers, and buyers. The incentive for landowners to participate in the process is to obtain a better price for their land, a result of the profits obtained by land developers selling unserviced land through an illegal or irregular subdivision process. Government policies that devote public resources to subsidise the provision of services to occupied lots influence the sale price of the land. The owners and land developers incorporate the value of the services that will eventually be provided into the land price, as it is known that the families will pressure the government to provide these services to the occupied lots. The land subdivision market operates in El Salvador without providing legal tenure for the lots, as the sales are made without full titles. Again, the actors anticipate that state policies will eventually regularise the property rights, a factor that contributes to the speculation already mentioned.

Other actors involved in the operation of this market and in the solutions to the problems it generates are the *Viceministro de Vivienda y Desarollo Urbano* (VMVDU) (Vice Ministry of Housing and Urban Development), as the national institution in charge of regulating urban and territorial development; the *Centro Nacional de Registros* (National Registry), which manages the Registro de la Propiedad (Property Registry); the municipalities, which have the responsibility to control the urban feasibility of the projects; the *Instituto Libertad y Progreso* (Institute of Freedom and Progress), in its activities that support the legalisation of land subdivisions; the *Ministerio de Medio Ambiente y Recursos Naturales* (Ministry of Environment and Natural Resources); the *Administración Nacional de Acueductors y Alcantarillados (*National Administration of Aqueducts and Sewer Systems); the *Consejo Nacional para la Cultura y el Arte* (National Council for Culture and the Arts); the *Ministerio de Agricultura y Ganadería* (Ministry of Agriculture and Livestock); and the electric energy distribution utilities. Other agencies that are involved include the national government agencies responsible for providing land subdivision permits; the NGOs, in their support of the improvement and legalisation of the communities living in illegal subdivisions; the *Fiscalía General de la República* (General District Attorney's Office), which processes legal actions against land developers; and the *Defensoría del Consumidor* (Counsel for the Defence of the Consumer) in its function as a source of information to buyers.

Regulatory Framework

In urban land markets, the information is usually imperfect and asymmetric, affecting the decisions of the actors. Also, in El Salvador there are few regulations that protect buyers in land transactions, leaving them vulnerable. In the land development market, the protection offered to the buyer is restricted to that regulating the buying and selling of goods, the Consumer Protection Law. According to the definition contained in the *Ley de Ordenamiento y Desarrollo* (Planning and Development Law) of the MASS, a land subdivision is the action and the result of dividing land into lots or parcels of land; however, as the majority of available land is outside the areas designated for urban use, this activity is framed by the regulations concerning the division of rural lands, or those designated for agricultural use and production with low population densities.[40] The land subdivisions are possible within the framework of the norms that set the technical requirements for parcelling land with incremental development of infrastructure and services. These regulations determine the minimum level of services required by the subdivisions and the public institutions that intervene in cases of breach. The specific legislation applicable to the land subdivisions is that concerning *Parcelaciones y Urbanizaciones Habitacionales* (Land Subdivision and Urbanisation) and that on *Ley de Urbanismo y Construcción* (Urban Development and Construction).[41] Other related norms are those that regulate the registry of the property rights and the environmental norms.

In the selling of lots, the legal relations among the different actors are regulated by general legislation, which is not adequate for the integral treatment of the phenomenon. The laws that regulate the rental-purchase agreements are important for this market, as this is the mechanism to finance the land purchases. The contracts are usually signed between the landowner (or land developer) and the buyer; in the agreement, one party commits to sell and the other to buy the lot. Due to its structure, it is considered a personal contract; that is, a promise between two individuals, and thus its fulfilment only needs the willingness of the parties involved. The rental-purchase agreement is like a deferred sale, which, once all the payments are made, obligates the land developer to issue a title under the name of the buyer (Article 1605, Clause 2° C, Code of Commerce). This means that it is possible to initiate judicial processes to grant the deed of sale; in this process the judge also acts as the legal representative of the owner of the subdivided real estate (Article 657, Clause 4°). Clearly, the practical problem in this structure is the lack of a formal document that would ensure a fast and secure process.[42]

Number of Land Subdivisions

Due to the lack of information about the land subdivisions market, the government has implemented the *Sistema de Información de Lotificaciones* (Information System on Land Subdivisions), which has the capacity

---

[40] The Ley de Desarrollo y Ordenamiento Territorial (Land Development and Planning Law) of the metropolitan area of San Salvador (MASS), and the bordering municipalities, was approved by the Legislative Decree 732 on December 8, 1993, and published in the *Diario Oficial* on January 26, 1994, and its respective regulation by *Acuerdo Municipal* N° 1 and published in the *Diario Oficial* on April 26, 1995.

[41] This law was approved by Executive Decree 70 on December 6, 1991, and published in the *Diario Oficial* 241, Volume 313, on December 20, 1991.

[42] The rental-purchase agreement has traditionally been dealt with in El Salvador as two different legal transactions: the rental and the purchase. The agreement can be substituted by one contract with the characteristics of a real contract, such as that of a real estate leasing contract, which consists of a single contract through which the property owner will transfer to the renter the ownership of a house in exchange for the payment of a periodic sum, or rent, for a fixed period of time. The real estate leasing mechanism can integrate into one contractual figure the rental and the purchase agreement.

Figure 3.1 El Salvador: Number of Lots per Year at the Start of Sales for Each Subdivision

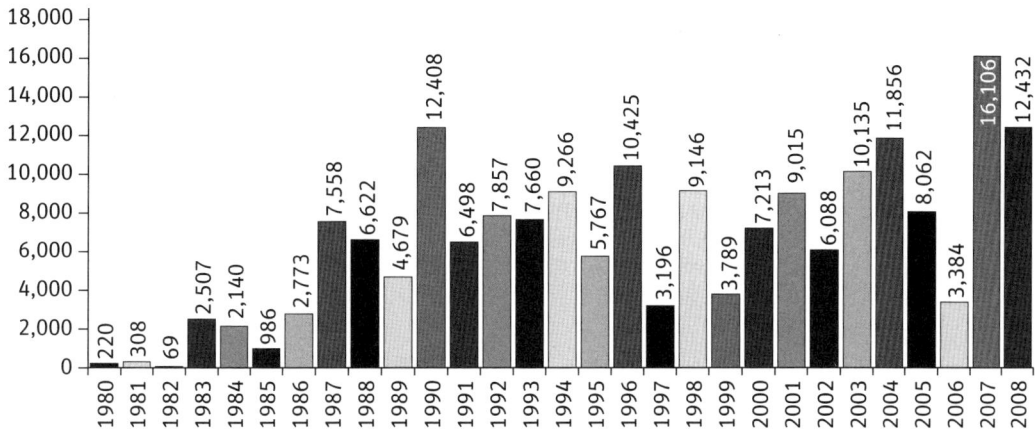

Source: VMVDU (2008).

to compile information relevant to the irregular land subdivisions.[43] In September 2008, the VMVDU had 812 irregular land subdivisions registered, which represents 100 percent of those reported by the *Asociación de Lotificadores de El Salvador* (ALES) (Association of Land Developers in El Salvador) and 27 percent of the ones that the government estimates to exist in the country (VMVDU, 2008). The information compiled on these irregular land subdivisions indicates that 80 percent of the subdivisions have not initiated an authorisation or regularisation procedure; 97 percent lack adequate drinking water services, while more than 83 percent have unfinished parks (many with only the land reserved for such use); and 70 percent have recreational facilities that have not been fully constructed, if they exist at all. Some 40 percent of the irregular lots are located in the Santa Ana, La Libertad, and San Salvador areas.

Although the number of new irregular land subdivisions has increased over time, Figure 3.1 presents the significant year-to-year variations and there are marked variations between 2006 and 2007. The decrease in 2006 may be due to the less tolerant attitude of the government, while the increase in 2007 may be due to the change in expectations generated by the discussion of a special law to regularise the illegal lots.

Impact on the Housing Situation

It is a common argument that urban informality is the result of poverty. But in the case of El Salvador, not all informality can be explained only by poverty. The municipalities with greater incidences of poverty are not

---

[43] This system aims to compile information on the characteristics of the irregular land subdivision, as well as to create a system that audits land developers and land subdivisions (http://www.evivienda.gob.sv/lotificaciones).

necessarily those areas with greater irregularity or with significantly higher numbers of informal land subdivisions, as such informality is due to the acquisition of housing lots through the practices described in this analysis.

Housing Conditions

The fact that almost 70 percent of homes in El Salvador have access to services is a good indicator that the housing situation in the country is acceptable in comparison with other LAC countries, where just over 50 percent of the housing stock is serviced. Table 3.1 illustrates the improvement in the housing situation in El Salvador between 1992 and 2007, a period in which public investment in housing decreased to just 0.01 percent of the gross domestic product (GDP).

At the same time, the number of households doubling up (calculated on the basis of the number of houses and the number of households) is quite low in El Salvador; in 2007, only 34,000 new houses were needed for every household to have a home, 20,000 fewer than in 1992.[44] Nearly 400,000 homes had at least one of the five deficiencies recorded in the census; nevertheless, this figure represents a reduction of almost 150,000 houses with deficits from the number recorded in 1992.[45] In 15 years, the percentage of homes with qualitative deficiencies in terms of the total housing stock descended to 21, a sign that, in spite of the population growth, 150,000 homes improved. During this period, the country built 16,000 houses over that required to accommodate the increase in the number of households. The geographical distribution of the qualitative housing deficit coincides with the municipalities having more irregular land possession.

Why Does Informality Continue to Increase in El Salvador?

In El Salvador, incomplete land subdivisions are the most affordable option since their developers offer loans to households without access to formal credit markets. Other factors behind the growth of informal land subdivisions include the absence of social housing programmes and the inadequate levels of public and private investment in urban infrastructure, which does not cover all urban services and is poorly targeted and uneven. Finally, the informal mechanisms of subdividing land are very profitable for its developers.[46]

---

[44] The difference between the number of households recorded in the census in 2007 (1,406,485) and the number of occupied houses (1,372,853) was 33,632 (Dirección General de Estadísticas y Censos, 2008).

[45] These include three deficits linked to the quality of the construction—floors, walls, and roofs—and two deficits concerning public services—potable water, and solid and liquid waste disposal.

[46] A 24,300 square metre rural piece of land without services was for sale for US$21,000 in 2008 (MundoAnuncio.com). If the land was subdivided with a sellable area equivalent to 65 percent of the total (15,795 square metres), it could still accommodate 79 lots (200 square metres each) that could sell for US$2,000 each. The total sale price would then be US$158,000 with minimum expenses.

Table 3.1 El Salvador: The Evolution of Housing, 1992–2007

	1992		2007	
	Homes	%	Homes	%
Homes lacking services	547,211	49.7	399,508	29.1
Households doubling up	50,127	4.6	33,994	2.5
Homes with services	503,376	45.7	939,351	68.4
Total	1,100,714	100.0	1,372,853	100.0

Source: VMVDU (2008).

The high cost of formally subdivided land with secure tenure drives households to buy into the land subdivisions market. On average, developers sell lots with basic services (as required by the urban development and building regulations) with their own financing in the form of 10-year loans with monthly payments that fluctuate between US$40 and US$60 for lots of 150 square metres (VMVDU, 2008). These payments are outside the reach of households with incomes below two minimum salaries. In contrast, developers of land subdivisions without basic services offer 200-square-metre lots that can be purchased through rental-purchase agreements with monthly payments between US$15 and US$30 for 12 to 15 years without a down payment required. This supply of long-term credit takes into consideration the paying capacity and the high regard held by many Salvadorians on the prompt payment of debts. Another factor in reducing the incidence of arrears in the land subdivision market is the easy repossession of the land by developers in cases of payment lapse; the contracts have clauses that commit the households to vacate the land after three missed payments. Confronted with the risk of losing the payments already made as well as their property, the households generally stay current in their payments. According to the data provided by the ALES, the arrears in this system are very low, between 4 and 5 percent.

A factor contributing to the growth of informal subdivisions are the urban development and building regulations that are often inflexible and unsuitable for the conditions of the country. The existing regulations in El Salvador set minimum lot sizes and require the provision of a variety of services that increase the cost of subdividing the land, making the serviced lots unaffordable for low-income households. The institutional weaknesses of the agencies in charge of controlling land use and subdivisions also contribute to increasing the cost of the serviced land, as they often take over two years to issue all the subdivision licences.

The households that purchase residential land in the incomplete subdivisions build their houses incrementally as and when they gather the resources to buy building materials and hire skilled labour to execute tasks they cannot do themselves. It may take many years to build a house this way, which explains why a high percentage of the houses have low-quality construction or services. Finally, periods of high inflation, underdeveloped or inaccessible

Figure 3.2 Government Interventions to Regularise Land Subdivisions

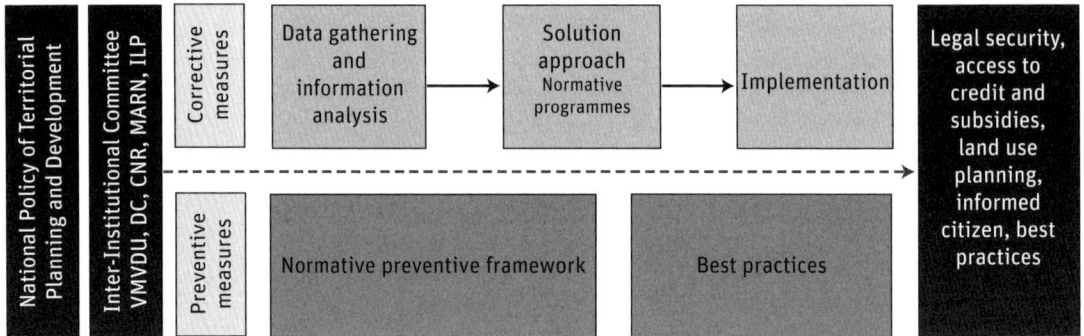

Source: VMVDU (2008).

financial markets, and the limited coverage of the social security system are factors inducing households to purchase lots as a value reserve and a capitalisation mechanism. Land purchases are one of the popular uses of money remitted from abroad, and this increases the demand for it.

Towards a More Efficient Market

The government of El Salvador, aware of both the problems generated by land subdivisions and their contribution towards solving the housing problem, seeks to enact norms and regulations to improve the functioning of the market for incremental land subdivisions. The VMVDU is in charge of implementing such preventive and remedial interventions, as described in Figure 3.2.

Among the remedial measures, it is important to set temporary norms for the provision of secure tenure for the lots sold and technical requirements (to be complied to by developers) to provide minimum living conditions in these subdivisions. Preventive measures include regulations that streamline the issuing of subdivision licences and a regulatory framework for rental-purchase contracts (house leasing) that grants legitimacy to the contracting system used in the land subdivisions market.

New Legislation

The draft Special Law on Land Subdivisions seeks to solve the insecurity of tenure of land buyers in two areas.

(i) *In relation to the contract:*

- In the rental-purchase contract, the debt is not tied to the lot being purchased, as the lot is not registered; the contracts include predatory clauses that leave the buyers unprotected.

- The management contract is signed between the landowner and the developer based on a power of attorney to manage and sell the lots; however, the obligations of the parties are not well defined.

(ii) *In relation to the lot:*

- The lands being subdivided often have liens, so during the validity period of the rental-purchase contract the lands may be transferred to third parties holding the liens; these parties hold no obligation towards the buyers.
- Finally, in a majority of cases, the subdivision does not have the required licences to issue the land ownership titles, leaving households with insecure tenure.

The draft legislation seeks to solve the problems of the market for land subdivisions and to establish a virtuous relationship among the actors in this market—which include the owners of the land that will be subdivided, the developers, and the buyers—and the lot as the good being purchased (see Figure 3.3). The legal solutions address the issues described in the preceding paragraph to correct the land market failures impacting the subdivision of land. The regularisation of the land tenure is needed not only for new undertakings but also in existing subdivisions. In the case of new subdivisions, the legislation will regulate the rental-purchase and land-management contracts to ensure they include a minimum set of clauses that protect the interests of the parties involved and strengthen the institutions in charge of issuing licences and enforcing compliance with the technical regulations.

The law also establishes fines for non-compliance with the regulations. In the case of existing subdivisions, the law contemplates rules to provide secure tenure to the buyers. When the subdivision is not in compliance with technical requirements (for instance, inadequate street width, lack of basic services or parks, lack of access roads, and so forth) a compensation mechanism operated by the local governments will help solve the problem by financing the investments to upgrade the subdivision to the set standards. Compensation for non-compliance with technical norms will be paid by the developer on behalf of the affected buyer and may be channelled through community organisations or the municipality. Such compensation does not affect the regularisation of tenure; that is, the sanctions that may apply for not paying the compensation will not prevent the households from getting title to the land if they have made all the payments. In the case of conflicts with third parties—and to protect lots from their demands—the law allows for the substitution of guarantees, allowing lien holders to get the cash flows generated by the subdivision (rent payments) as a guarantee. The technical requirements to be fulfilled by existing subdivisions are those in force at the time the subdivisions were started. Therefore, subdivisions initiated before 1998 do not need environmental licences, since the corresponding law was enacted after

Figure 3.3 El Salvador: New Structure for the Land Subdivisions Market

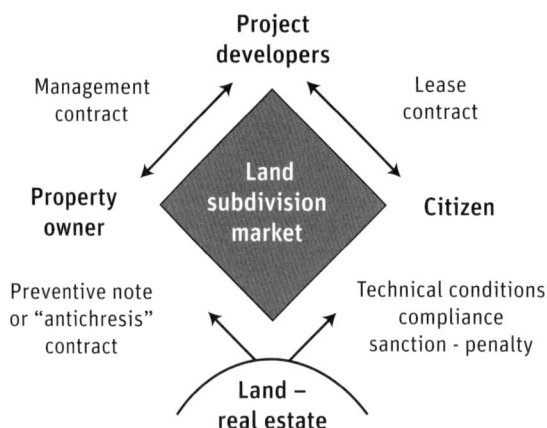

Source: Author's elaboration.

that date. Projects started after 1998 will use the self-regulation procedure contemplated in the environmental law.

Challenges for the Government

The proposed solutions pose diverse challenges to the actors involved. The Salvadorian government must sustain its political willingness to approve necessary laws and to set up the institutional and legal framework for the VMVDU to supervise the implementation of these measures. Among the most important action to take is establishing an efficient mechanism for managing compensation. Such a mechanism must rely on the information system on land subdivisions to ensure that buyers of lots are given transparent access to information concerning their land subdivisions. This process should be channelled through the Consumer Protection Agency, the municipalities, the government organisations, and the infocentre networks around the country.[47] The goal is effective oversight of the process by land purchasers, a basic condition for transparency on this market. The initiative succeeds as long as reliable information is available and municipalities are working in close coordination with communities. The involvement of these communities has the additional benefit of preparing them for the sustainable management of their neighbourhoods.

---

[47] The government organisations involved are: the Vice Ministry of Housing and Urban Development (VMVDU) and its decentralised offices, the Social Housing Fund, and the National Fund for Low Income Housing. Infocentres are non-partisan, non-profit social organisations that promote the use of new information and telecommunication technologies in El Salvador.

The government must promote a culture of gathering and disseminating information through the information system on land subdivisions that supports the efficient implementation of the public policies impacting this market. This information is also useful to assess the demand for future social housing programmes financed through the Housing Savings and Financing System of the VMVDU.[48] This information is useful for implementing housing policies based on the subsidiary principle—in which the state does not directly produce houses but instead facilitates the operation of markets—and for neighbourhood upgrading programmes, particularly to improve the living conditions in subdivisions developed before the enactment of the environmental law. These programmes have contributed to the reduction of poverty as they have improved the living conditions of the low-income households. Last but not least, there is a need to establish institutional mechanisms to regulate the housing policies; that is, to strengthen the VMVDU as the effective leading institution in the implementation of the National Housing Policy.

In sum, land subdivisions offer both a solution and a problem. They supply housing lots to low-income households and create a problem for the rest of society. But with adequate public oversight of new land subdivisions and regularisation programmes for existing subdivisions, it is possible to solve the housing problems of the poor while mitigating the impact on the environment and the urban development process. The solution requires a realignment of the incentives under which the key actors operate—landowners, developers, and buyers—so that part of the large profits obtained by the landowners and developers are channelled to investments in infrastructure and urban services. Also, it is important to introduce reforms so that the rental-purchase contracts provide security of tenure to the buyers from the beginning of the lease period.

The imperfections of the land markets, the multiplicity of institutions involved in the different phases of the process, and the lack of capacity among the institutions in charge of supervising compliance challenge the regularisation process in El Salvador. The solutions to such problems require the enactment of a special set of norms capable of controlling the central aspects of market operations and preventing the emergence of negative externalities without distorting their functioning. There is the need to define regulations for new subdivisions and temporary norms for the regularisation of existing subdivisions. Likewise, it is necessary to strengthen the capacity of supervising institutions and ensure that they are in compliance with the norms of the subdivisions regularisation programme.

---

[48] The Housing Savings and Financing System is the result of the joint efforts of the VMVDU, the German Agency for Cooperation (GTZ in its German acronym), and the government of Chile. The programme has the financial support of the IDB.

4 PREVENTING NEW INFORMALITY

EDUARDO ROJAS

Emerging Problems

In many cities across the Latin American and Caribbean (LAC) region, neighbourhoods developed by the formal sector and government-built social housing estates face problems similar to those of informal settlements. In these urban areas the lack of maintenance of the houses, shortages of infrastructure, and the weakening of the social relations in the resident communities combine to deteriorate the physical and social structures of the neighbourhoods. This problem is becoming evident in a variety of residential areas. For example, some homes built by the state over 10 years ago have deteriorated to the point that they can no longer serve their intended purpose. Many high-rise social housing apartment buildings are not adequately maintained and have badly deteriorated common areas: roofs, stairs, gutters, and supporting structures (foundations, supporting walls, beams, and columns). The commons of some social housing neighbourhoods have been abandoned, contributing to the neighbourhoods' overall decay and creating a locus for the antisocial behaviour of their inhabitants and groups from other areas of the city. The weakening of social relations compounds the gradual deterioration of housing and infrastructure. These problems represent a loss for the residents of these communities, who are forced to live in substandard conditions in homes that are losing market value, and also for the cities, which must absorb the negative impact associated with decaying neighbourhoods and deteriorating buildings. These are second-generation problems since they affect people with homes produced by the formal sector as opposed to those living in informal neighbourhoods or the homeless.

Formal neighbourhoods—often located on the peripheries of LAC cities—developed amid rapid urban expansion and generally lack adequate infrastructure and services. These shortages have different origins: in some cases, the developers managed to sell lots without full infrastructure; in others, the local authorities did not fully enforce the land subdivision regulations that were in place, or the municipality did not have sufficient resources to provide services and maintain infrastructure. Among the most pressing deficiencies are the low quality of access roads, which

Upper picture

Government-built housing estates, many located on the periphery of cities, often deteriorate rapidly. The physical structures and relations among the inhabitants tend to fall apart.
Social houses in San Pedro Sula, Honduras

Lower picture

Apartment buildings built by the government for lower-middle-income and middle-income households also deteriorate for lack of maintenance of the common property.
Villa Portales, Santiago, Chile

are either substandard or do not effectively connect the neighbourhoods to the rest of the city; incomplete drainage, sewerage, and storm water systems; irregular potable water supply; and a general lack of health and education infrastructure.

The informal settlements that are the focus of settlement upgrading programmes are often located in the same areas—on city peripheries. While upgrading programmes are specifically designed to solve the problems of informal settlements, they do not address the deficiencies in the surrounding areas, which means that the informal settlements end up with better infrastructure and more services than the formal ones. As stated by Jack Couriel in his analysis of the urban periphery of Montevideo, these substandard areas present a complex set of public policy and financing issues. The magnitude of the shortages requires significant investment, but the low density of some settlements brings their cost-effectiveness into question. Moreover, the heterogeneity of communities makes it difficult to use public resources alone for financing, as some of the beneficiaries are not poor but cannot be charged for the improvements.

The interventions required to effectively tackle these problems pose a planning, financing, and implementation challenge. The issues involved in the operation and maintenance of sewerage and drainage infrastructure are a key example. Public utilities often have few incentives to provide sewerage to low-density neighbourhoods comprised of low-income households. Similarly, households are reluctant to connect to these services and pay the accompanying tariffs, and instead use individual solutions such as latrines or septic tanks. Additionally, drainage infrastructure is expensive to maintain, and most of these neighbourhoods do not generate sufficient tax revenue due to their low property values. These factors dissuade municipalities from maintaining infrastructure—if built at the time of subdividing the land—or from building any infrastructure at all. Another inhibiting factor is the high cost and complexity of connecting these neighbourhoods to the infrastructure of the city, which may involve building trunk roads, bridges, water mains and sewers, and treatment plants. Municipalities and public utilities do not give these works priority, since they are often pressured to expand services in fast-growing high-income areas of the city. As a result, these neighbourhoods remain without services for a long time, which negatively impacts the residents' quality of life and property values. The government's lack of attention to these problems further undermines the willingness of communities to organise and get involved in neighbourhood affairs, which, as in informal settlements, devalues their social capital.

Reversing the physical and social deterioration of social housing neighbourhoods is costly and complex. This chapter discusses the Quiero mi Barrio (I Love my Neighbourhood) programme that has been implemented by the government of Chile to solve some of the problems confronted by low-cost housing estates built by the government over the past 30 years in many cities. As Maria de la Luz Nieto describes in her analysis of the programme, the physical deterioration of single-family homes, apartment buildings, and surrounding public spaces, as well as the attendant social disintegration, has fostered antisocial and criminal activity that impacts the rest of the city. As in informal settlements, the rest of the community broadly stigmatises the inhabitants of these deteriorated neighbourhoods, making it more difficult for them to join in the social and economic life of the city. To address these issues, Quiero mi Barrio uses lessons learned from similar programmes in Europe and the United States; it particularly recognises the need for intense social work in the communities before starting rehabilitation of the public spaces and common property of neighbourhoods and apartment buildings.

The Chilean programme differs from the European or U.S. models in that it does not provide assistance for the rehabilitation of the houses and focuses only on the rehabilitation of public spaces. This is a significant limitation since the programme does not address many of the factors that negatively impact inhabitants' quality of life and make it difficult for them to sell their homes in the market. This shortcoming of the Chilean programme can be explained in the difficulties encountered by governments to justify the use of public resources for home improvements whose benefits will finally translate into higher prices for the houses in the market. However, households living in these houses generally have irregular and low incomes, which prevents them from financing repairs with formal loans. Moreover, the insufficient maintenance of individual homes ends up impacting the other houses or condominiums in the neighbourhood. There is a need for incentives to encourage owners to rehabilitate their own homes, which would in turn benefit the rest of the community. The government can satisfy this need without a lot of spending: by guaranteeing the loans contracted by the households, by promoting microcredit schemes to finance the work, and by providing technical assistance to the communities to organise and contract the work with small- and medium-size construction companies.

A more detailed analysis of the European and U.S. programmes provides clues for how such social housing neighbourhood rehabilitation programmes could be set up in the LAC region. For example, the Generalitat, the government of the Catalonian region in Spain, has implemented a programme, the *Programa de barris àrees urbanes d'atenció especial* (Neighbourhoods and Urban Areas Requiring Special Attention), which provides subsidies to municipalities interested in rehabilitating neighbourhoods that are facing physical deterioration, service shortages, poorly integrated infrastructure, and related social problems (see Box 4.1).[49] This financing mechanism could easily be adapted to the situation in the LAC region, where the municipalities are usually financially and institutionally weak but are well positioned to confront neighbourhood problems.

---

[49] For more details on this programme, see: http://www10.gencat.cat/ptop/AppJava/cat/arees/ciutat/barris/index.jsp.

BOX 4.1 SETTLEMENT UPGRADING IN CATALONIA

JULI PONCE SOLÉ

Urban sprawl, the emergence of central neighbourhoods with social and urban problems, and the functional specialisation of the territories due to the segregation of land uses have been among the most significant changes occurring in Spanish cities in the second half of the twentieth century and the beginning of the twenty-first century. These growth patterns are at odds with the traditional Spanish city, which is compact and functionally diversified. These phenomena have fostered a growing urban segregation of residents (and urban spaces). The most clear physical expression of this trend is the proliferation of gated communities with high levels of services and urban facilities. Along with the growing incidence of the urban sprawl is the growth in the number of areas with dense concentrations of people who have difficulty integrating into the city, including immigrants from outside the European Union (EU). A report from 2000 indicates that between 4 and 5 million Spaniards live in troubled neighbourhoods, 12 percent of the total population of the country.

Law 2/2004 regulates improvements in neighbourhoods, urban areas, and towns. It promotes social cohesion by paying special attention to security issues from an urban development point of view. The law requires significant public policy interventions to rehabilitate deteriorated urban areas. An allocation of 800 million euros has been made to improve Catalonian neighbourhoods with an integrated and transversal approach that allows the efficient coordination of policies concerning urban development, housing, employment, and social assistance. The EU Council of Regions considers this norm and its implementation mechanisms as a European good practice. The law establishes a promotion fund for the neighbourhood programme with annual allocations from the budget and co-financing from the EU. Municipalities with areas requiring special attention (defined according to the criteria set by the law) can request funding for their urban rehabilitation projects for these areas. The promotion fund covers between 50 and 75 percent of the cost. Resources are allocated through competitions that give priority to the best-designed projects that benefit low-income households, with a large part of the financing coming from the community and the municipality.

Although the *Generalitat* mostly provides the financing, the municipalities are responsible for executing the projects. This level of government is closer to the community and responsible for the provision, operation, and maintenance of urban facilities and public spaces. Since 2004 this funding has benefited numerous neighbourhoods in Barcelona. The allocation of the funds is under the purview of the minister in charge of urban development, based on the recommendation of a commission with representatives from the regional government, the municipalities, and architects' and engineers' institutes.

The national and regional governments usually command more institutional and financial resources, so they would be in a good position to support the municipalities. The experience that LAC municipalities have in managing conditional transfers would facilitate the implementation of this type of programme.

There are numerous neighbourhood rehabilitation programmes in France, the United Kingdom, and the Netherlands that deal with the deterioration of the housing estates built after World War II.[50] These projects deal with neighbourhood problems in an integrated way and seek to rehabilitate homes through complex and costly interventions (partial demolition, major renovation, and opening up of public space) that may take a long time to complete. Although they are costly, these projects recoup the use and property value of houses that otherwise would have been demolished. LAC cities, endemically short of financing and facing multiple demands on their budgets, must mobilise additional resources—from current and future inhabitants—to undertake these projects. Innovation is required to leverage resources from the beneficiaries. Small loans backed by first or second mortgages (often households do not have debts and have clear title to their properties) are a way for owners to obtain resources for home rehabilitation. Municipalities can obtain medium- and long-term loans to finance the improvement of infrastructure and public spaces, which will benefit future generations (who will pay the loans) while improving the quality of life of current inhabitants. The improvement of neighbourhoods and houses recovers their use value and has a positive impact on real estate values and the attractiveness of homes in the market. In countries where municipalities charge real estate taxes, improved real estate value will lead to increased tax revenues in the short term. These revenue increases can be tapped to finance investments through mechanisms such as tax increment districts and the issuing of debt backed by this revenue. These resources can be further used to finance municipal investments—improvements in public spaces, infrastructure, and urban services—and to provide guarantees to mortgage loans contracted by the beneficiaries to improve their homes when financial markets are reluctant to provide this type of financing.

The physical and social deterioration in social housing and substandard formal neighbourhoods is growing and needs to be addressed, not only to prevent further spread of the problem and its negative externalities, but also to recoup the real estate value of the houses. Investing in a solution to these problems can have multiple benefits: homeowners will maintain or increase the real estate value of their assets and improve their marketability, liquidity, and horizontal or upward mobility; and the city can eliminate sources of physical and social deterioration that impact the whole population. Public intervention is justified given the complexity of designing and executing the required investments and the difficulty of coordinating the actions of all stakeholders. But the fact that the interventions generate private benefits also makes it necessary to use public-private co-financing mechanisms in these projects.

Preventing the deterioration of new neighbourhoods can also be efficient. It requires building neighbourhoods with better services and

---

[50] See, for instance, the Project La Caravelle in Villeneuve-la-Garenne in France http://www.sem-92.fr/index2.html.

PHOTO: MINISTERIO DE VIVIENDA, CONSTRUCCION Y SANEAMIENTO DEL PERU

higher-quality houses that do not easily deteriorate. Upgrading the quality of building materials and the design of houses can also improve their capacity to provide services for longer periods of time and give them greater real estate value. The construction of neighbourhoods that are dense, well connected to the city, economically diverse, and complete (with housing, commerce, services, employment centres, and recreation) not only improves the quality of life of the population, but also generates more tax income for the local governments and diversifies the range of social groups interested in maintaining them. This strategy involves larger initial expenses in the construction of houses and urban facilities and a higher cost of acquiring better-located lands. But considering the costs of retrofitting neighbourhoods shortly after construction—in 2008 Chile was spending US$5,000 per house to retrofit neighbourhoods containing houses that 15 years early cost US$15,000 to build—it is efficient to front load this expense and build better houses and neighbourhoods to prevent deterioration and provide better living conditions from the beginning.

Low-cost apartment buildings are often delivered to occupants without the condominium associations and financing mechanisms required to care for the common property, thus leading to their premature deterioration. **Low-cost residential apartments in Lima, Peru**

EDUARDO ROJAS   # The Deterioration of Social Housing

LAC governments have attempted for decades to solve the housing deficits afflicting low-income populations by implementing different social housing programmes. A widely used strategy has been the construction of housing by specialised public institutions. These houses are transferred in free holding ownership to low-income households under preferential financial terms. There are many public institutions in the region that manage public funds for housing with varying levels of efficiency and sustainability. Generally, the houses produced by the government are costly and, given the high levels of subsidies included in the loans (generally in the form of below-market interest rates) and the high incidence of arrears in their loan portfolio, the public housing institutions manage to recoup only a portion of their investments.[51] As a consequence, the public institutions in charge of financing and building the houses rapidly lose their capital and require a constant infusion of public funds. These resources are not used very efficiently, and in the majority of cases, public funding is insufficient to bridge this financial gap and meet the housing needs of all poor households. The classic problems inherent in a public bureaucracy, including complex contracting procedures and the incentive systems under which public servants operate—meet quantitative targets under tight budgets—typically, lead to the construction of costly and low-quality houses. This public housing policy has been largely unsuccessful in terms of equity and efficiency, producing a small number of quite expensive houses and benefiting relatively few households. Still, this funding mechanism has been responsible for the construction of a significant proportion of the housing stock in many countries and cities.[52]

The rapid deterioration of government-built social housing has resulted from several practices commonly used by the sector institutions. In order to build the maximum number of houses with limited resources, these institutions rely on five interrelated strategies: (i) constructing houses on the periphery of cities, where land is less expensive; (ii) shifting the responsibility for providing urban services to the municipalities; (iii) building a significant proportion of the houses in four-storey apartment buildings (usually the maximum height allowed without requiring an elevator); (iv) keeping the houses small (usually between 40 and 60

---

[51] It is not unusual for over 80 percent of the beneficiaries of these programmes to be behind by three or more monthly payments. There are many instances in which beneficiaries occupy the houses free for many years while awaiting their property title from the institutions, and generally face problems acquiring the land where the houses are built.
[52] For instance, the Argentinean Federal Housing Programme intends to build 150,000 new houses in 2009; the Ministry of Housing and Urban Development in Chile had contracted the construction of an average of 40,000 new houses per year between 2000 and 2005 for its basic and incremental housing programmes; and the São Paulo State Housing Secretariat and the São Paulo Municipal Housing Secretariat build an average of 20,000 and 10,000 houses each year, respectively.

square metres); and (v) building the houses with low-cost materials and minimal interior finishing. This results in the mass-scale construction of homes that are similar in type, size, and quality. These homes are allotted to those with similar income levels that end up living in vast neighbourhoods that lack adequate services and public spaces, and are located far from the urban centre.

The beneficiaries of these public programmes are usually low-income individuals that cannot afford houses produced by the private sector. They often work as employees in the formal sector, as public servants or as employees of private firms, although they may also earn their living in the informal sector. The specific demographic details vary from country to country and from city to city, but these populations often share a common story. Households in these neighbourhoods usually suffer from a high incidence of family disintegration, and the head of the household is usually poorly educated, not well paid, and frequently unemployed. These individual characteristics are at the root of many of the social problems that the neighbourhoods confront as a whole.

The houses and apartments in these public programmes are transferred to the individual owners with freehold tenure often without proper titles and legal provisions that define owners' financial obligations and responsibilities concerning the common property and with little information regarding condominium rules, owners' associations, and the proper registration of condominium rights. As a result, these communities usually lack formal tenant organisations or any other way to arrange for the maintenance of common property. This leads to negligent behaviour on the part of many households and the subsequent deterioration of common property (roofs, gutters, supporting structures, stairways, corridors, and so on) in the neighbourhoods or condominiums. Also, fees are not regularly collected to maintain and replace these components of the buildings. The municipalities, always short on human and financial resources, barely care for the roads and lighting and postpone the provision of equipment to maintain other public spaces (see Figure 4.1). Without preventive maintenance and repairs, the common areas in these buildings and public spaces rapidly deteriorate, and the flow of housing services to homeowners is reduced.

This combination of factors results in the proliferation of no-man's lands on city peripheries. Inhabitants do not feel responsible for any space beyond their front doors, while municipalities take responsibility for only sidewalks. The spaces that are left unclaimed—usually designated as community parks in the land-use plans—are eventually abandoned. Unemployed youth, felons, and other people on the social margins often congregate in these areas, and their antisocial behaviour affects the entire neighbourhood and the city as a whole. The rise in crime and the use of public spaces to conduct illegal activities, such as drug use and trafficking and gang violence, leads people to take refuge in their own homes. The control of the public spaces is thus further relinquished to delinquents.

Housing in neighbourhoods located far from city centres lacks urban services and employment opportunities and therefore meets only a part of the residents' needs. Projects often deteriorate rapidly and lose value.
Low-cost housing built by the private sector in Morelia, Mexico

Figure 4.1 Current Situation: Public Spaces without Responsible Entity

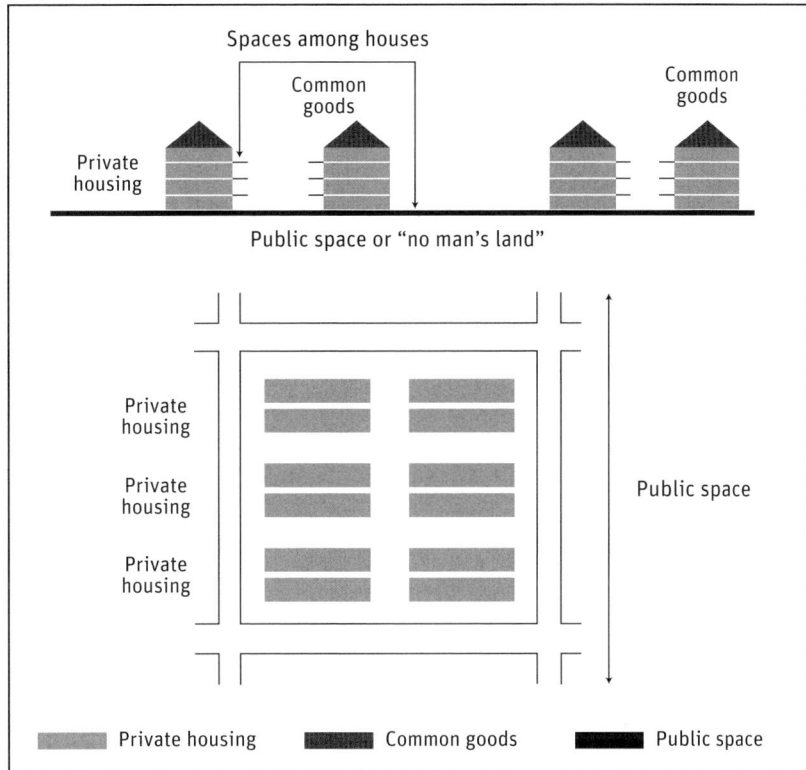

Spaces among houses

Common goods

Common goods

Private housing

Public space or "no man's land"

Private housing

Private housing

Private housing

Public space

Private housing   Common goods   Public space

In high-rise apartment complexes, the common areas are "no man's land" – no one takes care of them.

Source: Author's elaboration.

The process feeds itself, fuelling the rapid deterioration of community relations and the decay of public spaces. This deterioration discourages individual owners, who often allow their own apartments to fall into disrepair or who otherwise completely abandon them. Decay stigmatises the neighbourhoods and its inhabitants, impairing their opportunities to socially integrate into the city and find jobs.

Homeowners also end up with devalued real estate, which hampers their ability to move into larger and better-located houses in the future. Two economic problems emerge. The first is the loss in property value sustained by houses that, even shortly after construction, have a market value (when there is a market for them) that is lower than the cost of production. Second, the inflexibility that is introduced into the housing markets adversely affects labour markets. Workers are prevented from moving to cities or neighbourhoods with better employment opportunities since they cannot sell or rent the homes they received from the government.

The Public Policy Problem

Even though neighbourhood inhabitants feel most of the impact of the processes described in the preceding section, they do not, on their own, have the capacity to solve these problems. The rehabilitation of neighbourhoods and government-built apartment buildings turns into a public policy issue for the following reasons. The inhabitants can only repair their own homes, and they are often discouraged from doing so because of the deterioration of the common property in their buildings and the surrounding public spaces. Likewise, homeowners do not have incentives to organise themselves and to cooperate, and they do not have the means to prevent free riders from benefiting from the rehabilitation. Finally, the deteriorated neighbourhoods and buildings become enclaves of social problems, which in turn have an adverse effect on the rest of the city.

The urban development and housing challenge posed by deteriorated neighbourhoods and apartment buildings is a "second-generation" problem. It is present in cities of developed countries that had active social housing policies and also in developing countries where the public sector has been directly supplying houses to low-income populations for rent or freehold ownership. This situation can also arise in neighbourhoods and houses built by the private sector when market conditions or building regulations do not force developers to provide fully equipped public spaces or establish condominium owners' associations with sustainable financing to maintain the common property.[53] Consequently, the implications of this problem go beyond the more restricted formulation of the first section of this chapter that focuses on public housing estates and will be discussed in the third section, which analyzes the precarious urban neighbourhoods of Uruguay and proposes a unified solution for houses built either by the public or the private sector.

The Solution

Objectives

A solution to the urban development and housing problem under analysis requires public intervention. As stated earlier, this intervention is needed to resolve the coordination difficulties confronted by stakeholders and to tackle the negative externalities that the problem generates for the city.

---

[53] The success attained by the housing finance policy of Mexico in the 2000s has led to the production of nearly 150,000 new houses per year with private financing and demand-side support from the public sector. This massive production of houses is generating similar problems to those created by public housing construction. Many new neighbourhoods are being built without the full array of urban services and facilities and are far from employment and service centres. These neighbourhoods run the risk of rapid deterioration for reasons similar to those described here.

Public spaces that are not maintained by municipalities and are not under the care of the communities turn into "no man's land". Their abandonment hastens the deterioration of neighbourhoods.
Padre Hurtado neighbourhood, Santiago, Chile

The intervention should have a dual objective. For property owners, the objective should be to increase the market value of the real estate assets acquired by the households through public housing programmes. These assets should have a market value equal to or above the cost of construction, and they should be sold or rented in conditions similar to those of houses in other segments of the market in the same city. For the city, public intervention must turn around the negative externalities created by these deteriorated neighbourhoods, which have become centres of delinquency, violence, and crime.

The Structure and Sequencing of Interventions

The European and U.S. experiences in the rehabilitation of social housing and the Chilean programme indicate that the solution to these problems requires more than public intervention. Interventions must also be closely coordinated with homeowners.[54] The necessary interventions must go beyond investments in infrastructure and urban facilities that have characterised the settlement upgrading programmes to date. They also require a combination of public and private financing. Moreover, any attempt to reverse infrastructure shortages and rehabilitate public spaces and common property in condominiums will have little effect if it is not preceded by an effort to build social capital among the beneficiaries. These efforts must include the reconstruction of the community life of the neighbourhoods and the structuring of owners' associations to manage the common property in the condominiums. These necessary conditions make the rehabilitation of social housing neighbourhoods and apartment buildings more difficult. As discussed below, the required interventions are both complex and costly, and they must be executed in a strict sequence and coordinated fashion, and on a scale large enough to be effective.

The first condition for effective intervention is to implement the actions in the *correct sequence*. As stated before, community organisations must be capable of maintaining public spaces and common property for rehabilitation to be effective and lasting. There are prerequisite conditions for the rest of the interventions as well. For instance, little will be gained by rehabilitating the individual apartments in a building if the common property is left untouched. The following points outline the main components of a social housing rehabilitation programme and the sequence in which they must be put in place for maximum impact:

Rebuild the community life to set up a foundation for coordinated action by the households and establish institutional mechanisms to cooperate with the public sector. Building community organisations—and fostering cooperation among homeowners—contributes to the long-term sustainability of neighbourhood improvement efforts. In apartment buildings, these activities can help create condominium organisations that manage and maintain the common property. In neighbourhoods with single-family homes, community organisations must actively partner with the municipality in caring for public spaces. This is particularly important for the adequate maintenance of public spaces that are part of the neighbourhoods but are not recognised by the local government and the citizenry as public areas for general use.[55]

Connect the neighbourhoods to the city to prevent them from becoming isolated and deteriorating enclaves full of social problems. This type

---

[54] The Fiscal and Municipal Management Division (FMM) of the Inter-American Development Bank (IDB) commissioned two studies that document the experiences of neighbourhood upgrading programmes of several countries in Europe, Latin America, and the United States (Graham, 2007; Acosta, 2007). For more details on the Chilean case, see the corresponding section of this chapter.

[55] These spaces are commonly found in high-rise apartment buildings located in large lots on the periphery of cities. The municipality maintains the streets but does not provide furniture or maintain the spaces between buildings.

of intervention is crucial in facilitating residents' access to sources of employment and other services and amenities in the city. To be totally effective, this intervention must also ensure that the inhabitants of the city regularly use the streets and public spaces of the neighbourhood.

Provide basic urban facilities that lift living conditions in the neighbourhood up to the level of that in the rest of the city. The availability of primary, secondary, and technical education—depending on the size of the neighbourhoods—and the enrolment of the majority of the children and youth in these programmes effectively reduces antisocial behaviour and crime rates. Likewise, education increases the chances that residents will obtain gainful employment. Providing health and recreation facilities also improves the quality of life in neighbourhoods and makes them more attractive to new residents. In turn, the marketability of houses for sale or rent increases.

Rehabilitate public spaces in neighbourhoods and apartment condominiums with designs and furnishings that allow for the best use of these areas, either by the entire city (thus under the aegis of the municipality) or by the neighbourhood or condominium residents themselves (semipublic spaces, therefore mainly under the care of the community). It is crucial to clearly assign responsibility in the operation and maintenance of these spaces to ensure an adequate degree of social control over them and to clarify financial responsibility (see Figure 4.2).

Improve the quality, and thus the market value, of houses and maximise the flow of housing services provided to their owners. Particular attention should be paid to repairing bathrooms and kitchens, replacing doors and windows, and improving electrical wiring. As discussed later in this section, these improvements can be financed privately through bank loans, but the mobilisation of these resources may require and merit public support when households face restricted access to financing. Support may also be needed to coordinate the execution of the works in several houses to save on implementation costs and time.

The Coordinated Execution of Rehabilitation Interventions

The successful rehabilitation of social housing neighbourhoods or apartment complexes requires the coordinated action of several public and private actors. There are three main objectives that must be achieved through these coordinated efforts: guaranteeing the commitment of all relevant stakeholders, ensuring the timely availability of financing, and implementing a formal coordination mechanism.

Commitment of all relevant stakeholders. From the initial stages of the project, it is critical to have the full commitment of all stakeholders, which include:

Figure 4.2 New Communities: The Control of Public Spaces

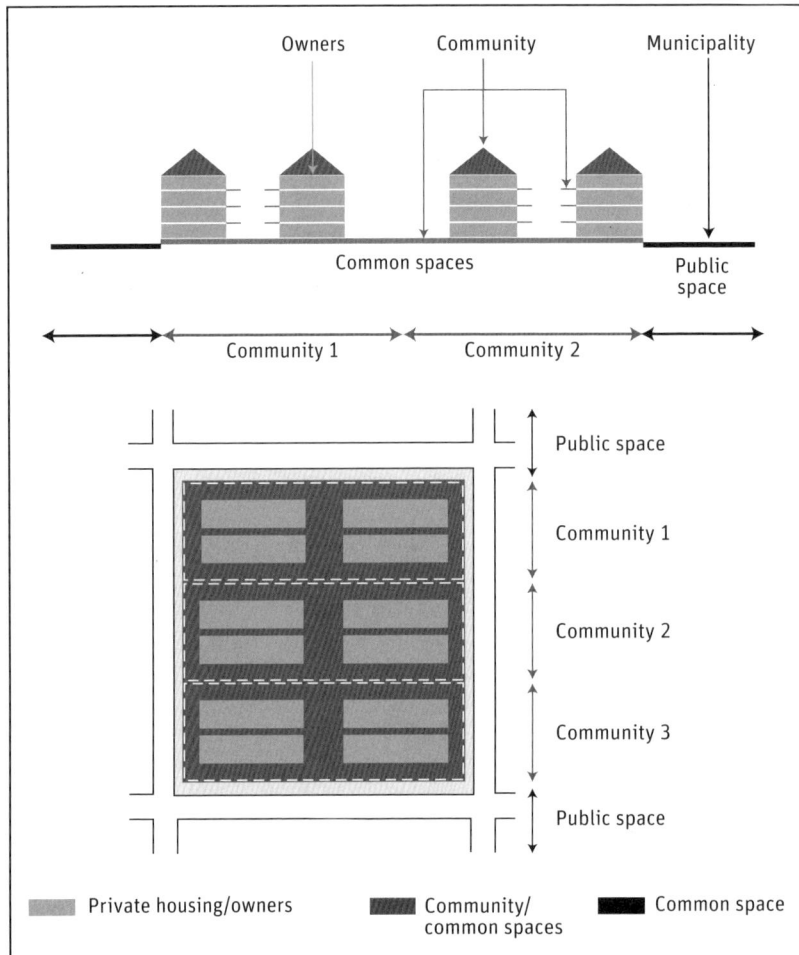

Community organisations can be encouraged to assume responsibility for public spaces and common property in high-rise buildings, leaving the municipality in charge of streets.

Source: Author's elaboration.

- The residents in the neighbourhoods or apartment complexes, whose involvement in the community or condominium organisations and role as partners in the public rehabilitation effort are crucial.
- The municipality, the public institution closest to the community, which should be responsible for the management of public spaces and the provision of urban services. The municipality is in the best position to identify the problems faced by the neighbourhoods and to design the most appropriate projects to solve them. In fulfilling its responsibilities, this branch of the government can get support from organisations of the civil society that specialise in housing issues.

- The central or regional government, which supports the munici-palities when they do not have sufficient institutional and financial resources to execute the required interventions.

Financing the interventions. The characteristics of the interventions and the distribution of benefits make it convenient to seek financing from dif-ferent sources. Generally, the interventions that generate private benefits for property owners should be financed with their own resources, either savings or borrowed funds. On the other hand, public funding should finance interventions that generate benefits for the whole city, such as providing public spaces for general use. Interventions in semi-public spaces require a combination of resources from the public budget and from the community members that use and directly benefit from these resources. This ideal allocation of funding sources may not be always possible or practical. As mentioned previously, homeowners may expe-rience difficulties in accessing commercial credit due to the instability or level of their income. They may benefit from public support in the form of guarantees or dedicated funding for these purposes. Likewise, commu-nities may lack resources to contribute to the rehabilitation of semi-pub-lic spaces. In these cases, the neighbourhood rehabilitation programmes may subsidise these interventions since they will benefit the city as a whole. The rehabilitation of public spaces for general use may also be too costly for some municipalities, and the central or regional government may need to step in with earmarked transfers. The majority of single-home or apartment neighbourhood rehabilitation programmes in Europe and the United States are financed with a combination of resources sup-plied by the national, regional, and local governments (Graham, 2007; Acosta, 2007). The financing must be structured according to the needs of each case and follow the principles stated here; but given the large amount of resources required, these programmes need significant finan-cial support from the central or state governments.

Adequate financing for and a culture of adequate operation and main-tenance of works are crucial to sustain the rehabilitation process. Within owners' associations, such a culture is essential for the continued main-tenance and operation of the common property. Legal measures, such as liens on property titles guaranteeing prompt payment of the owner's contributions to the association, are also necessary to support this effort. Such practices are particularly difficult to establish in low-income house-holds that have never contributed to the operation and maintenance of common property or urban services.

Formal management structure. Ensuring the coordinated execution of interventions by public and private actors with various funding streams is a complex problem that does not have a single solution. Whatever the solution, it should be capable of creating sufficient incentives to align the actions of different stakeholders towards the pursuit of a common objec-tive. The signing of a "neighbourhood contract" in the Chilean case, or

the execution of agreements between the autonomous regional government and the municipality in Catalonia, are both examples of mechanisms that can be used to reinforce cooperation. Financing agreements
need to stay in place for several years until all interventions are completed. The most successful programmes involve the transfer of financial resources from the national or regional levels of government on the
basis of open competition among projects sponsored by local stakeholders, usually municipalities. These systems of allocating resources give
priority to the contributions from the community and the municipality,
the existence of efficient implementation structures, and urgency of the
problems. These projects should be managed at the local level (that is,
at the level of the neighbourhood or apartment complex). Decentralised
management allows a better match between the interventions and the
needs of the neighbourhood and facilitates community relations. But
this decentralised model also presents the challenge of hiring qualified
personnel for projects at the local level, and the complexity and scale
of many of these projects make it necessary for municipalities to seek
technical assistance for their design and implementation. Over time, the
stability of the funding sources will promote the creation of social organisations and enterprises specialised in project management at the local
level.

The Challenge

The premature deterioration of houses and neighbourhoods presents two
interrelated challenges: on the one hand, the need to implement a new
generation of neighbourhood and public social housing upgrading programmes, and on the other, the need to reform land development regulations and urban development control practices to prevent the creation of
problematic neighbourhoods and communities (such as those emerging
due to the rapid growth of low-cost housing construction by the private
sector). These measures must ensure a good quality of life for residents
and prevent the premature deterioration of their real estate assets. They
must also ensure that neighbourhoods and public spaces are supplied
with all necessary facilities, and that the responsibility for their operation
and maintenance is evenly distributed among the municipality and the
beneficiaries. The operation and maintenance problem is not discussed
here, but it is a growing concern for integrated urban development policies aiming to provide a good quality of life to the population on a sustainable basis.

JACK COURIEL   # Interventions in Precarious Urban Areas of Uruguay

The social and spatial segregation of low-income households on city peripheries leads to their disengagement from the larger urban society. This section looks at the initiatives promoted by Uruguay's *Ministerio de Vivienda Ordenamiento Territorial y Medio Ambiente* (MVOTMA) (Ministry of Housing, Regional Planning, and Environment) to prevent these problems—initiatives that include urban and housing improvement and the establishment of community services. Such actions seek to involve the population in building an integrated society. After a short presentation of the characteristics of these areas in Montevideo and its surrounding metropolitan area, this section discusses a proposal to improve the housing standards of precarious urban areas: the *Programa de Rehabilitación Urbano Habitacional* (PRUH) (Urban and Housing Rehabilitation Programme) to be implemented in formal neighbourhoods, complementing the *Programa de Integración de Asentamientos Irregulares* (PIAI) (Regularisation of Informal Settlements Programme), which operates in informal settlements. The PRUH addresses the fact that precarious urban areas are made up of both formal and informal settlements and are thus complex pieces of the urban structure.[56] Its interventions, and specifically its zone-based approach, are framed by the *Plan de Desarrollo Territorial* (Territorial Development Plan) of the *Intendencia Municipal de Montevideo* (IMM), Montevideo's municipal government, in particular in its urban zone plans.

Social Fragmentation in Urban Areas

Sociologists and urban development specialists agree that, starting in the 1980s, the social fragmentation of cities accelerated across Latin America, each case with its own peculiarities. In several cities in Uruguay, for example, low-, middle-, and high-income households live increasingly far apart. Katzman (1999) characterises vulnerability using both indicators of assets and indicators of risk. Assets include the physical, human, financial, and social capital of households. The most at-risk populations are considered the young and uneducated (aged 8–15); unmarried young women with children (aged 15–19); and male youth that do not study, work, or actively seek work (aged 15–24). The growth of the vulnerable population on the urban periphery parallels the emptying of formal neighbourhoods, which are generally better endowed with urban infrastructure and services. To analyze the territorial correlation of these indicators in Montevideo, the spatial distribution of three population groups was plotted using the following categories: (i) high assets and low-risk behaviour, (ii) medium-level assets and medium-level risk behaviour, and (iii) low

---

[56] Irregular settlements are groups of 10 or more dwellings located in private or public lands, built without the consent of the landowner and without complying with land subdivision regulations. These settlements lack some or all public utility services and either lack or have very difficult access to other urban social services.

assets and high-risk behaviour. Map 4.1 shows that, except in the coastal area to the east, a population with low assets and high-risk behaviour can be found in most areas of Montevideo and its metropolitan area (MMA). But in Montevideo the population with low assets grows and the population with intermediate and high assets declines, while in the MMA the populations remain in more or less equilibrium. This is mostly the result of the rapid growth of the population with high assets and low risk behaviour in Ciudad de la Costa in the Canelones municipality, a majority of which migrated from Montevideo.

It is important to consider that vulnerable populations grow in the MMA because of two interrelated processes: migration out of consolidated neighbourhoods in the city centre and a higher birth rate. As youth move out of central areas in search of work and housing, Montevideo and its MMA face complex housing problems. The significance of this process is evident in the fact that 79 percent of people living in Uruguay's informal settlements are located in the municipalities of Montevideo, Canelones, and San José, with most informal neighbourhoods concentrated in the areas close to the limit of the city of Montevideo.[57] The residential location patterns of middle- and high-income households are voluntary decisions in search of space and good environmental conditions. Since the mid-twentieth century they have increasingly moved out of the city centre to the coast. On the contrary, low-income households settle where they find low-cost land. As a result, the social and spatial segregation of socially vulnerable households due to their low incomes—whether the result of low salaries or informal employment—is accompanied by precarious urban conditions.

The increase in neighbourhoods with low assets and significant shortages of urban services—which in turn contributed to the expansion of the urbanised area—took place during a period of economic growth (1980–1995). In this period, employment and social spending increased, inflation was in the single digits, inequality did not worsen, and the incidence of poverty diminished from 37 to 15 percent of urban households (Filgueira, 2004). But this picture, taken from the aggregate data, hides structural problems and definite trends fuelled by underlying economic and social processes, such as the growing spatial segregation of the urban population, which increased inequalities and weakened traditional social integration mechanisms (neighbourhoods, schools, public spaces) (Filgueira, 2004). In terms of employment, it is possible to observe an increase in informal and precarious jobs. In terms of family, the period saw the growth of low-income, single-parent households, particularly, among young mothers. At the periphery of the city, levels of primary educational achievement were low and many students deserted the system in the first cycle of secondary school. All studies agree that the concentration of the low-income population in precarious settlements contributed to the intergenerational reproduction of poverty.

---

[57] The built-up area included in the MMA is only a small portion of the total territory of the municipalities of San José and Canelones.

Map 4.1 Socio-urban Fragmentation in Montevideo

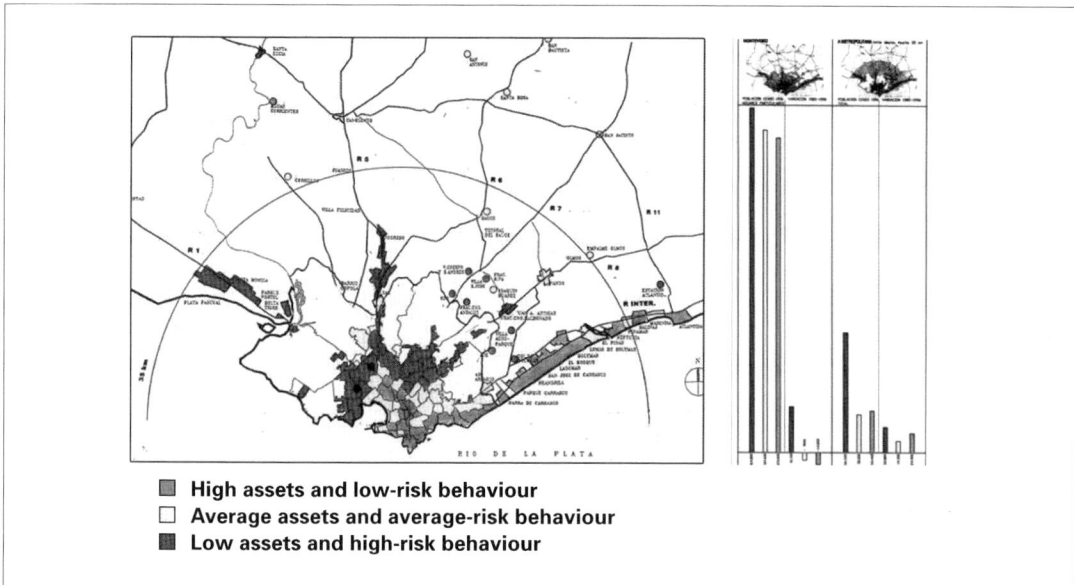

☐ **High assets and low-risk behaviour**
☐ **Average assets and average-risk behaviour**
☐ **Low assets and high-risk behaviour**

Source: Kaztman (1999).

Increases in territorial informality are due to both the populace and the public institutions. During the 15-year period under analysis, Uruguay underwent two major economic crises (1982 and 2002) that played an important role in the growth of informal settlements, particularly in Montevideo, where 11 percent of the population lived in informal housing (INE, 2006). The return to democracy in 1985 opened up channels of dialogue between the central government's sector agencies in charge of housing and the residents of informal settlements, allowing a better understanding of the economic and social forces fueling the growth of these settlements in Uruguay. The population moved to informal settlements to gain economic advantages: free access to land, no municipal taxes and fees, and free utilities (water and electricity). Public institutions tolerated the illegal occupation of lands to decompress social demands and tensions. The process ended up increasing a territorially fragmented and unsustainable urban development.

Interventions

To deal with the social fragmentation of cities, it is necessary to implement a coordinated set of urban development and housing programmes alongside settlement upgrading and informal settlement prevention programmes.

To tackle the problems described, the government should focus on "urban zones", critical problem areas of the urban periphery and also present in some intermediate areas of the city structure. Such areas would benefit from social and urban policies and programmes that are specific to their needs, flexible, integrated, and cumulative. Such programmes should address:

- Informal settlements eligible for investment by the settlement upgrading programme
- Informal settlements that need to be resettled in their entirety
- Government-built housing units that have deteriorated and are in danger of fostering criminal activity
- Formal residential areas with shortages of infrastructure and poor housing conditions
- Incomplete or precarious urban areas
- Shortages of infrastructure and social services

The solution to these problems is under the purview of the institutions with responsibility over the territory: municipalities, public utilities, and providers of social services, and, in particular, it is then necessary to coordinate the interventions of the local governments and those of the sector institutions with responsibility over the territory. The cross-sector nature of the PIAI is a good starting point because it works on three dimensions of the problem: society, housing, and urban infrastructure.

From the point of view of the city it is important to consider the problems of the urban zone when designing settlement upgrading projects. A recent evaluation of the settlement upgrading investment undertaken by the PIAI—designed and implemented without considering the scale of the urban zone—identified undesired outcomes of the public intervention (Interconsult, 2005). In one case, the *Nuevo Amanecer* project, a road was built to connect the neighbourhood with the rest of the city, which prompted the formation of two new informal settlements.[58] In another settlement, the *Sacrificio de Sonia Sur* project, the provision of access roads allowed the extension of the urbanised area with two housing complexes for low-income households, which increased the social and housing segregation problems of the city.[59]

Interventions in the Lower Pantanoso Creek, Montevideo[60]

This proposed approach is illustrated by the project implemented in the lower watershed of the Pantanoso Creek in Montevideo. The project cov-

---

[58] The informal settlement Nuevo Amanecer is located in Casabó, a neighbourhood that is part of the Rincón del Cerro area in the municipality of Montevideo. The settlement upgrading project executed by the PIAI in 2001–2002 benefited 81 households.

[59] The informal settlement Sacrificio de Sonia Sur is part of the Sacrificio de Sonia neighbourhood in the municipality of Rivera. A total of 117 households benefited from the project completed by the PIAI in 2004.

[60] The project is located in the Montevideo municipality and includes the La Paloma and Tomkinson neighbourhoods. A similar intervention is planned for the city of Pando in the municipality of Canelones.

ers 97 hectares, out of which informal settlements occupy 25 and formal land subdivisions the other 72. Of the 2,000 households in the area, 500 are in informal settlements and 1,500 in formal areas. There are 1,160 residential lots, 350 in the informal settlements and 810 in the formal ones. The project area comprises several social housing complexes, including the Municipal Neighbourhood 12 (La Paloma and Camino de las Tropas) and resettlement programmes resulting from the execution of the third phase of the Municipal Development Plan III (Verdún, Pernambuco and Vizcaya, Pasaje Martori). The formal and informal settlements in the area have several features in common, such as housing typology and construction quality, making it difficult to distinguish them at first glance.

The settlement upgrading programme in this part of the city is framed by an urban zone plan that extends beyond individual neighbourhoods.[61] The following interventions have been proposed:

- *Sanitation.* Expansion of the sanitation network to the whole area in order to serve the informal settlements that were not covered by the investments executed under the Municipal Development Plan III (implemented by the municipality using a loan from the Inter-American Development Bank).
- *Connectivity and integration.* Construction of cross-streets in the big urban blocks and the upgrade of existing streets to provide continuity with outside urban areas (see Map 4.2). The opening of new streets would require land acquisition by eminent domain, the realignment of property boundaries, and the enforcement of setbacks for new housing construction. This intervention also involves the realignment and improvement of road surfaces with asphalt, the construction of road shoulders, and the improvement of street lighting in the whole area.
- *Environmental mitigation.* This includes the rehabilitation of wetlands into public parks. This requires the physical demarcation of the boundaries of the area, the construction of pedestrian pathways, and the prevention of all situations that could alter the natural functioning of the ecosystem. Part of the population obtains income by processing solid waste collected from waste bins in the city. The project designates specific areas for these activities, whose management is the responsibility of individuals under the supervision of the municipal waste management service.

---

[61] According to the territorial plan of the IMM, zone plans are "plans covering the whole area of influence of the zone communal centres. These plans frame the urban interventions executed in the area and their main objective is to consolidate the key components of the urban structure of the area. Within the zone plans, special area plans and units of intervention can be defined, always within the provisions of the territorial plan and using its management tools. The management of these plans will be done in coordination with the responsible institution and supporting the actions of the technical teams, the local government and communal centres" (IMM, 1998: 235). Because there are different urban situations in the area, such as territorially grouped and isolated informal settlements, the interventions are based on different territorial scales, always retaining a focus on the whole zone.

Map 4.2 Interventions in Urban Areas with Shortages in Montevideo

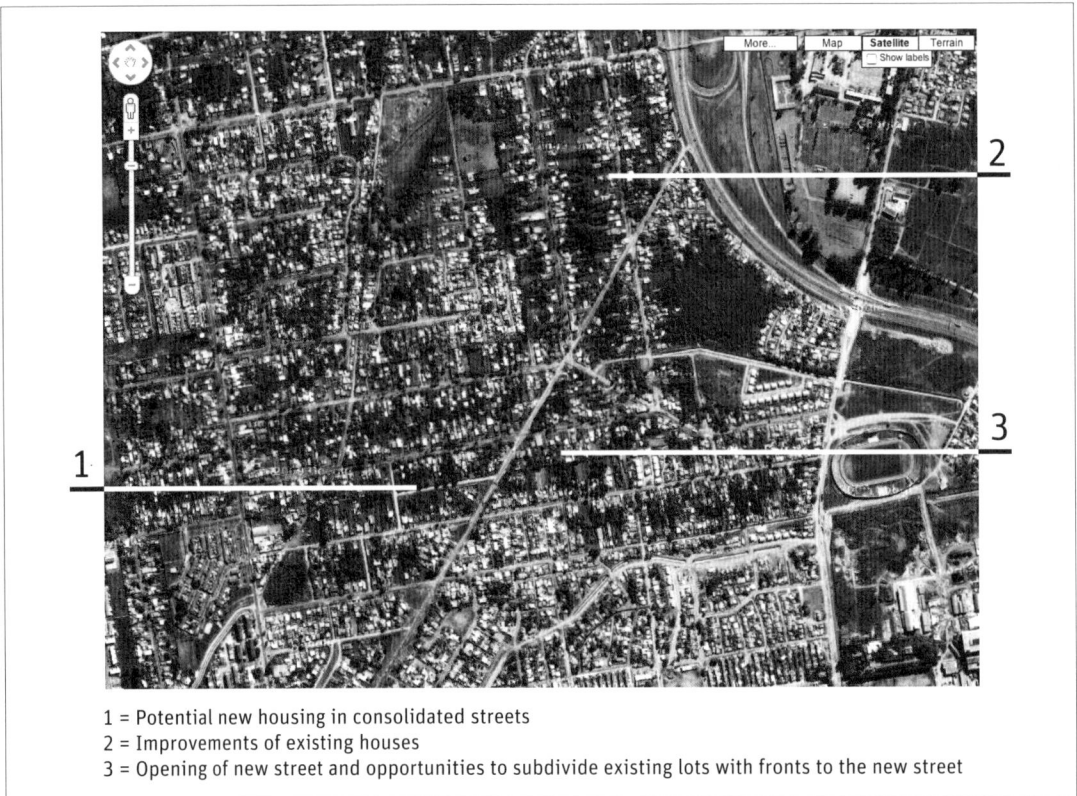

1 = Potential new housing in consolidated streets
2 = Improvements of existing houses
3 = Opening of new street and opportunities to subdivide existing lots with fronts to the new street

Source: MVOTMA.

- *Open space for recreation and sports.* Vacant and underused land will be utilised for neighbourhood facilities that can also serve other surrounding areas of the city. These interventions will expand the coverage of health and education services, and will rehabilitate and expand existing buildings to turn them into cultural, recreational, and informal education centres.
- *Resettlement.* The resettlement of 60 households as a result of opening new streets and the rehabilitation of public spaces.

The complexity of the issues present in the area result from the widespread practice of buying and using informally subdivided land and houses (which are then inherited by the next generation) generating neighbourhoods with severe shortages of services and low-quality housing. This process generates negative externalities that promote the deterioration of the urban structure and houses of the surrounding formal subdivisions. The problem is compounded by the fact that low- and low-middle-income inhabitants of the formal areas, who are paying for services, do not have the voice of those living in informal settlements that are organised in neighbourhood associations and capture the attention of the elected officials. It is necessary to implement the PRUH in order to solve the problems of the depressed formal residential areas and to improve their inhabitants' quality of life.

The road and public space improvement scheme shown in Figure 4.4 is proof of the programme's potential. Possible interventions range from improvements in existing houses and the rehabilitation of public spaces—streets, parks, and recreational facilities—to building new houses at the back of the formal housing lots, a scheme to increase residential density by opening new streets. The PRUH comprises two types of interventions: infrastructure and housing. The former comprises the consolidation of existing streets and the opening of new ones; the greening of public spaces; the construction and rehabilitation of sidewalks, bus stops, and signalling; and other urban facilities. The housing dimension includes a series of subprogrammes adapted to the needs of households and their financial capacity. The minimum intervention that may be fully subsidised by the programme is the improvement of the bathroom and kitchen with corresponding connections to the potable water and sewerage networks, and improvements in electric wiring. Other complementary interventions are also possible, including facade improvements to consolidate the urban image of neighbourhoods. At a maximum, the programme can help build a second house in the lot for rental or to share with family or friends.

For the community to take on this type of programme, it is necessary that multidisciplinary teams implement the entire process—planning through execution—including the follow-up and periodic evaluation needed to identify necessary adjustments to the programme. This requires the identification of indicators based on expert knowledge. The key to the programme's success is the coordination of existing social programmes by the municipality and sector institutions of the central government, in particular the ministries of social development and labour and social security. Institutionally, the PRUH will be executed under an agreement between the IMM and the MVOTMA, by which the IMM will execute the programme and finance the infrastructure, and the National Housing Directorate of the MVOTMA will finance the housing improvement component.

MARÍA DE LA LUZ
NIETO

Quiero mi Barrio, Chile[62]

How to Stop the Deterioration of Neighbourhoods

One of the characteristics of the rapid growth of Chilean cities—especially in the second half of the 1900s—was the spatial and social segregation of the population and the low building standards of the houses built or subsidised by the state to overcome the acute housing deficit. This led to the

---

[62] Literally, Quiero mi Barrio means "I Love my Neighbourhood".

deterioration of low-income areas, affecting houses, public spaces, and community infrastructure. Such areas have little spatial connectivity and poor road and public transport access to the rest of the city; a high incidence of environmental problems, such as dumping grounds for solid waste and other sources of pollution; and, in the most severe cases, a significant lack of public spaces, streets, parks, and community facilities. Residents of other city areas stigmatise these deteriorated neighbourhoods. Moreover, their inhabitants have very little sense of belonging and suffer from deteriorating social relations; low levels of social organisation and community involvement; growing security problems; and other social vulnerabilities, such as drug addiction, the microtrafficking of drugs, and other criminal activity.

The deterioration of such neighbourhoods—coupled with their isolation from urban amenities—creates a perception of social exclusion that weakens community relations. This, in turn, leads to a sense of disenfranchisement from the state and government, putting democratic governance at risk. Citizens do not see the benefits of development, but only a growing distance from the quality of life enjoyed by middle- and high-income households and that of the neighbourhoods in which they live.

Inclusive Public Policies

Inclusive public policies are necessary to improve social equity through the improvement of the quality of life in deteriorating and excluded neighbourhoods. Decisive actions to combat poverty, generate employment, and improve health, education, and housing services require a significant expansion of public and private investment. Initiatives should be targeted to specific territories and ensure that public institutions work in partnership with the beneficiary communities. The challenges confronted by neighbourhoods include the relaunch of community organisations, the development of links between the population and local and sector institutions, and the generation of a significant and observable improvement in the habitat.

To face the challenges described above, the *Ministerio de Vivienda y Urbanismo* (MINVU) (Ministry of Housing and Urban Development) executed the *Quiero mi Barrio* programme. The programme is based on an integrated and multi-sector approach that takes on both the social and physical aspects of neighbourhood rehabilitation projects, involving citizens in their design and execution. The programme aims to improve the social and urban integration of the neighbourhoods with rehabilitated public spaces, enhance environmental conditions, and strengthen social relations.[63] *Quiero mi Barrio* is executed by the MINVU in the framework of

---

[63] The *Quiero mi Barrio* programme was created by Decree No. 14 of January 22, 2007. The programme originates in the priorities of the national government that aim at improving the social safety net, creating conditions to accelerate the development process, improving the quality of life of the population, and combating discrimination and exclusion.

the three strategic axes of the government's housing policy: (i) to increase the production of housing solutions, (ii) to improve the quality of housing design and construction, and (iii) to promote social integration through housing solutions that are fully integrated into the city. The programme is also framed by the strategic objectives of the city agenda: (i) participatory and socially integrated cities; (ii) environmental sustainability; and (iii) competitiveness. The agenda seeks an integrated and sustainable urban development based on the real improvement of individuals' quality of life and the generation of quality employment and investment opportunities.

The majority of neighbourhoods face significant social problems. The *Quiero mi Barrio* programme does not attempt to solve all these problems; it is designed to implement interventions that reduce physical deterioration and social vulnerability. The programme's contribution is complemented by other government interventions and its actions are designed to coordinate with and induce the involvement of other programmes in neighbourhoods. The programme operates within a well-delimited territory and its focus is to strengthen the social networks of the inhabitants, improve the neighbourhood's image and identity, and rehabilitate the public spaces used by the community. Through *Quiero Mi Barrio*, the MINVU addressed the improvement and rehabilitation of the city's environment at the neighbourhood level for the first time. The improvement of the environmental conditions in the neighbourhoods and the strengthening of community involvement are key elements of the urban and housing policies pursued by the ministry. Execution of the programme began in 2007 with interventions in 200 neighbourhoods in all regions of the country. In view of the magnitude of the problem, it is expected that the interventions financed by the programme will become a permanent line of the MINVU investment.

Guiding Principles

The interventions carried out in the neighbourhoods are based on an integrated urban plan that links the physical works with social development initiatives from the early phases of diagnostics and sets up priorities for their implementation, operation, and maintenance. Exercising citizens' rights and improving community relations are two objectives to be attained through the implementation of each neighbourhood rehabilitation programme. Through this process, community members transition from being passive users of state resources into fully empowered citizens with both rights and duties. To attain these objectives, the programme promotes citizen forums to encourage involvement in the decision-making process. The formation of neighbourhood development councils is a central step to attain the objective of involving the citizens in the programme.

The implementation of integrated interventions requires coordination among institutions at the national, regional, and local levels. The multisector approach coordinates the different instruments available to the government, giving each responsibility for a different phase of the imple-

Figure 4.3 Intervention Strategy in the *Quiero mi Barrio* Programme

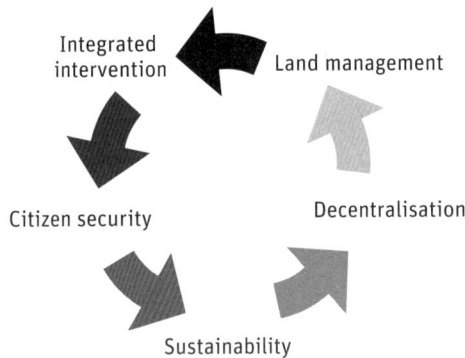

Source: Author's elaboration.

mentation process and pooling available resources for their optimal use to avoid duplication of efforts. This presupposes that the different actors have the capacity to adjust the services they offer to the needs of the project. Coordinating interventions across institutional levels is difficult given the complexity and lack of flexibility of the public administration structure. Added to this is the varied scale of intervention in neighbourhoods made up of between 150 and 5,000 houses. In the programme, 68 percent of the neighbourhoods had less than 500 houses, 28 percent had between 500 and 1,500 houses, 3 percent had between 1,500 and 3,000 houses, and only 1 percent had more than 3,000 houses.

Municipal Involvement in the Programme

The rehabilitation strategy of the *Quiero Mi Barrio* programme includes the active involvement of the municipalities as agents of local development and the coordination of the actions of various public and private actors in the neighbourhoods. Municipalities play a relevant role in the following project phases:

■ *Decision making*. Municipalities and programme administrators agree upon the execution mechanism for projects (direct execution, with municipal contributions, or public bidding). The municipality helps define the type of works that will be executed and the priorities for community work. The municipality also helps decide how resources are allocated between physical and social work.
■ *Allocation and management of resources*. The municipality is the executing agency for all the physical investments for which it has institutional management capacity.
■ *Dialogue with local actors*. Programme administrators approach communities through municipalities. The same is done with the

institutional and local actors that are included in the local development council.

■ *Adjusting the programme to the area*. Municipal authorities and professionals provide feedback to the programme administrators during the evaluation process and in defining future sector policies in neighbourhood rehabilitation.

The Programme

Objectives

The general objective of the *Quiero Mi Barrio* programme is to continue improving the living conditions in neighbourhoods experiencing urban deterioration and social vulnerability. The specific objectives of the programme are to rehabilitate deteriorated public spaces, improve the conditions of urban environments, strengthen community relations, and promote social integration.

Components

The programme has an urban and a social component, which are included in the interventions in each neighbourhood.

The urban component improves the physical connections between the neighbourhood and the rest of the city by extending and improving roads, and provides or expands community facilities, parks, street lighting, and other works required for the effective operation and maintenance of neighbourhood common areas or public spaces (see Table 4.1). This component is structured around an investment management plan that includes the portfolio of investments that the community prioritises. The equipment required for the functioning of the project (chairs, desks, sports equipment) is included in the total cost, including installation charges.[64] The investments may benefit public land used for general purposes, land owned by the *Servicio de Vivienda y Urbanización* (SERVIU) (Housing and Urbanisation Corporation) or the municipality, or land that is designated for condominiums.[65]

The social component is central to the implementation of an integrated model of urban rehabilitation. Its objective is to improve the social integration of neighbourhood networks and promote the involvement of neighbours in the rehabilitation of public spaces and the improvement of the neighbourhood environment (both social and physical). This component is

---

[64] The community can obtain other inputs required but not indispensable for the functioning of the project from other sources of financing during the execution of the programme.
[65] The SERVIU is an autonomous service of the central government attached to the Ministry of Housing and Urbanism (MINVU) and is responsible for the execution of the urban development and housing programmes of the central government.

Table 4.1 *Quiero mi Barrio* Programme: Urban Components

Component	Investments
Parks	Parks, street greening, water fountains, gazebos, exercise circuits, bicycle lanes, playgrounds, sand boxes, picnic areas, changing rooms, and multi-purpose playing fields.
Urban facilities	Multi-purpose rooms, sports centres, community centres, nurseries, and other basic neighbourhood equipment.
Accessibility	Rehabilitation of sidewalks, access roads and neighbourhood roads, pedestrian alleyways, parking areas, and pedestrian streets.
Complementary works	Urban equipment, retaining walls, absorption wells for rainwater, basic works to make land usable (drainage, landfills, land consolidation), repairs and improvements in potable water mains, sewerage, electricity, gas, irrigation networks, and equipment for community use.

Source: Author's elaboration.

structured around a social management plan that links social development initiatives to the physical investments included in the investment management plan, which include community control of the physical progress of the works, cleaning and beautification executed directly by beneficiaries, training of leaders, training of beneficiaries in topics connected with the use of community areas that have been improved or built by the programme, the strengthening of community organisations, programme dissemination activities, community meetings, programme follow-up and evaluation activities, and training that ensures residents will be capable of operating neighbourhood improvements and undertaking new projects on their own. The main focus of the social management plan is the neighbourhood development council, a functional organisation made up of representatives of community organisations from the neighbourhood, people with a stake in the development of the neighbourhood, and officials from the public and private entities involved in the neighbourhood, including the municipality and the regional secretariat of the MINVU.

In addition to these components, five types of *transversal activities* are implemented in all neighbourhoods:

- *Citizen involvement.* For neighbourhood rehabilitation efforts to achieve long-term sustainability, residents must actively participate in their design and implementation. Developing community organisations also helps to reduce many of the social vulnerability issues confronted by neighbourhoods. Furthermore, involving beneficiaries in the rehabilitation efforts helps to build their self-confidence and promotes the good use of their neighbourhoods' public spaces, one of the key components of improving the city's perception of informal neighbourhoods and eliminating the social stigma attached to them.

- *Cultural heritage and identity*. Activities that increase the knowledge of a neighbourhood's identity, promote the rediscovering of its culture, and create specific avenues for its members to connect to each other increase the level of trust among residents. Such activities should be geared towards both genders and all age groups as they try to reconstruct the history of the neighbourhood by identifying places, dates, events, rituals, and people that are important to the community.
- *The environmental variable*. The programme invites beneficiaries to view their surroundings with a critical eye, starting with identifying what is not desirable (for instance, the waste dumping areas, excessive trash in the neighbourhoods, the undeveloped parks) and then helping them to make improvements. This activity is a call for short-term action (cleaning streets, collecting litter, planting trees) and thus a mechanism to engage the interest of groups that are not easily motivated by ongoing community activities.
- *Citizen security*. This activity requires the coordinated action of several government institutions while still upholding the participatory model of intervention promoted by the programme. Activities geared towards crime prevention through environmental design are implemented to reduce both the feelings of insecurity among urban inhabitants and the incidence of crime.
- *Digital connectivity*. The programme increases digital literacy among residents, expands their access to opportunities, and strengthens the connections between the neighbourhood and the rest of the city.

These transversal activities are part of the project implementation process in neighbourhoods. They aim to modify long-established behaviours, improving the way residents regard and use their public spaces, mobilising local agents, and promoting dialogue and agreement around the projects.

Types of Neighbourhoods Covered by the Programme

The MINVU began the programme by allocating resources for work in 200 neighbourhoods. The ministry selected the initial neighbourhoods based on their urgent needs and the equitable distribution of investments in the territory. Municipalities with a minimum of 70,000 inhabitants and 10 percent of the population living under the poverty line made the first cut. Additional criteria were used to classify and select the 200 neighbourhoods according to the complexity of the problems they were facing. High incidences of urban deterioration and social vulnerability, shortages of infrastructure, and major deficits of urban services characterised the high-complexity neighbourhoods, which were highly stigmatised by the rest of society and accordingly showed low levels of social cohesion and self-esteem. Neighbourhoods with medium complexity had less severe shortages of infrastructure and services and required less intervention in their public spaces, urban facilities, and houses (see Table 4.2).

Table 4.2 *Quiero mi Barrio* Programme: Neighbourhood Types

Type of neighbourhoods	Number of houses	
	Medium-complexity neighbourhoods	High-complexity neighbourhoods
Type A	Up to 500	Up to 400
Type B	Between 501 and 1,500	Between 401 and 900
Type C	Between 1,501 and 3,000	Over 900
Type D	Over 3,000	—

Source: MINVU.

Investment by Type of Neighbourhood

The programme set a maximum amount of investment for each of the components for each type of neighbourhood. These resources could be used to finance any of the eligible investments within each component in conjunction with resources from other sources. The maximum investment for neighbourhoods was determined by budget considerations and the MINVU's experience in other urban programmes (see Table 4.3). The minimum amount allocated to each neighbourhood was always enough to build at least one good-quality neighbourhood facility.

Implementation

The Team

The team in charge of a project can consist of personnel from the regional offices of the MINVU, municipal workers, or private consultants hired by a public-bidding process. The team works from an office installed in the neighbourhood and includes, at a minimum, the following positions:

- *Neighbourhood team leader.* A professional who has experience in managing projects or programmes and knowledge of the functioning of the government. He or she is devoted full time to the project and is responsible for coordinating all aspects of it, including actions implemented by other stakeholders.
- *Social management plan coordinator.* A social worker with a background in community participation, experience in the design and management of urban development projects, and good leadership and conflict-resolution skills.
- *Investment plan coordinator.* A professional linked to the construction industry with a background in urban planning and management, the design of infrastructure projects, and community work.

Table 4.3 *Quiero mi Barrio* Programme: Maximum Investment Cost by Component and Type of Neighbourhood (in US$ as of 2008)

Number of houses		Number of neighbourhoods	Investment management plan	Social management plan	Technical assistance	Total investment by neighbourhood
From	To					
Medium-complexity neighbourhoods						
0	500	124	600,000	220,000	20,000	840,000
501	1,500	50	840,000	251,000	25,000	1,116,000
1,501	3,000	5	1,200,000	274,000	30,000	1,504,000
3,001	over	2	1,600,000	274,000	30,000	1,904,000
High-complexity neighbourhoods						
0	400	4	1,800,000	300,000	60,000	2,160,000
401	600	2	2,700,000	360,000	110,000	3,170,000
601	900	4	2,700,000	500,000	160,000	3,360,000
901	over	3	3,600,000	600,000	260,000	4,460,000

Source: MINVU.

In addition to the three coordinators, the neighbourhood team must have experienced community facilitators and other specialists as required by the social management plan. These specialists may work part time.

The Phases

The programme structures the projects in three phases:

Phase 1: Preparing the neighbourhood contract
Phase 2: Executing the neighbourhood contract
Phase 3: Closing the neighbourhood contract, evaluating the project, and setting the agenda for the future

The phases vary in length according to the complexity and needs of the neighbourhoods; however, there are maximum execution periods for each phase (see Figure 4.4 and Table 4.4). The following is a description of each phase.

Phase 1. Preparation of the neighbourhood contract. During this phase, trust is established between the neighbours and the team in charge of the project, and their collaborative work begins. The first activity is a technical study containing, at a minimum, a diagnosis of the urban and social environment and the safety conditions in the neighbourhood. The study identifies the most important shortages and the key actors, and proposes an integrated plan of action. Simultaneously, the team helps the community to make a self-diagnosis of its problems, promoting the involvement

Table 4.4 *Quiero mi Barrio* Programme: Duration of the Phases According to the Type of Neighbourhood (in months)

Phase of the project	High-complexity neighbourhoods	Medium-complexity neighbourhoods
Phase 1	6	4
Phase 2	26	18
Phase 3	4	2
Total time of intervention	36 months	24 months

Source: MINVU.

of all the social groups living in the neighbourhood and capturing their demands and expectations. The different interest groups of the neighbourhood conduct the self-diagnosis separately. This activity begins by collecting information to build the history of the neighbourhood and setting up a neighbourhood development council—the key participation structure—made up of representatives of the social and territorial organisations, the institutions with responsibility over the territory, including the municipality and community leaders. A shared diagnostic is developed, with information coming from the technical study and self-diagnosis done by the different interest groups. This diagnostic is the basis for designing the integrated plan for the neighbourhood. Projects and initiatives eligible for financing by the programme are incorporated into the investment and social management plans. Initiatives that are not financed by the programme are left out of these plans; the development council may seek alternative resources to fund them or incorporate them into the future agenda for the neighbourhood. An inaugural work, or "confidence investment", is planned and executed in the first phase to validate the government presence in the neighbourhood and generate trust among the beneficiaries.[66] The first phase ends with the signing of the neighbourhood contract by the neighbourhood development council, the municipality, and the MINVU.

Phase 2. Execution of the neighbourhood contract. In the second phase the physical works contemplated in the investment management plan are executed and the actions of the social management plan are completed. This involves the calling for bids for the construction of the physical works, hiring contractors, and supervising the execution of the project or projects. The investments linked to the transversal activities and multisector agreements are also executed in this phase. Among these activi-

---

[66] The inaugural event is mainly symbolic. It is specially designed for each neighbourhood to attract the attention of the beneficiaries of the project and to invite their participation in it. The inaugural event should require only a small investment of time and money while the investment and social management plans are being formulated.

Figure 4.4 Operational Model of the *Quiero mi Barrio* Programme

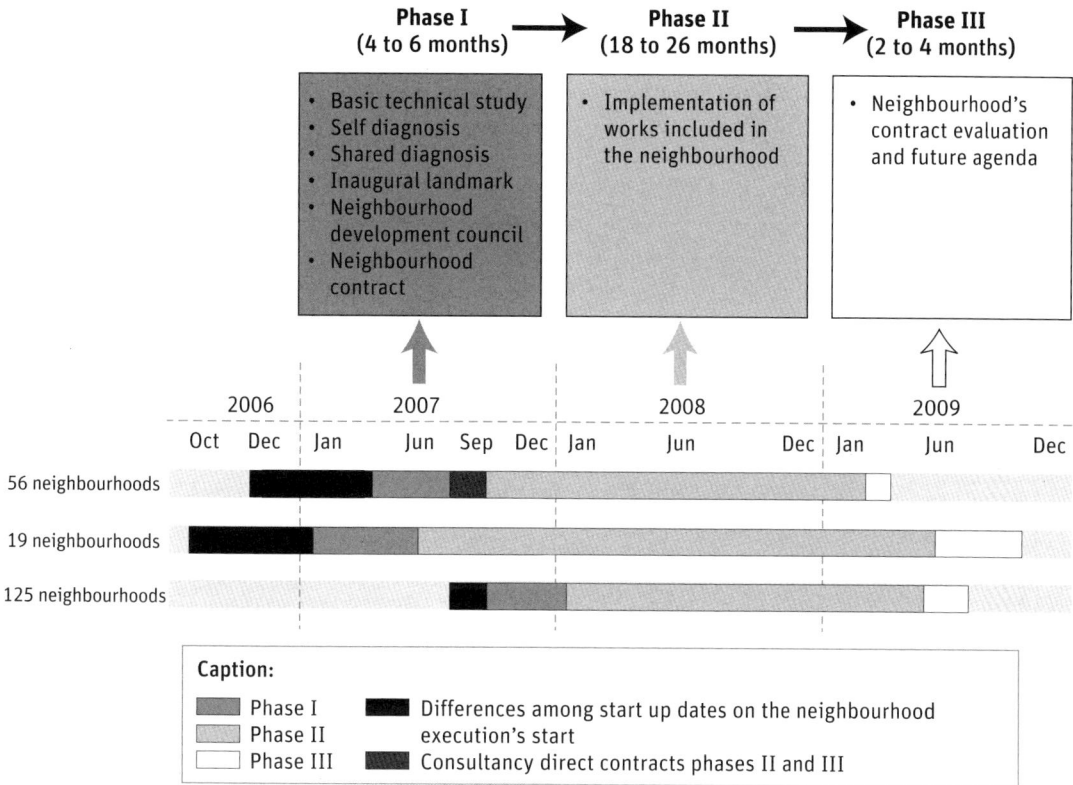

Source: Author's elaboration.

ties, it is worth mentioning those executed in coordination with the following government programmes:

- *Programa de Seguridad Ciudadana* (Citizen Safety Programme)—Ministry of the Interior
- *Barrios para una Sociedad de la Información* (Neighbourhoods for the Information Society)—Ministry of Public Works, Under Secretariat for Telecommunications
- *Creando Chile en mi Barrio* (Building Chile in My Neighbourhood)—National Council of Culture
- Various athletics projects—National Sports Council

Phase 3. Closing and evaluating the neighbourhood contract and setting the future agenda. The closing of the neighbourhood contract with the neighbourhood development council involves an evaluation of the programme, the systematisation of the experiences of the participants of the project, the formulation of the future agenda, the alignment of the community's

commitments with the facilities' operation and maintenance needs, and the formulation of new multi-sector projects. At a "closing event", the team and the community evaluate the process, achievements, experiences, and lessons learned from the project. The neighbourhood history compiled by the project is presented to the community to promote the continuity of the social and community dynamics initiated by the project and to strengthen the community organisations formed by the programme.

Recreational areas and parks built in the neighbourhoods are gathering points for young adults and children.
17 of September neighbourhood, Santiago, Chile

The Road Travelled

Quiero mi Barrio began operations in 2006 in 75 neighbourhoods and in 2007 in the remaining 125 new neighbourhoods; these were the 200 neighbourhoods included in the original budget. The implementation of the programme represents a big challenge for the MINVU given its participatory and integrated approach to the work, which takes into account everything that impacts the neighbourhood residents' quality of life and requires high levels of commitment, teamwork, participation, and coordinated management capacity on the part of all stakeholders. The results of the programme are becoming apparent. In neighbourhoods with projects initiated in 2006, the beneficiaries are rebuilding their social networks and have a new perspective towards their neighbourhoods. The programme had to overcome several obstacles to achieve these gains: the initial resistance of the beneficiaries, delays in reaching agreements, the difficulties of learning how to implement the programme, and, especially, the residents' fundamental lack of trust in the government. The programme executed inter-sector actions and investments, thanks to the capacity of the MINVU to attract other institutions; in doing so, MINVU benefited from the leverage provided by the resources allocated to the programme.

A key factor in the success of these programmes is the constant presence of the technical teams in the neighbourhoods. The teams have offices in the communities where the beneficiaries can contact them at any time to clarify issues, answer questions, and respond to complaints. Their presence builds trust. In addition, the neighbourhood development councils enable beneficiaries to participate in the rehabilitation of their neighbourhoods and work in close cooperation with government agencies. This form of involvement encourages residents to exercise their rights, to take responsibility for their neighbourhoods, and to defend their proposals with clarity, strength, and passion.

Quiero mi Barrio promotes a new way of living in cities, a new relationship among neighbours, and a new sense of pride regarding the quality of the neighbourhood's infrastructure and services. In short, the programme proposes a "new contract" between the individuals and the state, interlinking citizen coexistence and the provision of services and urban facilities. Coexistence and participation are promoted by access to good urban services and by improved communication and organisation among residents. These neighbourhoods will be more sustainable in the long run as their inhabitants know each other, help each other, and value their neighbourhoods as places offering a good quality of life.

There are also challenges to overcome, particularly in establishing lasting alliances with other institutions. The municipality and the beneficiaries are both central for the sustainability of the neighbourhood rehabilitation and the implementation of the future agenda. But it is also important to establish clear and complementary roles for the other sector institutions of the central or regional government to ensure their fruitful contribution to the improvement of the neighbourhood. A second challenge is to expand the participation of members of civil society in the rehabilitation plan, including school administrators, shop owners, local health-care workers, and the police. These actors can get involved through the neighbourhood development councils or through other ad hoc structures. Either way, their presence expands the diversity of stakeholders and the visions of the future of the neighbourhood, contributing to the sustainability of the rehabilitation effort. A third challenge is to make the improvement of houses a line of action of the programme; this has not yet been done. Finally, it is essential to provide more support to community organisations. A neighbourhood rehabilitation programme is sustainable only if the neighbours truly believe that they are responsible for ensuring that the improvements are executed and the results maintained.

5 NEIGHBOURHOOD UPGRADING PROGRAMMES: LESSONS FROM LATIN AMERICA AND THE CARIBBEAN

EDUARDO ROJAS

Building Collective Know-How

For more than 25 years, various countries and cities in the Latin American and Caribbean (LAC) region have been implementing programmes aimed at solving the problem of informal settlements. These efforts have provided valuable insight into the best way to design, execute, and assess such programmes, much of which is reported in the present volume. The knowledge born of this accumulated experience has been disseminated internationally through publications and congresses, and also through technical assistance given by international organisations. It has thus served to improve the conceptual and methodological design and the implementation of these types of programmes. Analysis of the experiences of the Inter-American Development Bank (IDB) highlights the challenge inherent in finding integral solutions to the problems of informal settlements. The challenge is complex because what seems at first to be a mere question of implementation—the need to coordinate the activities of many different public entities in a given territory within a specific time frame—also calls for sustainable and equitable financing.

Neighbourhood upgrading is an urban development activity that involves intervening in areas where the local government is traditionally responsible, but national governments also have a marked interest in financing this kind of investment. There are many reasons for this interest beyond the desire to reduce the number of people living in conditions of poverty.[67]

Integrating informal settlements into the city and solving their sanitation, drainage, and environmental problems greatly improve the quality of life of inhabitants and drastically change the urban image of the neighbourhoods. This can be observed in the before-and-after pictures of projects financed by the *Favela Bairro* Programme.
Fernando Carmin neighbourhood, Rio de Janeiro, Brazil

---

[67] For local governments, this objective is compatible with the need to eliminate the negative externalities that informal settlements generate for the rest of the city. A lack of

Mexico's *Programa Hábitat* (Habitat Programme) is run by the *Secretaría de Desarrollo Social* (SEDESOL) (Social Development Secretariat) and was conceived as an anti-poverty instrument within the government's larger social investment programmes. Argentina's *Programa de Mejoramiento de Barrios* (PROMEBA) (Neighbourhood Upgrading Programme) is another good example of a national government's effort to lessen the effects of the proliferation of informal settlements. These types of programme focus on the development of social capital and the integration of recipient communities into urban life.

In countries where central governments control the greater part of the public resources and municipalities control very little, these programmes are commonly financed by central government transfers to local governments. The neighbourhood upgrading programme that has been carried out by the Chilean government over the past 25 years exemplifies this financial model. Projects are financed by a national fund included in the annual budget of the central government, which the municipalities can access by way of open competition. The municipalities then take charge of project implementation under the supervision of the central entity responsible for the programme.[68]

National financing can either take the form of a matching grant, where funds are transferred on the condition that the municipality supply a portion of the resources required, or full grants that finance the total investment. In the first case, national resources leverage local resources, increasing the total volume of the resources available for programmes, but this system tends to discriminate against the poorest municipalities that are not able to finance their share. Full grants, on the other hand, benefit the poorer municipalities. A combination of both mechanisms could be employed, distinguishing between larger municipalities with sufficient resources to put up their share and poorer municipalities that are unable to do so. In either case, national programmes would have to allocate scarce resources to satisfy the multiple demands of the local governments. The fact that the grants need not be returned makes them even more attractive. The system by which funds are allocated on the basis of project merit balances the scarcity of resources with the high number of demands. A disadvantage of the allocation system is that some projects can get postponed for many years.

---

access to safe drinking water, hygienic methods of waste disposal, and health and education services gravely affects poor populations in informal settlements. These factors also have a negative impact on wider segments of the population, especially in terms of health and the environment.

[68] This programme received funding from the IDB at various stages in its implementation. It currently operates as a part of the Programa Chile-Barrios (Chile's Neighbourhoods Programme), which promotes the coordination of diverse social programmes in the territory (http://opensite.desarrollo.minvu.cl/opensite_20070212164850.aspx).

There are other modes of resource allocation. The Habitat Programme in Mexico operates on a territorial basis, focusing on those city blocks with the highest concentration of poor families (so-called habitat polygons). The PROMEBA initiative in Argentina attempts to promote territorial coordination among various public programmes with impact on the quality of the habitat of the poorest sectors of the population thus expanding the scope and size of its interventions. It allocates resources accordingly, with priority given to projects where the provincial or municipal governments contribute financing to the investments. Although they provide the majority of the financing, both programmes place the fundamental responsibility for project design and implementation on the municipalities themselves, and both emphasise community participation. These programmes ration the resources available for project implementation by precisely defining the components that are eligible for financing and by placing a ceiling on the amount to be invested in each family. Social and economic cost-benefit analysis methodologies are commonly used in determining these amounts since they help clarify the benefits that these investments will generate for the whole society (see Chapter 7).

The PROMEBA was one of the first programmes to coordinate the activities financed by social and urban development programmes with those carried out by other entities of the public sector. The *Programa Chile-Barrios* (Chile's Neighbourhoods Programme), which continued and expanded the activities of the settlement upgrading programmes financed by the IDB in the 1980s (see footnote 66), also employs this strategy. These programmes thus help municipalities diagnose the developmental problems confronted by informal settlements and enable them to draw resources from existing social and territorial development programmes that are financed by different agencies of the central government. In doing so, they utilise local governments' ability to coordinate resources coming from different sources in a timely and effective manner.

State or provincial governments may also participate in financing and executing these development projects. Some are drawn to do so for the same reasons national governments get involved; in other cases, the structure of intergovernmental relations determines their involvement. In Argentina, provincial governments help upgrade neighbourhoods not only to discharge their executive responsibility for social housing programmes, but also to provide financing that can attract additional federal funds through the PROMEBA. In other cases, provincial governments must work to solve the inter-municipal coordination problems that emerge from informal settlements. In such a way, the *Programa de Saneamento e Recuperação Ambiental da Bacia do Guarapiranga* (Environmental Rehabilitation of the Guarapiranga Drainage Basin Programme, further referred to as the Guarapiranga Drainage Basin Programme) carried out by the state government in the greater metropolitan area of São Paulo seeks to resolve environmental problems and counter the threat to water resources posed by the illegal occupation of lands located in the aquifer recharge areas.[69]

Municipalities have conceived and financed a large number of programmes across the LAC region. Since local governments have to deal most directly with the problems created by informal settlements, finding a way to solve these problems is always high on their agenda. Even when municipalities do not fully finance programmes, they play a key role in their implementation. The *Programa Barrios de Verdad* (the True Neighbourhoods Programme) in La Paz, Bolivia, is a typical neighbourhood upgrading programme fully designed and financed by a municipality. The programme also selects priority neighbourhoods through competitions in which community participation plays a crucial part. The selection mechanism thus rewards communities that make contributions or strive to minimise investment costs.

As previously mentioned, these financial complexities are coupled with operational ones, which are discussed further by José Brakarz in the following section of this chapter. Most neighbourhood upgrading programmes are alike in the types of investments they consider eligible. These include projects that upgrade urban infrastructure and facilities, improve public spaces, and strengthen community organisations. This similarity results from the similarity of the problems faced, which in turn leads to similar implementation challenges. Brakarz points out the risk of too much diversification in programme objectives, components, and activities: it can lead to an exponential increase in investment costs and in the complexity of implementation.

The examples presented in this volume provide a sense of the scope and diversity of the LAC experience in neighbourhood upgrading programmes. The lessons drawn can be used for the ongoing design and execution of such programmes, which are counted among the most effective ways of achieving the United Nations Millennium Development Goal of significantly improving the lives of 100 million slum dwellers by the year 2020.

---

[69] The Programa de Eliminação de Cortiços (Inner-city Slum Removal Programme) in São Paulo is a good example of how a state can deploy its greater technical capacity to solve the complex social and town planning problems resulting from a vast number of inner-city slums (http://www.IDB.org/projects/project.cfm?id=BR0298&lang=es). The expertise gained in this programme has since been employed, through the IDB, in solving similar problems in other cities, such as Colón in Panama (http://www.IDB.org/projects/project.cfm?id=PN0144&lang=es).

JOSÉ BRAKARZ   # The IDB: 25 Years of Neighbourhood Upgrading

The IDB's expertise in neighbourhood upgrading programmes is rich and varied, with 37 projects financed over nearly 25 years. The analysis presented in this part of the chapter includes a review of the projects and the amounts approved, as well as a discussion of general programme characteristics and common objectives, local counterparts, and implementation. The section concludes with a synopsis of the main findings and recommendations for the definition of objectives, challenges, and precautions to consider during implementation.

The IDB has been financing neighbourhood upgrading operations since the 1980s, although since 1994 there has been a significant increase in the number and scale of these operations. The Bank had previously financed programmes aimed at the development of specific urban areas. But the neighbourhood upgrading model—programmes targeted specifically at areas of extreme poverty, with interrelated social and infrastructure components—was established in its present form in the early 1990s. The first loan for the *Favela Bairro* (Urban Upgrading) programme, approved in 1995, is representative of this model. Since then, programmes have multiplied and become more complex in their objectives, design, and stakeholder diversity. The IDB has financed these kinds of programmes in 18 countries and in an even greater number of cities. This clearly demonstrates the demand for integrated urban interventions and also highlights the fact that this is a legitimate tool of local urban policy making. Table 5.1 lists the programmes financed by the IDB, including those that deal specifically with neighbourhood upgrading (as well as those that cover social housing or urban development, of which neighbourhood upgrading is a component). Table 5.1 shows that until 2009 the Bank had approved loans for more than US$3 billion and had financed programmes with investments totalling more than US$5 billion.

The volume of IDB loans in this sector has been irregular in terms of annually approved amounts, varying from a minimum of US$50 million in 2005 to a maximum of US$537 million in 2007, when neighbourhood upgrading programmes accounted for 8.3 percent of annual total loan approvals of US$8 billion (see Figure 5.1). It is worth noting that at least one neighbourhood upgrading programme has been approved every year over the past 15 years. The variations seen in the annually approved amounts are due mainly to political cycles in the larger countries, which tend to weigh heavily on the annual volume of lending.

A majority of large- and medium-sized countries in the region have implemented neighbourhood upgrading programmes, as seen in Figure 5.2. The larger countries—Brazil, Argentina, and Mexico—were among the first countries to adopt this model, not just for their capital cities, but for their large and intermediate-sized cities as well. Chile and Colombia—countries with a long tradition of innovation in the areas of town planning and housing—have launched nationwide programmes that involve

Table 5.1 Neighbourhood Upgrading Programmes Financed by the IDB, 1986–2008 (millions of US$)

Year	Country	Project name	Loan	Total
1986	Chile	Neighbourhood Upgrading and Sites and Services	40	90
1989	Trinidad & Tobago	National Settlements Programme	66	83
1994	Chile	Neighbourhood Upgrading Multiple Investment Programme	75	500
1995	Brazil	Favela Bairro, Rio de Janeiro Urban Upgrading	180	300
1995	Colombia	Social Protection Network for Housing and Neighbourhoods	157	300
1996	Argentina	Neighbourhood Upgrading Programme I (PROMEBA I)	102	170
1996	Brazil	Municipality of São Paulo, Singapore Programme	150	250
1997	Brazil	Programme Nova Baixada, State of Rio de Janeiro	180	300
1997	Uruguay	Municipal Development Programme III	55	78
1998	Bolivia	Housing Sector Reform Programme	60	71
1998	Brazil	Habitat Brazil Programme	250	417
1999	Guyana	Low-Income Settlement Programme	27	30
1999	Uruguay	Regularisation of Informal Settlements Programme (PIAI)	77	110
2000	Brazil	Favela Bairro II, Rio de Janeiro	180	300
2001	El Salvador	Housing Programme	70	94
2001	Argentina	Rosario Urban Rehabilitation Programme	43	71
2002	Ecuador	Housing Sector Support Programme II	25	40
2002	Trinidad & Tobago	Second Stage Urban Settlements Programme	32	40
2002	Nicaragua	Social Housing Programme	22	25
2003	Peru	Housing Sector Support Programme	60	75
2004	Mexico	Habitat Programme	350	500
2004	Panama	New Housing Policy Instruments	10	12
2005	Haiti	Urban Rehabilitation Programme	50	50
2006	Honduras	Social Interest Housing Programme	30	31
2007	Mexico	Habitat Programme II	150	300
2007	Ecuador	Integrated Neighbourhood Upgrading Programme	37	49
2007	Argentina	Conditional Investment Credit Line (CCLIP) Neighbourhood Upgrading Phase II	350	390
2008	Barbados	Housing and Neighbourhood Upgrading I	30	40
2008	Nicaragua	Multi-phase Low-income Neighbourhoods Housing Programme	15	32
2008	Brazil	Urban Upgrading and Social Inclusion, Fortaleza	59	99
2008	Brazil	Programme for Urban Development, Campo Grande	19	38
2008	Brazil	Programme for Urban Development, Belford Roxo	13	26
2008	Brazil	PROCIDADES, Programme for Urban Development, Curitiba	50	100
2008	Brazil	Programme for Urban Development, Nova Iguazu	34	57
2008	Brazil	Programme for Urban Development, Niteroi	32	44
2008	Brazil	Programme for Urban Development, Vitoria	39	65
2008	Panama	Programme for Improving Living Conditions	30	33
Total			**3,149**	**5,174**

Source: Author's elaboration based on IDB databases.

Figure 5.1 Settlement Upgrading Programmes Financed by the IDB, 1989–2008 (in millions of US$)

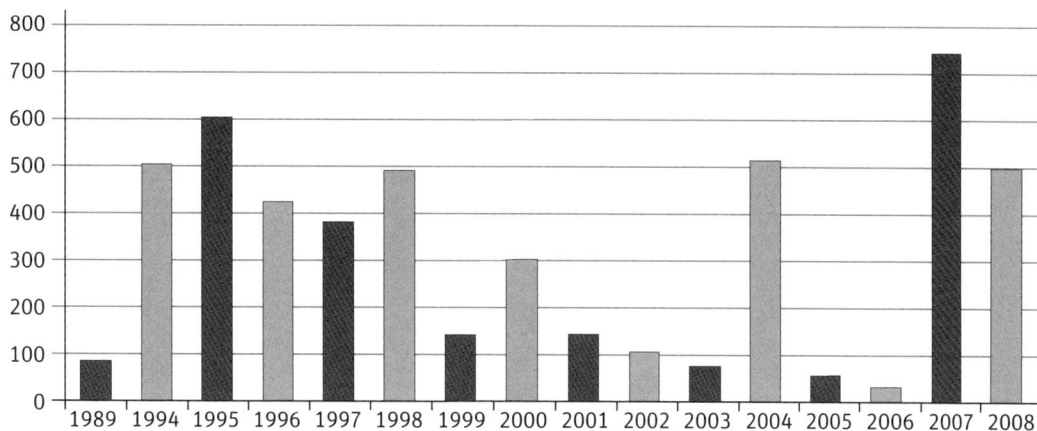

Source: Author's elaboration based on Table 5.1.

urban investment in poverty-stricken areas and have thereby contributed to the development of this model. Good examples of these innovations are found in the Chilean programmes (Chile-Barrio), which coordinate various public programmes focused on social housing policy, and in the Colombian programmes, which finance the urbanisation of irregular settlements as part of their social support network. The smaller countries in Central America, such as Panama, Nicaragua, and Honduras, have only recently begun to implement nationally based programmes. The broad implementation of such programmes could be due the widespread recognition of their value in meeting one of the gravest problems faced by cities today. The demonstrated success of these projects and the work undertaken by international and national institutions, including the IDB, has helped disseminate this model around the world.

In sum, neighbourhood upgrading programmes are recognised as efficient tools of urban public policy that yield high social and economic returns. These programmes are particularly relevant in the developing world, where 60 percent of the population lives below the poverty line and half of those live in extreme poverty (Fay, 2005). Cities are facing severe problems in informal neighbourhoods, where the urban poor are concentrated and which lack urban infrastructure, face deteriorated environmental conditions, and suffer from social and public security problems, among others. Governments across the LAC region—and municipal governments in particular—have come to the conclusion that investing in neighbourhood upgrading is a viable strategy. The beneficiaries themselves have been satisfied with the improved living conditions that result from these programmes. In turn, neighbourhood improvement programmes have gained legitimacy as a type of urban inter-

Figure 5.2 Volume of IDB Loans for Settlement Upgrading by Country, 1989–2008 (in millions of US$)

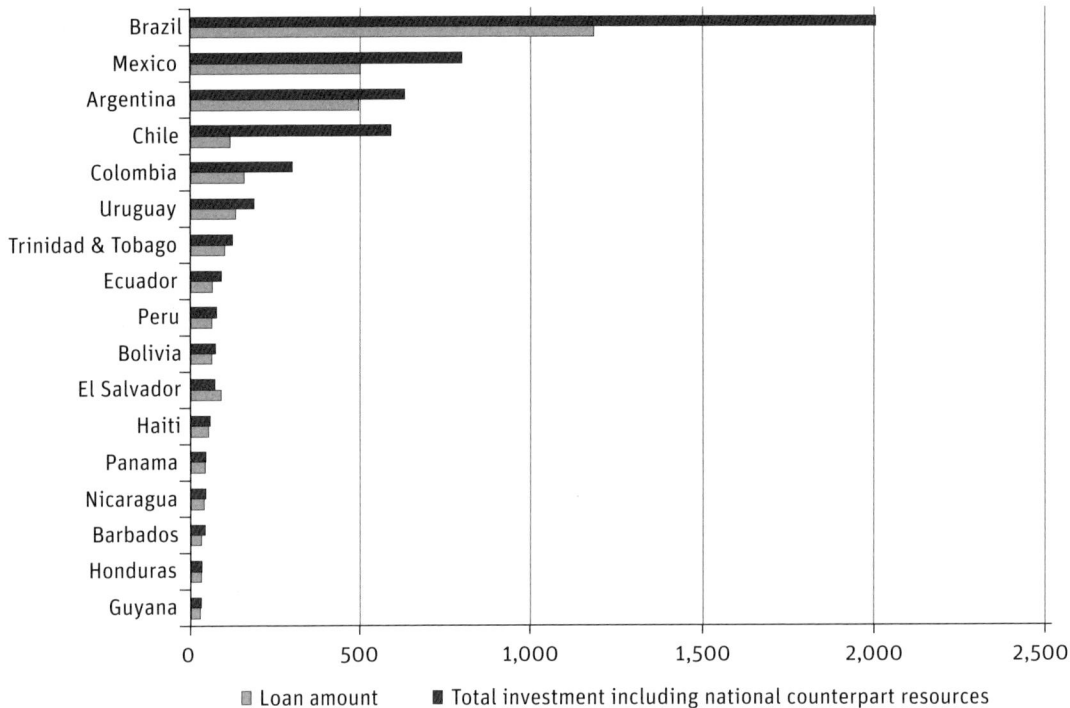

Loan amount   ■ Total investment including national counterpart resources

Source: Author's elaboration based on Table 5.1.

vention with a distinct methodology and set of operational principles. Government interest in implementing such interventions has grown at both the national and local levels, and is reflected in the growing demand for IDB loans to finance these types of social and urban development projects.

Even though the magnitude of the challenges faced is enormous, and the historical shortfall of investment in LAC cities will take decades to reverse, investment in neighbourhood upgrading is a significant improvement on previous approaches, which favoured the relocation of informal settlement residents into new housing estates that were expensive and located in areas distant from the city centre.

Programme Typologies

As previously mentioned, neighbourhood upgrading programmes respond to a variety of needs and objectives. They have been used to implement many policies, at both the local and national levels. Figure 5.3 shows the distribution of projects funded by the IDB, divided according to the level

Figure 5.3 Total Lending Amounts and Number of Loans Granted by the IDB for Settlement Upgrading Programmes, 1998–2008 (in millions of US$)

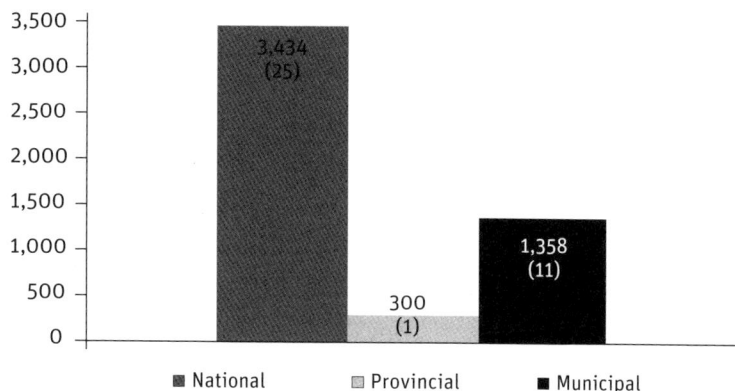

Source: Author's elaboration based on Table 5.1.

of government implementing them. Although neighbourhood upgrading programmes are investments in urban development and therefore fall into the local government's sphere of action, national governments have managed a majority of the projects financed by the IDB. Of a total of 37 loans, 25 (68 percent) have been granted to national governments, 1 to a provincial government (2 percent), and 11 to municipal governments (30 percent). Lending amounts follow the same pattern, with 67 percent and 26 percent of the volume lent to national and local governments, respectively. This is due to the fact that the central governments are the primary clients of the IDB and also wield far greater financial power.

Although national governments initiate most programmes, they do not always manage their implementation, which instead frequently happens at the municipal level. Resource allocation mechanisms, implementation agreements, and financial responsibility are shared among various levels of government. But practically all LAC countries acknowledge that the problem of urban poverty and the investment needed to fight it are not merely local issues. The solution requires large investments and collaboration between local and central governments.

National Programmes

Central government programmes financed by the IDB have responded to different criteria and have been conceptualised as part of different areas of government policy. From the national governments' point of view, the neighbourhood upgrading programmes have been conceived as part of the following areas of public policy:

Urban policy. Programmes have been included in many national urban policies, usually with the goal of improving the quality of life in cities, fostering orderly development, and solving infrastructure deficits. Although these are usually the responsibility of local governments, central governments acknowledge that there are national objectives involved in these aspects of the urban development process. The neighbourhood upgrading programmes are direct ways to materialise the support of national governments for urban development projects, since these investments make it possible to generate agreements with local government based on clear goals and measurable outcomes.[70]

Housing policy. Neighbourhood upgrading programmes have also been included in comprehensive housing policies. This approach grew out of the understanding that housing deficiencies are both quantitative (insufficient numbers of dwellings) and qualitative (poor-quality dwellings). Studies done by the IDB during the loan assessment process for housing programmes have shown that the qualitative deficiency is generally larger than the quantitative one. Policies that tackle the qualitative deficit seek to improve the infrastructure of neighbourhoods where the dwellings are located, promote the regularisation of tenure, and help households improve their houses by facilitating access to building materials and technical assistance. There are various ways in which these services can be offered: programmes aimed at improving housing markets that include the provision of direct subsidies to households—such as those of Ecuador and Honduras—operate as a form of collective subsidy, in contrast to the individual grants provided to partially finance the cost of a new house for qualifying households.[71] In other cases, housing programmes may include a specific upgrading component, in addition to the traditional direct subsidy components.[72]

Social policy. Neighbourhood upgrading programmes have also been included as components of social policies, specifically as mechanisms of investing in areas where poverty is high. Expanding the level of services offered to households in these neighbourhoods increases the value of their assets and reduces poverty in terms of unsatisfied basic needs. Similarly,

---

[70] Examples of this kind of approach include the Habitat Brazil Programme (http://www.IDB.org/projects/project.cfm?id=BR0273&lang=es) and the Programa de Aceleração do Crescimento (PAC) (Growth Acceleration Programme) (http://www.brasil.gov.br/pac/) in Brazil and the Programa Regularización de Asentamientos Irregulares (PIAI) (Regularisation of Informal Settlements Programme) in Uruguay (http://www.IDB.org/projects/project.cfm?id=UR0123&lang=es).

[71] Ecuador, Housing Sector Support Programme II (http://www.IDB.org/projects/project.cfm?lang=es&id=ec0207&query=&project=ec0207); and Honduras, Social Interest Housing Programme (http://www.IDB.org/projects/project.cfm?id=HO-L1007&lang=es).

[72] Bolivia's housing programme, Apoyo a la Política de Vivienda (Support for Housing Policy) (http://www.IDB.org/projects/project.cfm?id=BO0008&lang=es) and El Salvador's Housing Programme (http://www.IDB.org/projects/project.cfm?id=ES0087&lang=es) contain these kinds of components.

providing social services to the urban poor, for example, in the form of nursery schools or health centres, contributes to eliminating conditions that contribute to the intergenerational reproduction of poverty. The spatial concentration of poverty, especially in the cities, turns neighbourhood upgrading programmes, which invest in the most poverty-stricken areas, into effective mechanisms for targeting public investments towards the poorest segments of the population. They benefit informal settlements, whose populations have fairly homogenous low-income levels, so it is difficult for subsidies to be siphoned off towards more affluent beneficiaries. Examples of neighbourhood upgrading programmes that are part of social policies are Mexico's Habitat Programme and Argentina's PROMEBA, which are discussed in detail later in this chapter.

Provincial Programmes

The only example of a provincial programme financed by the IDB is in the state of Rio de Janeiro, which benefits four municipalities in the Baixada Fluminense (part of the metropolitan region of Rio de Janeiro).[73] The Guarapiranga Drainage Basin Programme in São Paulo is discussed in this chapter as another example of a settlement upgrading programme financed by this level of government (with partial financing from the World Bank). This paucity of provincial programmes demonstrates the reluctance of many regional governments to acquire debt to take on the responsibilities of their municipal counterparts, although many of the programmes implemented in the period under consideration have benefited from the active involvement of provincial governments. It is worth noting that in the cases of the PROMEBA and Mexico's Habitat Programme, provincial governments did take a leading role in project selection and in providing technical support for municipalities during the design and execution phase and, to a varying degree, in financing the investments.

Municipal Programmes

The larger municipalities, and those with previous experience working with the IDB, were the first to borrow to finance their neighbourhood upgrading programmes. The cases of Rio de Janeiro and Quito (discussed further in Chapters 6 and 7, respectively) are worthy of note. It may be that fewer municipalities borrow from the Bank because they lack agile mechanisms to access this source of funding.[74] Municipal-level projects

---

[73] Programme Nova Baixada (http://www.IDB.org/projects/project.cfm?id=BR0242& lang=es).

[74] Recently, the number of direct operations with municipalities has increased, especially since the establishment of a municipal finance mechanism in Brazil's Programa de Desenvolvimento Urbano (PROCIDADES) (Programme for Urban Development) to finance urban development investments by Brazilian municipalities. There are neighbourhood upgrading programmes included in practically all of the PROCIDADES projects.

Table 5.2 Neighbourhood Upgrading Programmes: The Advantages and Disadvantages of National and Local Programmes

National programmes	Local programmes
Greater financial capacity; more stable financing when part of the national policy	Better targeting through the identification of priority neighbourhoods in each city
The programme can be applied to more cities and eventually reach more beneficiaries	The objectives can be adjusted according to the specific problems encountered in each city
Greater demonstration effect; potential multiplier effect	Easier to manage technically due to a direct working relationship with the executing agency
Implementation problems due to complex transfer mechanisms and the distance between the central government agency and the implementation agency	Enhances coordination in implementation, as there is only one level of government involved

Source: Author's elaboration.

are clearly on the rise, either because they attend to the concrete and urgent needs of the local population or perhaps because municipalities are more efficient when it comes to implementation (as will be discussed later). The aims and objectives of the municipal programmes are usually directly associated with urban development problems and social issues. The objectives include:

Urban development. Neighbourhood upgrading programmes are a fundamental part of local urban development policy. They contribute to the regularisation of informal settlements by integrating them into urban utilities networks and municipal public services. The IDB encourages municipalities to formulate far-reaching urban polices, containing strategies to tackle the problems of informal settlements through investment and urban development measures that lead to definitive and sustainable solutions.

Specific social policies. The fight against urban poverty is frequently seen as the prime objective of municipal neighbourhood upgrading programmes due to their ability to target investment in the areas where the poor are concentrated. Key benefits for this population include improved living conditions (by satisfying basic needs such as access to sanitation and urban services) and an increase in the value of their homes. Other objectives include protecting vulnerable groups (such as young people at risk) and decreasing urban violence. Although it was generally expected that physical and social improvements would improve security conditions, neighbourhood upgrading programmes were not originally designed with this specific objective in mind. This trend parallels recent changes in programmes aimed at reducing violence and improving security, which include measures to improve living conditions in the targeted communities as a way of tackling the problem of violence at its root. Out of this convergence, a new kind of programme has emerged featuring environmental prevention measures (such as the elimination of unsafe areas and increased community control over public spaces) directed at reducing some of the conditions that create insecurity, as well as preventive social actions targeted at those groups most likely to become the victims of violence (women) or its perpetrators (youth, especially school dropouts). These themes are covered in more detail in Chapter 2 of this volume.

Urban-environmental measures. Regularising urban conditions in informal settlements improves the environmental conditions of the city as a whole, particularly when the rehabilitation of degraded—or otherwise invaded and illegally urbanised—areas is part of an integrated approach to solving the neighbourhood problems. This often happens around the riverbeds and other water bodies within the city that are informally occupied and in protected aquifer recharge areas, as in the case of the Guarapiranga Drainage Basin Programme. Total settler eviction from these areas is not always viable, either due to the high level of consolidation of the settlements or the high cost involved. But a variety of creative solutions within recent neighbourhood upgrading programmes have managed to relocate families, thereby freeing up land for the creation of urban parks alongside rivers, as in the *Programa Social e Ambiental dos Igarapés de Manaus* (PROSAMIM) (Social and Environmental Programme for the Creeks of Manaus, further discussed in Chapter 6). Active monitoring systems have also been set up to prevent the settlements from expanding further (which has met with some success in the *Favela Bairro* [Urban Upgrading] programme, also discussed in Chapter 6) and to reclaim mangrove swamps and other fragile areas.

Income generation. As mentioned in Chapter 2, neighbourhood upgrading programmes have made only modest contributions to improving the income of programme beneficiaries. There are only a handful of programmes that have sought to integrate beneficiaries into the labour market or foster the development of enterprises in the community. In these cases, there has been an increase in the number of businesses (especially home-based businesses) in beneficiary communities in the wake of a project's implementation. Similarly, as the legal standing of beneficiaries improves (because they now have a permanent address and documents attesting to their tenure), these residents are less stigmatised and their chances of entering the formal labour or credit market increase, thus improving their ability to get a job or a loan. The regularisation of tenure is a contributing factor here, although it is difficult to track whether the newly legalised properties are subsequently used as loan collateral. The best outcomes are seen in school-support programmes, which are targeted at young adults or youth already outside the education system. By being encouraged to finish their elementary or secondary education, their opportunities in the job market improve.

Table 5.2 compares the national and local programmes and clearly identifies the advantages and disadvantages of each.

Objectives: Specific and Few, or General and Many?

The fact that neighbourhood upgrading programmes attend to a variety of objectives makes it difficult to define priorities. Attempting to meet multiple objectives increases costs and adds complexity to the implementation process. The dilemma of attaining various objectives and ensuring adequate implementation, while keeping a tight rein on investment costs, is a recurring theme in project design—one that can only be resolved case by case. Obviously, certain objectives must be prioritised over others. Neighbourhood upgrading programmes must complete the infrastructure networks and provide basic public services. Other objectives depend on public policy priorities and the availability of resources to finance activities, or the technical capacity of institutions to implement them. The most urgent problems faced by a city—whether they be environmental issues, urban infrastructure shortages, or violence—should be the focus. Meanwhile, adding objectives and components to a programme has two consequences: it raises the investment costs per household (meaning that fewer families benefit from the available resources), and it makes programme implementation more complex.

Achieving a balance between simplifying implementation and meeting objectives is an important part of the design process, but there seems to be no general rule for doing so. The general social and urban development policy goals of the implementing agency and the living conditions of the beneficiaries must be considered. The technical capacity of the executing agency, which determines the level of functional complexity and the number of components a programme can maintain, is one of the most significant variables in this equation. Without this capacity, there is the risk that the project will fall short of reaching its multiple objectives.

Implementation: Operational Challenges

As design and implementation methodologies have improved, neighbourhood upgrading programmes have grown both in investment volume and in complexity. Because the field is still new to many local governments, programme development has required extra effort on the part of technical teams, both in promoting integrated intervention shared among beneficiaries and decision makers, and in establishing adequate organisational schemes for its implementation. Similarly, the diversity of physical works, services, and systems put in place by a programme demand that special attention be paid to their sustainability, especially in the operation and maintenance of infrastructure and services. The following challenges have been identified based on the design and implementation experiences of IDB-financed neighbourhood upgrading programmes:

Technical capacity for the implementation process. From a technical standpoint, neighbourhood upgrading projects are very difficult to implement because they involve investments in multiple sectors and must be executed in inhabited areas. The following institutional resources are necessary for their implementation: technical implementation teams with a variety of expertise, a sustained inter-institutional coordination effort, good monitoring and control mechanisms during implementation, and adequate information systems. A change of administration at any level of government (which usually involves changes in priorities) has a significant impact on projects with long implementation periods. One way to compensate for this potential instability is to contract a specialised consulting firm to provide technical support throughout implementation. This is customary in Brazil, where such firms are frequently called *gerenciadoras* (managers). The *gerenciadoras* have specialised personnel and equipment for complex programme management at their disposal and, although they represent an additional programme cost, provide crucial technical and management support.

Sustainability. The challenge of sustaining neighbourhood upgrading programmes has three dimensions:

- *Investment policy.* When they were first introduced, these programmes represented a novel form of public urban policy to project implementers. The programmes are successful to the extent that they can establish themselves as a permanent sphere of municipal government intervention. Ambiguous results have so far been observed as the commitment to continue with the programmes varies across countries or different levels of government. Although there is substantial interest in this type of investment at all levels of government, the continuity of government interest and the commitment of resources cannot be generalised. Continuing investment in these programmes depends to a large extent on external factors, such as continuity in the housing and urban development policies, the strength and stability of the urban planning apparatus, and prevention measures directed against the proliferation of new settlements.

- *Operation and maintenance.* The majority of neighbourhood upgrading programmes have problems operating and maintaining newly established urban systems and services. The degraded physical and social conditions in the areas where projects are implemented hamper the extension of the urban services and of good operation and maintenance in general. Public utility companies are also not used to (or interested in) working in these areas. The institutions in charge of maintaining and operating urban services in these neighbourhoods find it difficult to provide services, as do the municipal social sectors, which find it hard to maintain their technical teams and services in these areas. This issue goes beyond the scope of most programmes' sphere of action because it involves public urban management activities of a permanent nature. A realistic and careful analysis of the institutional capacity of service suppliers (and its enhancement, if necessary) is required to prevent these problems. This analysis must be undertaken at the very beginning of the design stage, and formal cooperation agreements with the other institutions need to be established and their compliance enforced by the public authority during implementation of the projects and after completion of the works.

■ *Social actions.* The following social actions stand out: i) *Community development*: Programme methodologies recommend that the implementation of projects should be preceded and accompanied by community development and organisational activities. The best results are obtained when these activities are included as specific components of the programme and are sustained for a reasonable length of time (at least a year) after the physical works have been brought to a close. Inadequate community development may cause the community not to value the investments, which can seriously affect a programme's sustainability. This theme is further examined in Chapter 6 of this volume. ii) *Social services*: The continued good quality of the social services set up by a programme is as important as their presence. Experience shows that it is easier to ensure the efficient and continuous provision of services such as schools, health centres, and nurseries when they are already integrated into the regular system of social service provision in the municipality, state, or province. The greatest problems tend to occur in facilities designed for community use in which fewer institutionalised activities take place, such as community centres or centres used by non-governmental organisations (NGOs). These facilities and services require special attention and they should be included in a programme only if adequate resources for their permanent operation are guaranteed.

PATRICIA PALENQUE   # Settlement Upgrading Programme (PROMEBA), Argentina

Most cities in Argentina have well-defined streets and public spaces and acceptable standards of urban services.[75] But the impact of the severe economic crises experienced in recent decades has resulted in periods of high unemployment, a decline in access to urban land, and a fall in the production of housing for the lower-income sectors of the population. These factors have given rise to the informal occupation of residential land, so-called *villas*, and informal settlements. At the beginning of the 2000s, approximately 350,000 households—or 3.9 percent of the total number of households in the country—lived in these *villas* and settlements, which were characterised by a lack of infrastructure, housing deficiencies, and irregular land tenure (INDEC, 2001).

The responses of the national government to these problems and to demands for housing and the provision of public services and infrastructure have been channelled through programmes with federal financing.[76] The national government implemented a strategy to group and efficiently manage public resources by coordinating investments across various habitat policies, strategies, and programmes (including the PROMEBA, the main focus of this section) that attempt to solve the housing problems of the poorest sections of society.[77] These programmes have tackled the problems of deficient infrastructure and housing, and have also focused on strengthening social networks, improving the environment, and regularising land tenure.

Financing for these programmes is provided by funds from the national treasury and international financial institutions.[78] Similarly, through the

---

[75] Argentina is a federal republic comprised of three levels of government: national, provincial, and municipal, each with its own powers. The national government coexists with 23 provincial governments and the autonomous city of Buenos Aires. The country also has 2,198 municipalities differing in importance, size, and population.

[76] These programmes are promoted by the *Subsecretaría de Desarrollo Urbano y Vivienda,* (Subsecretariat of Urban Development and Housing), part of the *Secretaría de Obras Públicas del Ministerio de Planificación Federal, Inversión Pública y Servicios (*Public Works Subsecretariat of the Ministry of Federal Planning, Public Investment, and Services).

[77] These include the following programmes: *Provisión de Agua Potable* (PROPASA, Drinking Water Provision), Desarrollo Social en Áreas de Frontera NEA-NOA (PROSOFA, Social Development in Border Areas), *Federal de Construcción y Mejoramiento de Viviendas* (Federal Housing Construction and Improvement), *Emergencia Habitacional* (Emergency Housing), and *Urbanización de Villas y Asentamientos en el Gran Buenos Aires* (Settlements and Slums Upgrading in Greater Buenos Aires) (http://www.vivienda.gov.ar/).

[78] At the beginning of 1997, the Argentinean government contracted an IDB loan worth US$102 million to integrate into the total amount of US$170 million earmarked for the PROMEBA. Later, during the crisis of 2001, the PROMEBA was one of the programmes that increased its activity to alleviate the social emergency, and an additional US$164 million was injected. In 2007 the second stream of the programme (PROMEBA II) was implemented with a total finance amount of US$390 million, of which US$350 million came from the first tranche of the Conditional Investment Credit Line (CCLIP). This amounted to a total of US$1.5 million approved by the IDB in 2007, to be implemented over the

Most settlements on the peripheries of cities lack basic infrastructure and urban services.
Informal settlement in the northwest region of Argentina

Sistema Federal de la Vivienda (Federal Housing System), the federal government provides funding for the *Fondo Nacional de Vivienda* (National Housing Fund) that is allocated to the provincial housing institutes. These funds come from a percentage of the tax imposed on liquid combustible fuels, the recuperation of previous investments in social housing, and contributions from the provinces themselves. Provinces and municipalities are responsible for implementing infrastructure works, providing urban services, and financing the operation and maintenance of infrastructure and services (street lighting, roads, public space and park management, waste disposal, and so on) included in the budget of each corresponding level of government.

Objectives

The objective of the PROMEBA is to improve residents' quality of life and to contribute to the social and urban integration of Argentina's poorest households. Investments concentrate on the *villas* and informal settlements, and seek to improve living conditions in a sustainable fashion. The programme stimulates social organisation and community development

following 25 years. The CCLIP would support the sub-secretary's strategy to find a solution to the problems posed by the slums and informal settlements around the country, with an aim of gradually taking care of all existing demands.

The regularisation of settlements in inner cities poses complex relocation issues, as it is necessary to move some households to make room for infrastructure, create public spaces, and improve accessibility. **Informal settlement in the Avellaneda Municipality of metropolitan Buenos Aires, Argentina**

and works to promote the communities' active participation in setting priorities and designing works.

Implementation

A specialised unit of the subsecretariat implements the PROMEBA II, the second phase of this programme. Project implementation is organised in a decentralised way through municipal and provincial executive bodies. The management model adopted includes financing for integral projects, resources for participative management of the design and execution process, investment monitoring, and community support for the duration of the work through an interdisciplinary group of professionals (see Figure 5.4). Contracted private companies carry out the works themselves. The non-returnable funds are transferred to the subcontractors, provinces, and municipalities, and the national government is responsible for the total cost of the interventions.

Table 5.3 lists the components financed by PROMEBA and Table 5.4 illustrates the volume of investment by component. The projects are integrated and cover all necessary basic infrastructure and, as required, home improvements and the construction of new homes and internal sanitary units. Works carried out inside the privately owned lots are financed by other sources, either from the national government or its municipal or provincial counterparts.

Figure 5.4 PROMEBA: Stakeholders' Negotiation Table

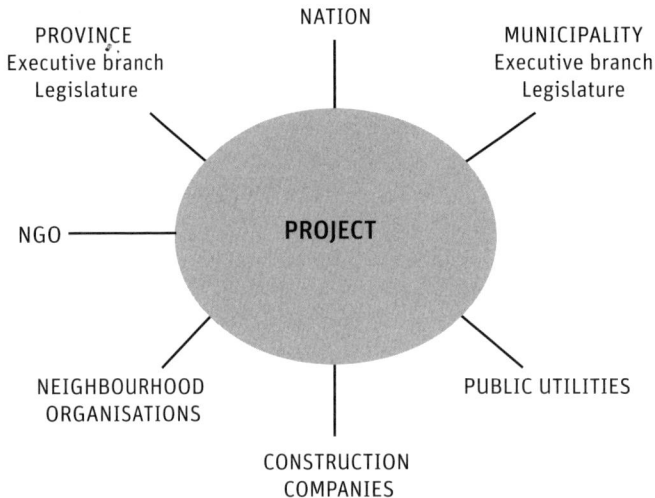

Source: Author's elaboration.

Results

The PROMEBA I has implemented 175 integral projects that have bene-fited 59,345 households. The new goal is to help 250,000 additional households over the next 20 years with IDB financing for four consecu-tive phases of implementation. The PROMEBA II will contribute to reach this goal by financing the implementation of roughly 100 projects that will benefit 47,500 families between 2007 and 2012, as well as by financing the design of new projects. In 2008 the PROMEBA had 65 projects either at the implementation stage or awaiting approval, which would provide assist-ance for 17,800 families.

The PROMEBA (with 11 years experience in implementing integrated projects based on the work of multidisciplinary technical teams and the involvement of residents and social organisations) focuses on improving efficiency in the use of the public resources allocated to the neighbour-hood upgrading programmes. The PROMEBA's integrated approach has had a synergetic effect on other programmes. The field teams financed by the programme to carry out work in the settlements are the fundamen-tal instruments that support coordination among different stakeholders, which include governments, participating institutions, contracting com-panies, and the communities themselves. Other positive effects of this integration include:

Table 5.3 Argentina, PROMEBA: Components

Line of action	Interventions
Regularisation of land tenure	Financing of legal studies and land surveys. Support for legal and physical regularisation of land tenure and delivery of registered ownership titles to beneficiaries.
Provision of infrastructure and urban amenities and environmental rehabilitation	Financing of technical, economic, legal, environmental, and social studies for integrated implementation projects. Investments in sanitary networks, electricity, rainwater drainage, gas distribution infrastructure, roads, pedestrian networks, connections to main road, urban and community amenities, green areas, community development projects, environmental impact mitigation, land acquisition for settlement consolidation, and relocation of households.
Social and human capital development	Financing of fieldwork by multidisciplinary teams for the urban, social, environmental, and legal support to residents in the area. Help for the management of independent initiatives by residents, and articulation of relations among residents, state organisations, and NGOs; finance and support for projects for the development of the community's human and social capital aimed at containing and preventing the risk of vulnerable groups (through recreation, sport, training in job skills, and solid waste treatment).
Enhancement of management capacity	Financing of training activities, urban planning, and new illegal settlement prevention plans. Setting up of monitoring, assessment, and management systems. Nationwide illegal and informal settlements registry.

Source: Author's elaboration.

- *Improved sanitation networks*, which involves the connection of sanitary units in the individual dwellings to city networks through projects executed by subcontractors paid with municipal or provincial resources.
- *The provision of land*, provided that the projects are carried out on municipal or provincial land, or on lands owned by the occupiers or cooperatives acquired with members' contributions.
- *Environmental impact reduction*, as when projects are supported with municipal contributions for the construction of network connections (access roads, drinking water, rainwater, and sewerage drains), the building of parks, and other small-scale works (funds from provincial governments cover large-scale works) to reduce the environmental impact.

Table 5.4 Argentina, PROMEBA II: Costs and Financing by Component (in thousands of US$)

Investments	IDB	Local	Total	Percent
Legalisation of land tenure	6,624	736	7,360	1.9
Infrastructure, urban amenities, and environmental rehabilitation	307,694	32,666	340,360	87.3
Social and human capital enhancements	20,142	2,238	22,380	5.7
Empowerment of management capacity	9,000	1,000	10,000	2.6
Administration	6,540	3,360	9,900	2.5
Total	**350,000**	**40,000**	**390,000**	**100**

Source: PROMEBA.

- *Social promotion activities* that foster sporting and cultural activities, skills training, and other activities executed in coordination with community organisations.

The human resources and institutional structures required for setting up execution units are usually mandatory contributions of the municipal and provincial governments. The PROMEBA assists the municipalities and the provinces to finance the preparation of projects. It is customary for public utilities—the majority of which are privatised—to contribute resources to the design of projects under their administration. Works financed by the PROMEBA are implemented by contracting out to private companies, which provide professional and technical support during the implementation process.

Consequently, the PROMEBA promotes urban development policies, giving priority to those neighbourhoods included in a strategic municipal plan. This exchange enhances public management and increases municipal management capacities. Through various streams of financing from different levels of government, it is expected that every beneficiary neighbourhood will attain acceptable standards of sanitation, environmental sustainability, urban integration, security of tenure, and enhanced human capital. This way of articulating actions and financing has permitted the programme's integration into local policymaking and a slow, but lasting, assimilation of its management model.

The PROMEBA design, implementation, and supervision process has yielded many lessons. On an operational level, it must be emphasised that it is a flexible programme that can adapt to the different realities existing across communities and institutional setups. This flexibility is built into the programme's implementation scheme, which on a territo-

Interventions provide sanitary units for houses. **House improved by the PROMEBA Programme, Argentina**

rial scale, aims to forge links with local stakeholders and allows for the incorporation of local regulations and procedures, applying existing policies and rules in order to achieve its objectives. These characteristics are evident in tenure regularisation actions and in the executive agreements and complementary actions made between municipal and provincial agencies and their counterparts. Detailed plans of action that specify both individual and combined actions ensure that necessary resources are available for project completion, thereby guaranteeing their adequate implementation.

ELISABETE FRANÇA ## Environmental Rehabilitation of the Guarapiranga Drainage Basin Programme, São Paulo (Brazil)

The drainage basin feeding the Guarapiranga reservoir covers a wide area in the metropolitan region of São Paulo (Brazil) (see Map 5.1). This region includes seven municipalities where approximately 750,000 people live (IBGE, 2000) in substandard housing. The water catchment area supplies a reservoir whose waters satisfy the needs of 3 million inhabitants (20 percent of the total water supply for the metropolitan area) and is the second largest water provider in the metropolitan area of São

Map 5.1 The Guarapiranga Basin in the São Paulo Metropolitan Region

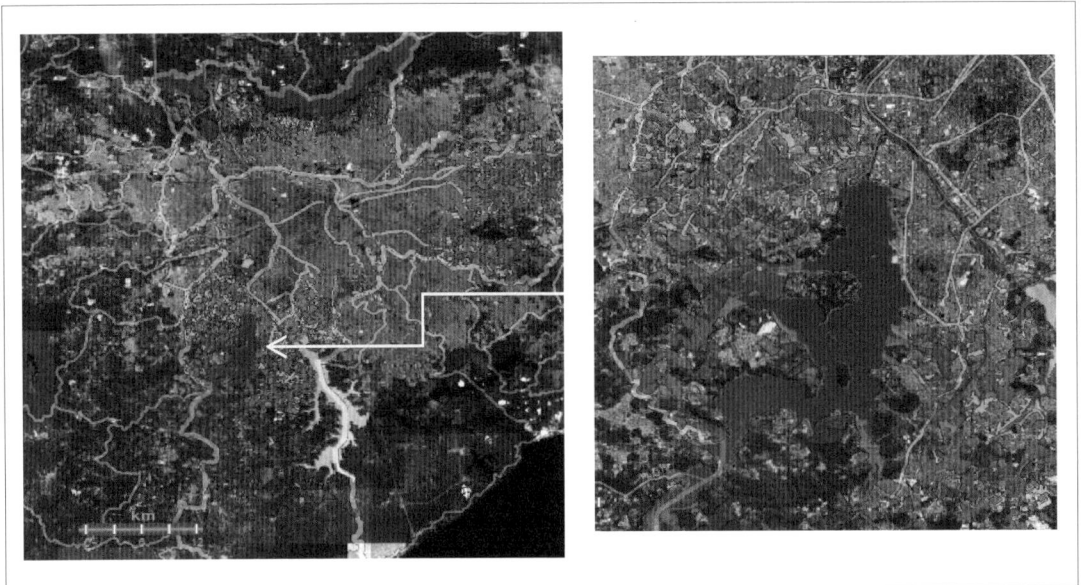

Source: Author's elaboration based on satellite images from Google® Maps.

Paulo. The last vestiges of the typical flora and fauna of the *mata atlán-tica* ecosystem are to be found within this territory. This area, considered since 1975 to be of strategic importance for metropolitan development, is regulated by state legislation (Laws 898/1975 and 1,172/1976) that was intended to establish protected zones and regulate land use in order to protect the aquifer recharge areas, the riverbeds, and other reservoirs of importance to the metropolitan area of São Paulo. This legislation limited the expansion of industrial activities and the urbanisation of lands in these protected areas. This caused a fall in land prices that unintentionally favoured a process of uncontrolled urbanisation, which created a large number of informal settlements from land invasions (so-called *favelas*) and illegal land subdivisions. This type of land use is incompatible with the preservation of the aquifer recharge areas.

From the 1960s the advance of illegal urban occupation increased at an alarming rate. Great swathes of the population moved towards this region and began to occupy areas that were not suited to residential use, attracted by new jobs in the vicinity of the protected area. Today around 20 percent of the population of the drainage basin lives in informal settlements. There are more than 200 *favelas* in the São Paulo municipality alone and an equal number of irregular settlements with an estimated total population of about 380,000 inhabitants. This process, in addition to the poor quality of life of the residents, has created a variety of urban and environmental problems. Some areas are prone to flooding, landslides, and raw sewage spills. Moreover, garbage is discharged into the rivulets that feed into the reservoir, and there has been an increase in the sedimentation rate in the artificial lake. The effect of this process has been a gradual deterioration of the water quality in the reservoir and the rivers that feed into it, potentially endangering a principal resource for supplying water to the São Paulo metropolitan area.

Objectives

To solve these problems, which affect several municipalities in the metropolitan area, the government of the state of São Paulo has developed a regional environmental rehabilitation programme aimed at mitigating the negative consequences of the occupation of these lands. The Guarapiranga Drainage Basin Programme, inaugurated in 1992, is primarily concerned with preserving the environment and cleaning up the areas of the rivers feeding into the Guarapiranga reservoir. It seeks to control the disorderly occupation of the aquifer recharge areas and to develop social activities and environmental rehabilitation measures within neighbourhoods that already exist in the area. The environmental, sanitation, and housing branches of both the *Governo do Estado de São Paulo* (State Government of São Paulo) and the *Secretaria Municipal da Habitação e Desenvolvimento Urbano de São Paulo* (São Paulo Municipal Housing Secretariat) collaborate in the programme's implementation. The first phase of the programme, with financing from the World Bank, ended in 2000, but upgrading activities continued until 2007 with financial support from the Municipality of São Paulo.

Many people settle on the recharge areas of aquifers.
Settlements on the Guarapiranga watershed, São Paulo, Brazil

The main objective of the Guarapiranga Drainage Basin Programme is to conserve the aquifer recharge areas that supply the metropolitan region of São Paulo, an area already suffering from water scarcity. Consequently, it seeks to maintain the operational conditions of the aquifer recharge areas by controlling further occupation of this territory and improving the living conditions of the residents already in the area, particularly with regards to sanitation infrastructure and housing in the poorest neighbourhoods in the protected areas. The investments have directly benefited approximately 38,000 low-income families, 16,000 in the *favelas* and 22,000 in irregular settlements. Among the programme's achievements are the construction of 1,000 new dwellings in the *favelas* and the relocation of 2,000 families to residential complexes outside of the protected areas.

Table 5.5 The Guarapiranga Drainage Basin Programme: Implementing Agencies and Interventions

Subprogramme	Implementing agencies	Interventions
Water supply and sewerage services	*Compañía de Saneamiento Básico del Estado de São Paulo* (SABESP) (São Paulo State Sanitation Company)	Expansion of the water supply and sewerage systems, improvements in the sewage water treatment plants, use of flotation techniques to improve large bodies of water, wetlands restoration, improvement in the operational capacity of sewage systems, solid waste collection, and solutions for the final disposal of wastes.
Solid waste	São Paulo Municipal Government	Waste collection and final disposal.
Urban rehabilitation	São Paulo Municipal Government and the Urban and Housing Development Company	Neighbourhood upgrades, infrastructure provision for informal settlements, and construction of new dwellings for relocated families.
Environmental protection	Environmental Secretariat	Construction of parks and rehabilitation of urban greenery and degraded areas.
Administration and management of drainage basin	Environmental Secretariat, São Paulo State Sanitation Company, São Paulo Municipal Government, and The Environmental Sanitation Technology Company	Implementation of the new basin management legislation; studies to attract new investment and design of new urban developments in the region.

Source: Author's elaboration.

Execution

The Guarapiranga Drainage Basin Programme consists of five subprogrammes, each with actions coordinated by the diverse project implementers listed in Table 5.5.

The central problem that arose during the programme's initial design phase (1992) was that of identifying viable options for the relocation and resettlement of families occupying irregular settlements with inadequate sanitation infrastructure. Two factors influenced the solutions that were adopted: (i) the cost of urban rehabilitation versus the cost of moving thousands of families out of the protected areas and (ii) the social, economic, and affective ties that families had established in the area over time. The programme opted to let residents stay in the region and to improve their living conditions through neighbourhood and settlement upgrading programmes. The *Secretaria da Habitação do Estado de São Paulo* (São Paulo State Housing Secretariat) carried out these actions.

The main improvements undertaken in the illegal neighbourhoods included the construction of water supply and sewage networks, the consolidation of the main roads to allow easier access to public services, the construction of drainage systems, the mitigation of natural risks, the paving of roads and stairways leading to the settlements, and the construction of recreation areas. Families occupying the zones most at risk were resettled in new dwellings in the same zone or in settlements built outside the perimeter of the aquifer recharge area. The Municipality of São Paulo adopted as its guiding principle the concept that all urban and environmental rehabilitation measures in informal neighbourhoods should not only tackle the problem of pollution, but also make all beneficiaries partners of the public sector, with a shared interest in maintaining the environmental quality needed to ensure the conservation of the aquifer recharge areas.

Based on the limited results obtained in upgrading the first seven neighbourhoods, where projects focused on providing basic infrastructure networks, the programme began implementing more complex projects. Subsequent projects were based on the concept of integrated urban upgrading: ensuring that when the works were completed, not only would there be new infrastructure but also a neighbourhood that was fully integrated into the city. The neighbourhoods benefited from the development of new water supply and sewage networks, paved roads, channelled water courses, drainage systems, and more than 30 new recreational areas, as well as the elimination of environmental risks.

Results

The programme established novel public management approaches, which were capable of reconciling the private appropriation of natural resources for urban development with the social imperative to preserve the public interest. The most important step was to acknowledge, as a central point of urban public policy, the possibility that a vital natural resource—water—might become exhausted. This threat has catastrophic implications for the future of the metropolis and prompted the need to coordinate the activities of the various municipal governments to ensure the protection of the water supply. As the São Paulo state government was taking action in a conservation area situated next to one of the most densely populated areas in the world, it had to define a clear, central objective: to restore in the medium term the quality of the water supply of a large part of the metropolitan population. This objective was easy to measure objectively and also gave clear, defined goals for the various programme implementers. Furthermore, the clear demarcation of the area of intervention, defined by the physical limits of the drainage basin itself, facilitated coordinated action within the territory.

Various actions were implemented that were linked to complementary strategies. One was to develop the technical, financial, and institutional capacities to manage the drainage basin by integrating state and municipal governments and civil society organisations. This resulted in a new juridical status for the area. Another included the enhancement of the quality of life for residents of the irregular settlements by improving and extending the basic sanitation infrastructure, rehabilitating the most densely populated urban areas, improving unhealthy housing conditions, and building more open public spaces.

The implementation approach adopted by the programme led to a coordinated management model for multi-sector interventions that was innovative compared with traditional models of public sector management. This model is based on the establishment of a management unit comprising the various state and municipal agencies. The implementation unit imposed a culture of effective implementation focused on coordinating complementary interventions and making optimum use of resources. The management unit represented a first step towards a new institutional structure that would take administrative responsibility for the drainage sub-basin, a model that has since been successfully reproduced in similar situations.

The expansion of the objectives of the programme after the first seven projects led to the implementation of an integrated upgrading programme in the *favelas* based on the idea that controlling water pollution and improving the quality of life of the resident population were fundamentally inseparable, and that the relocation of people out of the area should be undertaken only as a last resort, since it involved high economic, social, and political costs. The urban regularisation of the *favelas* represented a significant component of the Guarapiranga Drainage Basin Programme given that it helped solve the problems of sanitation infrastructure, improved the roads and the geotechnical stability of the land, eliminated unhealthy living conditions, and satisfied the demand for social facilities.

In spite of these positive results, the programme could not fully contain the spread of illegal land occupations in the area, due to a failure by government and civil society organisations to establish a coordinated monitoring programme. For the programme to be successful, investments in upgrade initiatives needed to be complemented by preventive measures that validated land use controls and implemented actions for the social inclusion of low-income families by providing them with legal access to housing.

During the development of the Guarapiranga Drainage Basin Programme, fundamental concepts of urban management were brought up to date, especially those involving the environment. Environmental concerns became a central component of public policy making in recognition of the gravity of this issue for the inhabitants of cities. Multi-sector actions based on institutional integration were also implemented as part of a new culture of public policy design and execution. This approach encouraged agility, complementariness, and the optimisation of technical and financial resources. It also promoted the adoption of transparent management mechanisms—which allowed all segments of society to access information about the programme—and established result assessment and monitoring procedures.

RAMIRO BURGOS   # True Neighbourhoods Programme, La Paz (Bolivia)

According to the 2001 census, the municipality of La Paz (Bolivia) had a population of 793,000 inhabitants. The population is growing at a rate of 1.1 percent per year, lower than the national average. The poverty map of the city—drawn up by the municipal government based on the indicators of unsatisfied basic needs—shows that 61 percent of the population faces deficiencies that place them in a condition of poverty. This segment of the population suffers from housing problems, high levels of illiteracy, and poor access to services such as water, electricity, and sanitation. The majority reside in recently established neighbourhoods that are generally perched on very steep slopes and are therefore more vulnerable to natural disasters. These are unplanned settlements with very little land available for public spaces, poor access to the city, and limited pedestrian access. Most of the dwellings are self-built, offer precarious living conditions to their inhabitants, and are overcrowded. Although the majority of the population has some form of property deed, a large percentage of the deeds are not legally validated because they have been acquired from third parties—usually the informal developers of municipal land. The majority of the inhabitants are immigrants from rural areas, particularly from the Bolivian highlands, although there are some members of the poverty-stricken middle class that have been expelled from the formal areas of the city due to economic problems. The programme developed by the municipality seeks to benefit 100 neighbourhoods that find themselves in a position of urban marginality due to grave infrastructure deficiencies and high poverty.

Objectives

The *Programa Barrios de Verdad* (True Neighbourhoods Programme) was started in 2005 based on neighbourhood upgrading activities promoted by the IDB and is one of the components of the *Programa de Reforma del Sector Vivienda* (Housing Sector Reform Programme). The general aim of this programme was to improve the quality of life of the city's marginalised by promoting their participation in the integrated upgrading of their neighbourhoods. Several specific objectives were: (i) to promote resident organisation and participation, thus ensuring social control of the project and its long-term sustainability; (ii) to mobilise and organise the community to protect its living environment; (iii) to train and organise the community to respond adequately to emergency situations; (iv) to give legal security of tenure to families by regularising their property rights; (v) to provide urban infrastructure to upgrade the neighbourhood; (vi) to construct road networks to improve access; (vii) to improve basic and environmental services and risk prevention; and (viii) to provide urban amenities for all neighbourhoods.

The True Neighbourhoods Programme recognises that this population's poverty is related not only to economic inequality, but also to factors

The majority of the informal settlements of La Paz are located on the hillsides, the result of the illegal subdivision of municipal land.
La Paz, Bolivia

such as social exclusion. This affects the people who live on the slopes surrounding La Paz, and especially indigenous people within these communities. Consequently, the programme aims to help the people who live in situations of poverty or marginalisation by giving them access to economic, social, cultural, and political resources. The programme's methodology is based on an integrated approach that takes into account gender, culture (by recognising the ethnic diversity of the country and the bilingual condition of its people), and age, and seeks to promote organised resident participation.

Execution

The resources are allocated through open competition among neighbourhoods to finance works selected from a list of eligible investments (see Table 5.6). This method not only prioritises investments in accord with community demand, but also motivates the residents to participate in the preparation of the projects and contribute to its financing (as the alloca-

Table 5.6 True Neighbourhoods Programme Components

Components	Interventions
Road networks	Streets, avenues, pedestrian passages, and stairways to improve the neighbourhood's internal and external connections.
Risk control	(i) Rainwater drainage: improvement, substitution, or implementation of new rainwater collection and conduction systems (underground channels, canals, culverts, flushwaters, and drainage basin control); and (ii) stabilisation works: longitudinal and transversal containment walls, dikes, banks, floodways, and gabions.
Community amenities	Sports, social, and cultural facilities: sports fields, clubhouses, nurseries, squares, parks, recreational areas, overlooks, public footpaths, and green areas.
Basic services	Installation of in-house sanitary modules; provision of sanitary appliances and accessories for houses lacking in basic services and indoor toilets.
Electrification and street lighting	Provision of lampposts and electrical and lighting accessories, as well as the civil works necessary to provide the services.
Urban furniture	(i) Bus stops: localisation and construction of public stops at various points on the roads; and (ii) murals and sculptures: creation of murals and/or sculptures reflecting the neighbourhood culture to embellish public spaces.
Social support	Activities aimed at enhancing residents' social and human capital, so that they get involved in the implementation process and comply with their counterpart contributions. Empowerment of community organisations and participation to guarantee appropriation of programme investments in community development and physical works.
Regularisation of property rights	Regularisation of land ownership to increase physical capital and create a sense of belonging and identification with neighbourhoods. Issuing of property title in both names of a couple, in order to protect the woman's rights, irrespective of marital status.
Environment	Creation of community awareness about ecosystem fragility and the need for collective and individual responsibility for environmental preservation and rehabilitation. Actions include neighbourhood clean-up, reforestation, park maintenance, and residents' health care.
Sustainability	Community involvement to promote the appropriate use of urban and social facilities, to assume responsibility for the maintenance of social infrastructures, and to carry out initiatives that benefit the entire neighbourhood.
Disaster and emergency prevention	Develop skills in residents of all ages that permit them to identify, reduce, and be ready to deal with emergencies and disasters.

Source: Author's elaboration.

tion rules give priority to projects solving critical needs and that include community contributions). Similarly, it allows the municipal government in La Paz to select those neighbourhoods where investments are likely to have greater social and economic impact. The competition rules are

based on a participatory planning methodology—put into practice follow-ing the *Ley de Participación Popular* (Popular Participation Act)—and seek to stimulate residents' participation and commitment through a process of mobilisation, reflection, and consensus building. The residents them-selves and their leadership prepare the application for funds after gath-ering the necessary information to comply with the competition rules. This information must include data regarding access to services and the physical, geographical, socioeconomic, cultural, organisational, and environmental status of the neighbourhoods. These data help prioritise neighbourhoods that exhibit both the highest poverty levels and the best degree of organisation.

The programme implements, monitors, and assesses the results achieved through the logical framework designed for each project. Activi-ties are systematically organised by time frame, indicators, and verifica-tion methods. Community action—the tasks carried out by the residents to benefit the neighbourhood as a whole—is the voluntary contribution that residents offer as a counterpart to infrastructure improvements carried

Inhabitants of informal settlements often solve their housing problems through incremental construction.
La Paz, Bolivia

Inhabitants of informal houses built on hillsides face severe risks and pose a complex problem for neighbourhood upgrading programmes. **La Paz, Bolivia**

out in the neighbourhoods by the municipal government in La Paz. These tasks and activities include reforestation and urban tree planting and clean-up campaigns aimed at eliminating garbage dumping areas or removing debris. This kind of community work is not new in these neighbourhoods as residents have been working in this way for years, in keeping with a long-established practice in rural areas (whence a majority of the residents come), where works destined for collective use are usually built with communal help.

Results

The neighbourhoods that have benefited from the programme show visible signs of improvement. The installation of sanitary units inside the dwellings and the regularisation of property rights have done much to improve the beneficiaries' quality of life and increase the value of their assets, respectively. In the environmental sphere, permanent sources of pollution have been eliminated and recreational spaces constructed in their place, thereby improving the neighbourhood's urban image considerably. The impact on job creation has also been significant because building companies executing the works have contracted both male and female workers from within the neighbourhoods themselves. Quality of life for women has also improved, since they are now able (and feel confident and secure) to rely on nurseries to take care of their children while they work at home or elsewhere. Young people, too, have benefited from the large investments made in sporting facilities.

PHOTOS: BARRIOS DE VERDAD PROGRAMME

Neighbourhood community organisations have been strengthened. This has led to greater participation in activities organised by the community, greater credibility for community leaders, and greater participation by women in activities within the neighbourhood. The monthly meetings that update residents about their programme's physical and financial progress have become effective social control mechanisms through which the community can gather information, take part in debates, and make decisions.

Although the programme has not directly intervened in the provision of drinking water and sewerage, it has helped those lacking these services negotiate the connection from the networks to their dwellings, thereby substantially improving basic service coverage in the neighbourhoods. Another immediate and very significant effect has been the improvement of housing conditions, both in the building extensions carried out and in the increased use of better-quality building materials. Surveys completed by the municipality show that the population living in upgraded neighbourhoods also has a greater sense of belonging and higher self-esteem.

The process of implementing this programme made evident that the majority of projected activities required the close collaboration of residents, authorities, the implementation agency, and the municipality. For most of these stakeholders, the activities were largely new and unknown and therefore required adaptation and learning.

The community contributes directly to the implementation of the Barrio de Verdad Programme.
La Paz, Bolivia

MARÍA EUGENIA
GONZÁLEZ ALCOCER

Habitat Programme, Mexico

The Habitat Programme is designed to tackle the problems faced by poor households living in urban zones with high concentrations of poverty.[79] According to the most recent population and housing sample (INEGI, 2005), 73,700,000 people were living in Mexico's cities in 2005, representing 71.4 percent of the national population. This population is growing at an annual rate of 1.5 percent, which is higher than the national average. The *Consejo Nacional de Población* (National Population Board) predicts that in the next 25 years, 90 percent of the national demographic growth will take place in the cities. The *Consejo Nacional de Evaluación de la Política de Desarrollo Social* (CONEVAL) (National Board of Assessment for Social Development Policy) estimated that in 2006, 35.6 percent of inhabitants in urban areas (26.2 million people) were living in conditions of poverty. [80]

This high poverty rate goes hand in hand with other indicators portraying the low quality of life of this population: 44 percent of the urban population (32.4 million people) had no access to health services, 4.7 percent (3.5 million people) were illiterate, and 20 percent of the homes had a female head of household (14.7 million people). Similarly, 4.4 percent of the dwellings (762,000 units) had dirt floors, 7 percent (1.2 million units) had only one room, 5.9 percent (1 million units) had no running water, 3.8 percent (666,000 units) had no sewage connection, 5.3 percent (920,000) had no electricity, and approximately 34 percent of the dwellings (5.9 million units) were situated on unsuitable land, which increased construction costs by 50 percent (INEGI, 2005). Furthermore, 37.3 percent of poor urban households, amounting to 1,900,000 units, lived in highly populated areas (CONEVAL, 2007). Those city blocks with the highest poverty concentration levels, the habitat polygons, are the main focus of the programme's activities.

Objectives

The Habitat Programme, which has operated since 2003, was designed by the SEDESOL with the aim of coordinating the objectives of the social policy with those of the urban and territorial development policies. The Habitat Programme seeks to address the shortages and deep social contrasts

---

[79] Any locality with a population of more than 15,000 inhabitants is considered to be an urban zone, and the combination of all the 358 cities meeting this criterion are grouped into the *Sistema Urbano Nacional* (SUN) (National Urban System). The SUN is made up of 56 metropolitan zones, taking in 656 municipalities, including the 16 delegations of the federal district.

[80] The CONEVAL defines three levels of poverty: (i) *food poverty:* insufficient income to acquire a basket of basic food, even if all the disposable income of the household were used to buy only the goods in the basket; (ii) *capacities poverty:* insufficient income to acquire the value of the basket of basic food and to pay for basic health and education needs, even if all the household income were dedicated to this end; and (iii) *patrimonial poverty:* insufficient income to acquire the basket of basic food, and to meet the necessary health, education, clothing, and transport costs, even if all household income were used exclusively to acquire these goods and services.

found in the cities and metropolitan areas and to turn them into secure, orderly, and liveable areas. It also promotes "city building" by constructing spaces with local identity and social value and aims to integrate marginalised neighbourhoods and informal settlements into the urban structure, to promote the rights of the citizens settled in those areas, and to raise the quality of life of city inhabitants. The programme seeks to ensure the concurrence and integration of all the efforts directed at supporting poor households in marginalised urban zones. This is accomplished through targeted actions aimed at improving amenities and basic infrastructure, community development, and basic services provision. The SEDESOL has identified 3,166 city blocks with high concentrations of poverty-stricken households. The habitat polygons represent the programme's sphere of action, where federal resources—complemented by state and municipal government funds and contributions from the beneficiaries themselves—are employed in a coordinated fashion. The municipalities are the prime project implementers.

Execution

Due to its integrated approach, the Habitat Programme contributes to skills training, social capital formation, environmental improvement, land use planning, and the strengthening of the municipal and local governments' management and planning capacities. This is achieved through three main courses of action described in Table 5.7.

The *Unidad de Programas de Atención de la Pobreza Urbana* (UPAPU) (Urban Poverty Attention Programmes Unit) is the national coordinating body for the Habitat Programme. In each of the chosen cities, the programme identifies, selects, and targets its interventions to one or more of the habitat polygons. The federal government, the entities of the state and municipal governments, and the recipient communities participate in the financing and implementation of the projects according to their respective competence levels. Similarly, the programme promotes the implementation of other programmes within the habitat polygons, either from the social development sector, or from other departments and entities of the public federal, state, or municipal administration. These include public security for persons and patrimony, education for adults and young people, schools, public health programmes, financing for entrepreneurs, housing upgrades, and the provision of nurseries to help working mothers. The programme's implementation follows the stages set out in Table 5.8.

Results

Since its launch in 2003 and through the end of 2008, the Habitat Programme has financed 50,000 projects. Periodic evaluations of the programme show that it does respond adequately to the problems for which it was created and that it has obtained good results, which include the

Table 5.7 Mexico's Habitat Programme: Components

Components	Interventions
Social and community development	i) Skills training ii) Building, extension, renovation, and rehabilitation of equipment and buildings to be used for social services provision iii) Social services provision for the target population iv) Promotion of interventions by other programmes and government agencies
Upgrading the urban environment	i) Construction or renovation of benches and shelters, parks, gardens, and sports facilities within the habitat polygon; basic urban facilities and street furniture; dedicated transport corridors and roads for internal transit and connections with the city ii) Improvement in public transport access; establishment of routes, footpaths, and secure stops for pedestrians; installation of street lighting with special features for increasing public security in high-risk areas; identification and control of garbage dumping grounds[a] iii) Integrated strategies for disaster prevention through the preparation of studies and maps detailing natural risks iv) Disaster prevention through investments designed to mitigate risk, and the relocation of families living in zones where risks cannot be mitigated v) Support for poor households affected by natural disasters through the replacement of a basic package of goods and furniture vi) Orientation and awareness concerning environmental rehabilitation vii) Construction of plant and equipment for solid waste collection, recycling, and final disposal viii) Environmental conservation and rehabilitation measures, including actions aimed at water purification, clean-up campaigns, restoration of river-beds, and tree planting
Promotion of urban development	i) Support for the formulation or updating of municipal development plans and programmes ii) Creation and enhancement of urban development agencies and urban observatories iii) Promotion of social involvement, intersectoral coordination, and municipal association for the identification, planning, promotion, and execution of strategic projects aimed at ending urban poverty iv) Strengthening of local capacities in matters of social and urban development planning, administration, and management v) Acquisition of land for social services facilities vi) Support for state and municipal governments to acquire land to be set aside for urban development and social housing, providing building plots with basic services for households living in conditions of poverty[b]

Source: Author's elaboration.

[a] These investments were discontinued in 2009.

[b] This action was discontinued in 2009.

Table 5.8 Mexico's Habitat Programme: Implementation Phases

Phase	Activities
Grant allocation for states or municipalities	Definition of budgetary ceilings by the state and municipality. A formula is applied that takes into consideration the incidence and concentration of poverty, lack of basic infrastructure, and continuity of the interventions in the marginal urban zones. This is formalised by coordination agreements. These instruments define the cities and polygons selected for intervention, as well as the amount of the contributions from the federal government to the state governments and the municipalities.
Selection of "Habitat Polygons"	Targeting of the investment in the territorial areas identified by the SEDESOL in agreement with the local authorities, or in areas proposed by state or municipal governments that satisfy the basic requisites laid down in the programme's operative rules.
Actions	Grant allocations are executed by the SEDESOL delegation in the States. Proposals are drawn up and presented to the SEDESOL delegation by the programme's executing agencies.
Authorisation and execution of works and actions	The implementing agency identifies the projects and its interventions, draws up the relevant technical dossier, places it in the *Sistema Integral de Información de los Programas Sociales* (Social Programmes Integral Information System), and presents it to the SEDESOL for authorisation. In order to maximise the impact of the interventions, integrated projects are designed, including all the necessary works and interventions in each polygon and an implementation plan for each. The local delegation gives final approval after assessing each project's budget. The executing agency is responsible for managing the corresponding payments until the end of the project and is responsible for preparing and signing the formal acceptance in the case of works or the results assessment report in the case of other interventions. It must also provide documents attesting to the project's successful completion.
Reallocation of subsidies	All grants awarded to municipalities participating in the programme not taken up within the given time frame are subsequently reallocated to other municipalities or states that have submitted proposals.

Source: Author's elaboration.

concentration of resources in urban zones described as having a high or very high degree of marginalisation; upgrading of investments in marginalised settlements that would not otherwise have had access to public works or social investment; improved access to labour markets; increased opportunities for women; and better institutional conditions for the implementation of the investments and for preparing community development plans, thus preventing the dissipation of efforts and resources. State, federal, and municipal officials, from both the delegations and the SEDESOL central office, all agree that the primary strength of the Habitat Programme lies in the integrated nature of its activities, which increases its poverty-reducing effects. On the other hand, they acknowledge the scale of the urban poverty problem goes far beyond the project's scope.

From 2009 until 2011, a multi-annual impact assessment process will measure the benefits of the Habitat Programme by using representative indicators from all three of its investment areas. The classification of the habitat polygons will also be brought up to date by utilising information contained in the 2005 population and housing sample, which will allow an expansion of the programme's coverage into areas that need priority attention.

The assessment taken on by the Habitat Programme in 2007 of the estimated property appreciation generated by investment in infrastructure found that investments in road paving, street lighting, electrification, water supply networks, drainage, sewerage, benches, and shelters have had a significant effect. For every Mexican peso invested, the value of properties of households in the recipient areas went up by 2.85 pesos.

The Habitat Programme has successfully tackled most of the problems in terms of quality of life for the poorest people within the *Sistema Urbano Nacional* (SUN) (National Urban System) of Mexico. By focusing on a well-defined set of actions that are complementary to sector interventions, it has contributed to the battle against poverty in the territory. As in other neighbourhood upgrading programmes discussed in this volume, combining support for improvements in urban development with social and community development has been an effective strategy for tackling the problem. The multidimensional approach of the Habitat Programme has had a positive impact on the social, economic, environmental, and administrative spheres of urban development, while responding to local demand and developing new institutional and human capabilities (Vittrup, 2004).

The specific territory involved is a determining factor in the generation of poverty and in the definition of its characteristics, as well as a key factor in the implementation of policies designed to fight poverty. The Habitat Programme was designed as a local solution to work with poverty-stricken households in urban areas of the country. Due to its structure, the programme could not be effectively applied in areas with fewer than 15,000 inhabitants, since the wide dispersal of inhabitants in these towns greatly increases the costs of providing basic goods and services. But the goal of combining support for neighbourhood upgrading and urban development with social and community development can be applied to any LAC country that must adapt programme designs and implement them within existing political and administrative systems.

6

COMMUNITY PARTICIPATION: MORE THAN GOOD INTENTIONS

EDUARDO ROJAS

Community Involvement as a Basis for Citizenship

The communities living in informal settlements suffer from multiple deficits and vulnerabilities. As discussed in the preceding chapters of this volume, the solution to their problems require multiple and well-coordinated interventions by agencies from different levels of government. But no matter how well financed and implemented, the solutions will not be effective if the beneficiary communities are not involved. The participation of the beneficiaries in settlement upgrading projects is crucial for many reasons. At the basic level, community involvement is necessary to facilitate construction work in densely occupied areas where conflicts can easily arise. The planning of the construction process must be carefully coordinated with the community to minimise the disruption to daily life and to avoid accidents and material losses.

Community involvement allows the inhabitants, who are aware of their own problems, to take part in selecting the most appropriate interventions for their neighbourhoods. Community members feel a greater sense of ownership of the solutions when their opinions are taken into account during the design phase of the projects, and this involvement will be a key factor in the effective operation and maintenance of the infrastructure, facilities, and services provided by upgrading programmes. Community involvement is also crucial if the resettlement of community members becomes necessary. Most upgrading projects require the displacement of some of the beneficiaries, either to move them from environmentally vulnerable areas or the make room for the construction of roads, public facilities, and other infrastructure. An organised and involved community will help disseminate information among the beneficiaries regarding resettlement options and provide support to households during and after the resettlement phase. The involvement of the community is also important after programme implementation. Neighbourhoods with strong, highly involved communities tend to have more efficiently maintained and operated public spaces, facilities, and infrastructure. Local governments often hire community members to operate and maintain neighbourhood

Upper picture

Officials responsible for implementing settlement upgrading projects explain the type of work that can be executed within the budget ceiling in a community participation exercise. **Belem, Brazil**

Lower picture

The community's contribution to construction work reduces costs and enhances the social capital of the beneficiaries. **El Alto, Bolivia** facilities as community organisations have the capacity to oversee the work of public utilities and government entities in charge of maintaining infrastructure and providing services, as well as the capacity to press for better services when needed.

The advantages of community involvement and its supporting role in the efficient implementation of settlement upgrading projects are evident from the perspective of the individual settlement. Their importance is even greater for the city as a whole. The creation and development of community organisations in informal settlements builds social capital, which helps residents effectively exercise their rights as citizens. This process is reinforced as inhabitants of the improved neighbourhoods continue to make collective decisions and to work towards common objectives after the implementation phase. Community participation therefore yields multiple benefits, not only during the design and execution of settlement upgrading programmes, but also in sustaining the urban development process by facilitating the physical, social, and economic integration of the settlements and their inhabitants in the city.

Most settlement upgrading programmes include community involvement as a key activity cutting across all sector interventions that is supported with human and financial resources. In many programmes, such as the *Programa de Mejoramiento de Barrios* (PROMEBA) (Neighbourhood Upgrading Programme) in Argentina and the *Programa Barrios de Verdad* (True Neighbourhoods Programme) in Bolivia, community involvement is a central objective. This chapter analyses the community participation process and discusses its practical implications as a central axis of the design and implementation of interventions and its role in facilitating the resettlement process, sustaining the presence of the state, and maintaining services in the neighbourhoods.

The first part of this chapter argues that community participation is a complex activity; it is not politically neutral, and it requires balancing the perceptions and interests of the different social actors involved. After discussing the main conceptual approaches towards community participation, this section analyses the methodological and institutional developments that have allowed for the establishment of complex community participation programmes.

The practical implications of these arguments—and the complexity of the community participation process—are evident in the accomplishments of two projects financed by the Inter-American Development Bank (IDB). Ecuador's *Programa de Mejoramiento Integral de Barrios* (Integrated Neighbourhood Improvement Programme) has exemplified the importance of community involvement in the effective design, implementation, and financing of interventions. The involvement of the beneficiaries in the projects—in developing social action plans and contributing to their financing—has gradually bolstered their confidence in the programme and its benefits. In Brazil's *Programa Social e Ambiental dos Igarapés de Manaus* (PROSAMIM)(Social and Environmental Programme for the Creeks of Manaus), the community played an important role in a mass relocation programme. Through extensive consultations with the community, it was possible to identify their preferences and receptivity regarding different relocation options. In regular meetings, workshops, and consultations, the beneficiaries were informed of their various options, with different degrees of involvement from the project promoters ranging from the beneficiaries purchasing a home in the city with the help of a voucher provided by the programme to relocating to a new home built with programme resources in a neighbourhood close to their original settlement. Technical teams worked with the community and provided beneficiaries with support before, during, and after the relocation.

Although the sustainability of a committed level of community participation after programme implementation is still unknown, a Rio de Janeiro case has shown that the difficulty of consolidating a state presence in the *favelas* (informal settlements) is not necessarily an obstacle to sustaining significant forms of citizen involvement. In the *Favela Bairro* programme of the Rio de Janeiro municipality and the *Nova Baixada* programme of the government of the state of Rio de Janeiro, garbage collection is contracted with the community, with training and supervision provided by public service personnel. The *Postos de Orientaçâo Urbanística e Social (*POUSO) (Social and Urban Orientation Posts) in the *favelas* is another component of the *Favela Bairro* programme that has brought the municipality closer to the community and opened new channels of cooperation.

The experiences discussed in this chapter cover community participation during the project implementation phase. More research on the impact of community participation on citizenship building in beneficiary communities after the completion of projects is still needed. There are, however, signs that involvement does continue. Many community organisations maintain a wide and sustained commitment to their members even after upgrades are completed, which indicates that beneficiaries value the role of collective action and voluntary cooperation in finding solutions to many of their problems. Likewise, the fact that many of these organisations participate in training and income-generating activities shows that they support the beneficiaries' social and economic integration into the city. Analysis of these experiences provides insight into the challenges inherent in trying to expand and maintain the involvement of a community in the different phases of a settlement upgrading programme, including the post-implementation period. The lessons learned may reveal the best way to approach those processes central to the efficient implementation of projects and the building of citizenship in the neighbourhoods.

BOX 6.1 COMMUNITY INVOLVEMENT IN THE OPERATION AND MAINTENANCE OF URBAN SERVICES IN BRAZIL

ADERBAL CURVELO

Favela Bairro

From 1995 to 2006, the *Favela Bairro* (Urban Upgrading) programme in Rio de Janeiro (partially financed by the IDB) benefited 108 favelas (450,000 people) with interventions to improve infrastructure, urban facilities, education, employment, and other income-generation activities. The community was included in the project preparation stage itself through workshops, door-to-door visits from community leaders and assemblies, and events in which the community debated and approved settlement development projects. The social action plan, which provided a framework for community involvement, was formulated in the second phase of the programme and implemented in parallel to the urban development project. The social action plan also provided the framework for the implementation of education and other activities that were the responsibility of the local authorities.

The responsibility for waste management was transferred to community associations through an agreement with the municipal company in charge of the service. The associations were made responsible for contracting and managing the teams in charge of collecting waste in the settlements. There was one manager for each neighbourhood, and several employees were hired from the communities according to the needs of the neighbourhoods. The municipal company trained the neighbourhood teams and supervised the provision of the services.

In the second phase of the programme, the municipality established the *Postos de Orientaçâo Urbanística e Social* (POUSO)

(Social and Urban Orientation Posts), which were offices located in the neighbourhoods that provide technical assistance to the population for regularisation of land tenure, house construction, maintenance of urban facilities and infrastructure, environmental education, and community supervision of the service providers. These offices were part of a key institutional arrangement and allowed the municipality to maintain a relationship with the community upon completion of the upgrade programme.

Programme Nova Baixada

This programme was designed, financed, and implemented by the government of the State of Rio de Janeiro. The programme upgraded eight neighbourhoods in four municipalities in the metropolitan area of Rio de Janeiro. The community participation activities promoted by the programme were noteworthy for their scope and depth. During the design stage of the projects, technical teams visited each household to complete a detailed diagnosis. The programme also held training workshops for community-based health agents, street cleaners, and community leaders.[a] Community-based management commissions worked hand in hand with municipal units in charge of the services to maintain and operate them. Neighbourhood management committees received support from the municipalities and played a major role in the entire project cycle, mostly in controlling the quality of the infrastructure and services.

---

[a] The programme organised 30 workshops to prepare communications materials, 32 to train health agents, and 240 to train community leaders.

SONIA FANDIÑO   # Community Participation and the Sustainability of the Settlement Upgrading Process

Conceptual Framework

The settlement upgrading programmes implemented in the Latin American and Caribbean (LAC) region have made a significant contribution to the reconstruction of the social fabric of the beneficiary communities. Their implementation has required going beyond the vertical, sector-based structures of urban management. They promote cooperation among very diverse actors, including government entities and civil society organisations, leading to the greater sustainability of the services provided. Likewise, they provide a unique opportunity for the beneficiary communities to integrate into the rest of the city. Regardless of this progress, it could be argued that there is still much to do in further consolidating participation and making it integral to the democratic life of cities. This assertion is particularly true when community participation is conceived as a way to exercise democracy and help decentralise the state.

Democracy, widely understood, is a form of social coexistence in which all members of the society are free and equal before the law, and social relations are established by contractual mechanisms. Democracy can be direct, indirect, or representative. Democracy is direct when decisions are made directly by the people; indirect when decisions are made by representatives of the people; and representative, or participatory, when the political model empowers people to enter into association and organise to directly influence decisions.

Several theorists argue against representative democracy. According to Weber (1968), citizens have little influence in public decisions in this type of democracy, and Velásquez (2003) states that representative democracy relegates citizen involvement in decision making to a secondary and marginal role. Bobbio (1986) puts forth the counter-argument that in a complex and large society, representative democracy is the only form that allows the interests of different social groups to be taken into consideration, but acknowledges that it excludes a significant part of the society. Held (1996) argues that it is possible and desirable to find a democratic model that includes both representation and participation.

Habermas (1995) stresses the importance of the processes of dialogue, substantiation, deliberation, and consensus building in establishing democratic societies. Likewise, he supports a participative form of society in which individuals—women, workers, racial minorities—can discuss, in public, conditions of inequality in the private sphere. The author states that these public actions allow individuals to question their exclusion from political arrangements through a rational discourse in which the only valid norms are those that have won the assent of all the participants.

From Habermas' argument it follows that participation is only possible through an understanding that originates not from individual interests, but from a collective consensus on the results to be obtained. The participants pursue their particular interests by articulating them in a mutually defined context. The author also makes a distinction between an action oriented towards success and one oriented towards consensus; the first is individual and strategic and manipulates the intentionality of the subjects, while the second implies an agreement among subjects through shared language. These agreements must be accepted as valid through rational processes that provide the basis for the concerted coordination of individual action plans (Habermas, 1988). Velásquez (1986) elaborates on the intentionality of the participation processes. The author argues that through a process of participation, different social forces intervene directly or indirectly in the collective life to transform or sustain the political or social systems according to their interests.

Participatory democracy modifies the relationships among actors, especially those who are traditionally marginalised, by creating opportunities for them to intervene in the public arena and contribute to the definition of collective goals. Also, it allows the community to intervene in areas that affect the citizens' quality of life, and it fosters the formation of an organised civil society that is accountable, capable, and well-informed. Participatory democracy promotes consensus and unified action, while recognising the gender, cultural, political, and religious differences that exist among its members. It also engenders trust between the citizens and the state, which in turn strengthens governance.

The IDB (2004: 4) defines citizen participation as "the set of processes through which the citizens, directly through the governments, influence the decision-making process on activities or objectives. Citizen participation does not involve making the decisions but having influence on the decisions that in each case must be adopted by the rightful authorities".

In recent decades, community participation has gained in importance in many spheres of public action, including the settlement upgrading programmes discussed in this volume and the participatory budgeting processes implemented by municipalities in southern Brazil (IDB, 2005). This is a result of the growing confluence of actors involved in the management of public affairs and the increased awareness among citizens of their rights, duties, and capacity to make decisions that can affect their situations. The methods by which different social actors can participate have evolved alongside new theoretical frameworks. The technical and scientific rationale that supported top-down planning processes has fallen out of favour in many decision-making arenas, especially in complex situations like settlement upgrading programmes. Success in planning and managing such programmes requires the recognition of "other" actors.

Effective citizen participation requires three conditions:

- A committed government that opens spaces and establishes institutions and mechanisms capable and willing to take on new proposals;

- An organised civil society that transcends individual interests, linking them to the general interest of the society; and
- Simple, efficient, and transparent procedures to manage the process.

It is not possible to discuss community participation without acknowledging the role played by the territory, the symbolic and physical place where everyday life takes place. The existence of different social relationships and perspectives on the territory makes participation particularly relevant in urban planning. Most confrontations take place in the territory, which is also where agreements for peaceful coexistence take place.

Participation in Projects

The quality of the participation process depends on the political willingness of elected officials to involve the community in decisions and to establish institutions and the hiring of committed technical teams with the knowledge, abilities, and managerial capacities to conduct the process. Successful participation also requires community organisations that are capable of voicing their aspirations and proposals while they work in partnership with elected officials and other stakeholders.

As they work together, elected officials and community organisations begin to understand each other. Political leaders become more aware of the need to keep community organisations informed and involved in planning public interventions. They also become more sensitive to the fact that coordinating the actions of different government agencies promotes the efficient use of scarce resources, and they learn to take advantage of potential synergies with the actions of private agents. Moreover, they learn to integrate interventions rather than implement them in isolation, and not to burden beneficiaries with an excessive level of involvement that would prevent them from fulfilling their normal obligations. Community organisations in turn become more conscious of their rights and more effective in fighting for them due to a greater knowledge of intricate government procedures and the rules of the democratic game. Instead of locking themselves out, community organisations form alliances with the government and other social actors.

The establishment of a community participation component in a settlement upgrading project and its implementation are not spontaneous acts. Also, as it can be observed in Figure 6.1, the involvement of the community is required in different implementation phases of the projects. In participation processes, it is useful to know the capacity of the municipal teams, as they often need training to respond to the community's needs. The technical teams, on their part, need to be aware of their own interests in the programme, as well as the characteristics of the communities involved. This will ensure that the diagnosis of the situation and any existing expectations will be more realistic.

Sustainable public policies require coordinated action between the state and the beneficiaries, but social groups also must be able to effec-

Figure 6.1 Community Involvement in Different Phases of the Design and Implementation Process in Settlement Upgrading Projects

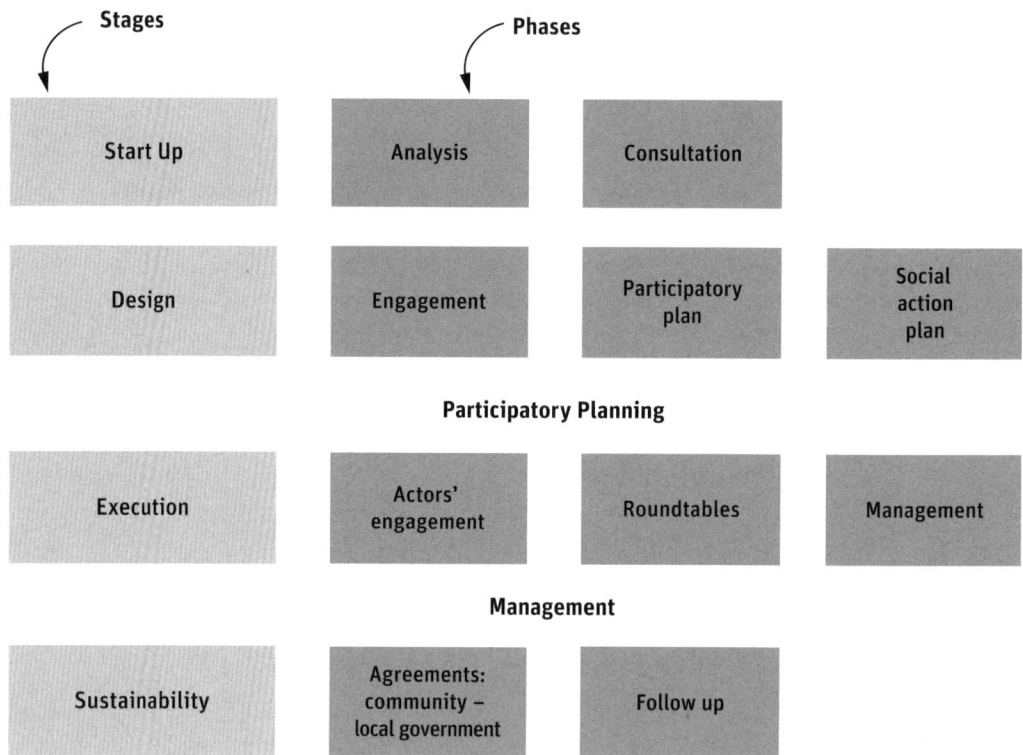

Stages	Phases		
Start Up	Analysis	Consultation	
Design	Engagement	Participatory plan	Social action plan

Participatory Planning

Execution	Actors' engagement	Roundtables	Management

Management

Sustainability	Agreements: community – local government	Follow up

Source: Authors' elaboration.

tively participate. The inhabitants of informal settlements often lack self-esteem and need help in overcoming this deficiency. This factor accounts for the passive attitude of many beneficiaries, who often expect the state to solve all problems instead of actively participating in finding a solution. The neo-liberal model of society also fuels this attitude by promoting competition in the marketplace, which leads the state to support vulnerable individuals and groups with monetary subsidies, rather than valuing the concerted action of the community.

Finally, although community participation is mostly territorial, it is necessary to transcend a fragmented vision of the territory and understand each neighbourhood as part of the city. Community participation involves multiple neighbourhoods and municipalities working together to solve conflicts throughout the city. In sum, the neighbourhood scale of intervention must be well aligned with the dynamics of the whole city.

MARGARITA ROMO   # Integrated Neighbourhood Upgrading Programme, Ecuador

The *Programa de Mejoramiento Integral de Barrios* (Integrated Neighbourhood Upgrading Programme) in Ecuador was designed to assist municipalities of large and medium-sized cities to set up management models to upgrade informal settlements located in the urban periphery. The inhabitants of these settlements were very poor (earning money mostly from informal activities) and lacked secure tenure over their dwellings. Neighbourhoods were characterised by low-quality infrastructure and access roads. The programme promoted a model of intervention aimed at integrating these informal settlements into the formal city by assigning neighbourhood communities a major role in their own development. The programme was notable in its integrated approach to the problems of the informal settlements and the fact that it incorporated the community in the design and implementation process and assigned the responsibility of executing the interventions to local governments. This approach ensured the sustainability of the interventions and had a significant impact on overall poverty reduction, with outcomes superior to those achieved by traditional public works programmes.[81]

To attain the objectives of the programme, the project cycle included the following phases and community participation mechanisms:

- *Neighbourhood improvement.* Projects were formulated on the basis of agreements reached with the community and using low-cost and innovative approaches. They included an urban plan that gave priority to public spaces that promoted community interactions and the development of potable water and sewerage networks, rainwater drainage, roads, and basic urban facilities. The project preparation stage also included the preparation of social, environmental, tenure regularisation, and resettlement plans.
- *Contracting and implementation.* Projects were contracted out through a bidding procedure designed with the IDB and implemented by the municipal contracting committees with the support of the national programme implementation team. In each of the committees there was a representative of the community to ensure the transparency of the process.

---

[81] The programme had a demonstration phase executed in several municipalities throughout the country where the participation-based modes of intervention—involving the community, the central government, and the municipality—were designed and implemented. In this phase, the programme benefited approximately 3,600 households in neighbourhoods selected by the municipalities. The average investment per household was US$2,100. The Ministry of Urban Development and Housing (MIDUVI) supplied a voucher for US$1,000 per household with resources from the Integrated Neighborhood Upgrading Programme. The municipalities and the beneficiaries (who contributed US$100 per household) provided the rest of the resources.

■ *Operation and maintenance (sustainability).* This was a shared responsibility of the municipality and the community.

The implementation of the programme includes activities to strengthen the capacity of the actors to participate in all the project phases. These activities were the backbone of the implementation process and ensured support from the community. Table 6.1 presents the contents, scope, and results of the project training, implementation, and follow-up activities.

Table 6.1 Training, Implementation, and Follow-Up Process for the Integrated Neighbourhood Upgrading Programme in Ecuador

	Module 1	Module 3	Module 5
Teaching modules	Conceptual aspects	Socialisation: participation plans (project fair)	Socialisation of the project design process
	Experiences from other countries: Colombia, Brazil, Mexico	Design experiences from other countries	Operation and maintenance experiences
	Project cycle: eligibility, instruments, participation plan, methods and tools	Project cycle: design; low-cost experiences; social, environmental, and tenure regularisation plans; contracting and implementation	Project cycle: community involvement in implementation, operation and maintenance agreements
	Module 2	**Module 4**	**Module 6**
Practice modules	Local team uses neighbourhood eligibility criteria	Municipal team designs the project with the community	Municipal team supervises the implementation of the works
	Municipal team prepares the community involvement plan	Community involved through delegates to the contracting committee	Community executes the social, environmental, and land tenure regularisation plans
	Support from the social monitor	Advice to the committees	Social and legal monitor
	From modules 1 and 2	**From modules 3 and 4**	**From modules 5 and 6**
Outcomes	Municipal team organised and operational	Project dossier completed	Works and other interventions implemented
	Community organised and participating in the diagnosis	Settlement and neighbourhood improvement voucher	Local team and the community in charge of operation and maintenance
	Diagnosis and priority setting completed	Works contracted	Municipality–community partnership strengthened
	Community involvement plan completed	Social plan executed	Land titles issued

Source: Authors' elaboration.

Informal settlements
on the hillsides of the
Pichincha volcano.
Quito, Ecuador

There are three key actors involved in the Integrated Neighbourhood Upgrading Programme: *the community members* as the main beneficiaries residing in the neighbourhood improved by the programme; *the municipality* as the government level closest to the community and the one that coordinates the relationship between the national government and the community; and the *Ministerio de Desarrollo Urbano y Vivienda* (MIDUVI) (Ministry of Urban Development and Housing) as the national agency promoting the programme. These three actors contribute to the development and improvement of the Integrated Neighbourhood Upgrading Programme through the activities shown in Figure 6.2. The programme has adopted a management model, which achieves the following:

- Coordinates the contributions of the national and local levels of government
- Promotes the involvement of the community in the design of the neighbourhood plan and the upgrade project, and (later in the process) in the contracting, implementation, operation, and maintenance of works
- Arranges the shared financing of the projects among MIDUVI, the municipalities, and the community
- Seeks the integrated improvement of the neighbourhood and promotes the regularisation of the land tenure and the execution of investments in infrastructure, urban facilities, environmental protection, and social development actions
- Develops induction projects that help to perfect the programme and design and train officials that will replicate the model

Figure 6.2 Strategy for the Participation of Stakeholders in the Integrated Neighbourhood Upgrading Programme Project Cycle

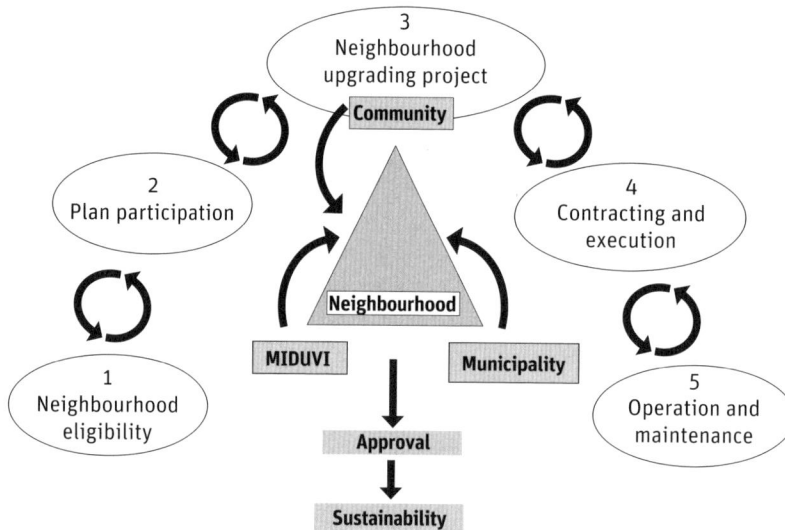

Source: Author's elaboration.

The success of the Integrated Neighbourhood Upgrading Programme has resulted from the confluence of institutional, methodological, and social factors that have promoted the effective involvement of benefici-aries in the projects. Several specific factors contribute to a successful culture of community involvement: the political and institutional willing-ness to act, the capacity of technical teams to implement the projects, the use of a participatory budgeting process, the follow-up of a national pro-gramme implementation team, the dissemination of training procedures, and an open line of communication to stakeholders that fosters a sense of mutual confidence and credibility in day-to-day interactions (CG Consult-ing Group, 2007).

The high level of community satisfaction is another positive outcome of the participation process. But the challenge of involving the commu-nity does not end with the best practices generated by the programme. It is essential for the community to stay involved in activities that increase citizen awareness, strengthen community organisations, and consolidate the alliances established among the stakeholders. The evaluation of the Integrated Neighbourhood Upgrading Programme highlights the need to strengthen the urban management model and efficiently train munici-pal teams to reproduce the projects promoted by the programme. It also shows that the projects have facilitated social and community integration by improving degraded public spaces, which supports the overall process of improving the quality of life.

BÁRBARA ARAÚJO
DOS SANTOS

The Social and Environmental Programme for the Creeks of Manaus (PROSAMIM), Brazil

The *Programa Social e Ambiental dos Igarapés de Manaus* (PROSAMIM) (Social and Environmental Programme for the Creeks of Manaus) is an urban development intervention undertaken by the government of the State of Amazonas in the capital city of Manaus, Brazil, with financing from the IDB. The programme attempts to solve the social and environmental problems in certain areas of the city caused by informal settlements that occupy the creeks (*igarapés*) that cross the urbanised area and provide it with rainwater drainage to the Rio Negro (see intervention areas in Map 6.1).[82] The informal settlements originated during a period of rapid growth experienced by the city between 1970 and 2003, a period in which the urban population quintupled from 300,000 to just over 1.5 million, increasing at a much more rapid pace than the rest of the Brazilian cities.[83] The rapid population growth in Manaus was not accompanied by necessary investments in infrastructure or controls on land use and illegal invasions. This shortfall, combined with the lack of affordable housing for low-income households, fuelled the emergence and expansion of illegal settlements in environmentally vulnerable areas, particularly on the banks of the *igarapés* in and around the downtown area.

In 2003 there were at least 7,000 households (36,000 inhabitants) living on the banks of the *igarapés* of the Educandos watershed; over 90 percent of these households had monthly incomes below the minimum salary (equivalent to US$100 in 2008). The creeks' drainage function was obstructed because of the houses on stilts (*palafitos*) linked by narrow bridges and walkways occupying its banks. The occupation of these highly vulnerable environmental areas, unsuitable for urban use, created an environmental and social problem for the city. Flooding, bad odours, and the proliferation of mosquitoes and rats in the downtown area led to the abandonment and deterioration of neighbouring areas. Dropping real estate values resulted from the degradation of buildings and public spaces near the *igarapés*. The supply of water and electricity in the occupied lands was accessed illegally. These problems had a negative impact—both direct and indirect—on the entire population of Manaus (Magalhâes and Rojas, 2007). Despite these difficulties, illegal settlers still benefited by living in the downtown area near employment centres with easy access to public transportation, public services, educa-

---

[82] *Igarapé*—from the Tupí language—is a creek, narrow body of water, or canal. There are several in the Amazon watershed.

[83] This growth accompanied the expansion of the commercial and manufacturing activities connected to the Manaus Free Zone and the growth of public services and government activities. The population growth resulted from migrations within the State of Amazonas and other regions of Brazil, particularly the northeast. The city of Manaus represents more than half of the population of the state and generates over 90 percent of its internal gross product.

PHOTO: FERNANDA MAGALHAES

The inhabitants of the *igarapés* have very poor living conditions. They suffer from frequent floods and lack potable water and sanitation.
Igarapé Mestre Chico, Manaus, Brazil

tion, and health facilities, as well as other facilities present in the central area of the city.

The objective of the PROSAMIM was to restore the environmental function of the creeks and make them compatible with the urban development needs of the downtown area. The strategy adopted had four components, two of a corrective nature and two of a preventive nature: (i) construction of macro- and microdrainage infrastructure to regulate the impact of rains and the regular rising of the Negro river; (ii) relocation of the population living in the *igarapés* to alternative housing on suitable land with basic services; (iii) usage of the more vulnerable lands for roads, avenues, and parks to keep them from being occupied again; and (iv) greater allocation of land for residential use at prices affordable to low-income populations and implementation of land use controls in accordance with the city's Urban Development Master Plan. The programme offered several resettlement options, which were designed with input from the community.

Approach and Methodology

The complexity of the environmental and urban problems in the programme area and the large number of people directly affected by the interventions demanded close collaboration with the community to find solutions acceptable to all the stakeholders. The work with the beneficiaries was organised in a community participation plan with an aim to:

Map 6.1 Intervention Areas of the PROSAMIM

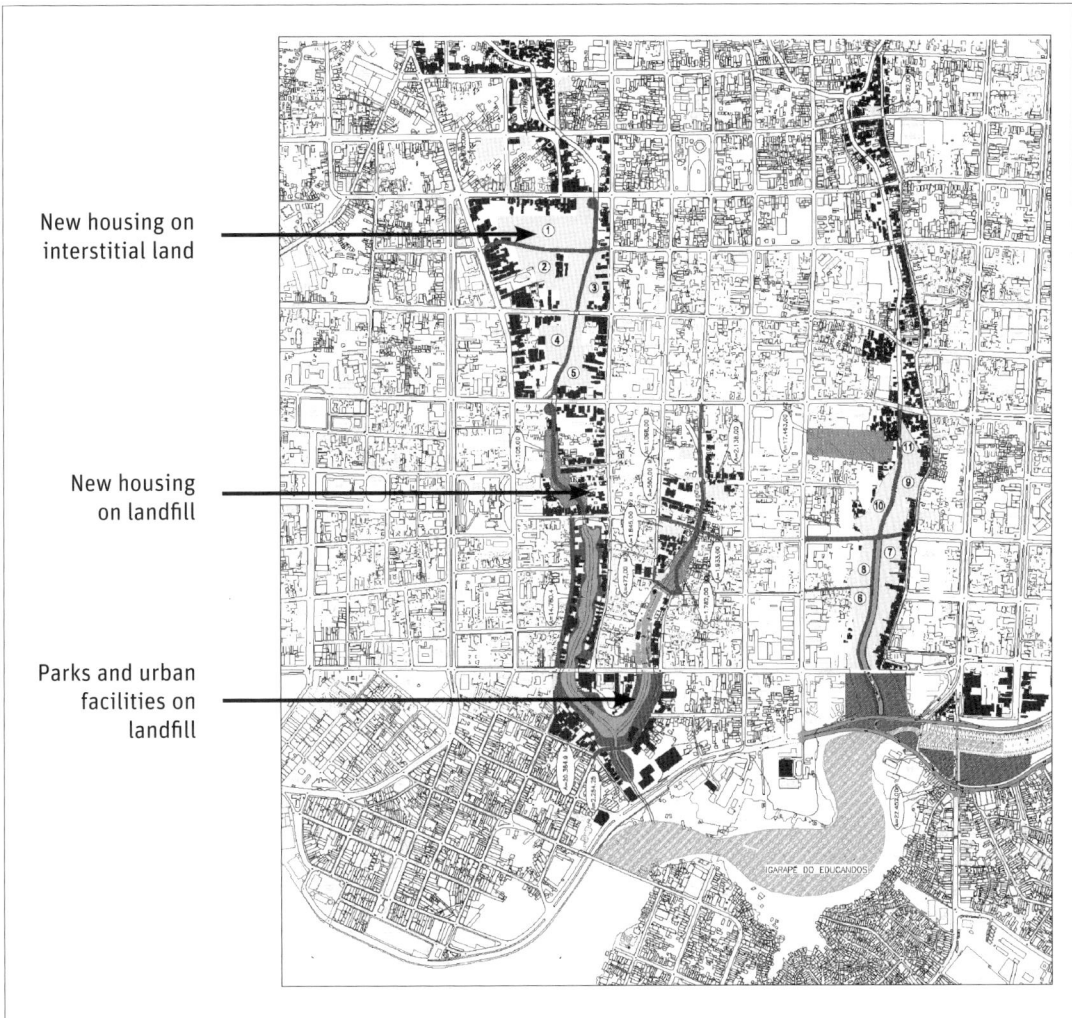

New housing on
interstitial land

New housing
on landfill

Parks and urban
facilities on
landfill

Source: Author's elaboration.

- Put into place mechanisms to facilitate communication with community members and encourage them to participate in the project
- Set up a participatory management style in all stages of the project, including the planning, implementation, monitoring, and evaluation phases through a committee representing the community and local support groups
- Establish communication channels to ensure that all inhabitants were well informed about the project

- Ensure the involvement of the households in the decisions concerning their new neighbourhoods, the assistance they would receive, and resettlement options
- Recruit and train new community leaders to manage community affairs and the development of social groups
- Implement environmental and sanitary education programmes to improve individual and collective attitudes towards environmental and health sustainability
- Implement skill-training activities (with emphasis on gender issues) to create new opportunities for accessing existing income-generation programmes
- Strengthen the social capital of the communities, particularly by promoting community solidarity and assistance to the elderly
- Implement monitoring, evaluation, and follow-up activities, after the completion of the civil works, to strengthen self-management capacities for the sustainable use of the new neighbourhoods, the control of urban development, and the efficient operation and maintenance of investments

The programme promoted community involvement as a way to ensure a better quality of life for the population. To encourage community members to express their opinions, the project promoted training activities to increase the awareness among residents of their rights and duties as citizens. The concept of participation was closely connected with that of citizenship, since it emphasised the democratisation and socialisation of knowledge. This methodology led to a shared management of the decisions that greatly empowered the community.

The programme proposed several resettlement plans for those living in the *igarapés,* allowing them to choose the one that most closely suited their needs and preferences. The resettlement options included:

- *A new house*. New houses were built on land that was reclaimed from the igarapés or in nearby areas with good access to existing infrastructure and urban services.[84]
- *Housing voucher*. A government voucher of US$8,000 was given to households for supervised resettlement into houses for sale in the local and regional market.
- *Housing complex*. Displaced households were offered homes in the state or municipal social housing programmes.
- *Compensation*. Cash compensation was given to those households who were able to resettle independently within the framework set up by the national legislation and IDB policies.

---

[84] The houses were built of locally produced bricks and followed the building codes of the city regarding minimum size and number of rooms. They had a total area of 54 square metres with two bedrooms, a living area, kitchen, and bathroom. The houses were built in groups of 6, 12, and 24 individual units; one-third were single-storey houses and the rest had two floors.

Due to the difficulty in finding homes for the households that chose to live in the same area, the programme established a housing support subsidy to assist them in renting a house until new houses were built (the first option above). The programme also financed all the resettlement expenses of the families.

Implementation

To promote the involvement of the community, the project has opened shared management offices in the intervention areas of the *igarapés*. The offices work under the supervision of the project management unit of the Housing and Urban Development Secretariat of the government of the State of Amazonas. There are two offices under operation, one to work with the population of the *igarapés* of Manaus and Bittencourt and the other for the Mestre Chico *igarapé*. A multidisciplinary team that includes social workers, lawyers, psychologists, engineers, surveyors, and administrators staffs the local offices. The social workers are in charge of the community participation activities and are key in contacting, engaging, and orienting the beneficiaries to mitigate any negative effects of the resettlement process financed by the project. The team organises community meetings, house visits, and individual interviews before presenting the beneficiaries with the resettlement options. The engineering team appraises the houses that will be removed from the *igarapés* and negotiates compensation for the residents. The lawyers prepare the legal documents upholding the resettlement option chosen by the beneficiaries, and finally, the social work team responsible for the relocation process organises and implements the transfer of the households to their new homes.

The project has also implemented social development activities in the new housing complexes to assist the population after resettlement, by welcoming beneficiaries to their new neighbourhoods and implementing the social insertion activities laid out in the community participation plan to ease the process of relocation. These activities include skills training that trains women for jobs in the hotel services industry, leadership training, promotion of school enrolment, adult literacy campaigns, and activities that help applicants prepare for university admissions tests in partnership with the *Universidade Federal de Amazonas* (Federal University of Amazonas).

The project recommends the creation of vigilance agents, who are selected residents trained to facilitate communication between the inhabitants of the new housing complexes and the project administration. These agents work under the guidance of the project team and assist the PROSAMIM to manage the post-relocation process. Each neighbourhood block has an agent and a substitute who keeps a logbook to record the block meetings and decisions adopted. The participation effort is geared towards formally organising the community into resident associations that manage the public spaces, promote neighbourhood activities, and organise production groups to generate employment and income.

FOTOS: PROSAMIM

Results

The PROSAMIM has adopted an innovative approach to the relationship between civil society and the programme's beneficiaries and advocated a participative management model that has departed from the classical top-down management approaches. This has resulted in both high levels of community support for the project and a high degree of community involvement. By mid-2008 the project had completed the voluntary relocation of more than 5,600 households (see Table 6.2). Each family was involved in at least three meetings before the relocation, which allowed them to understand the project, its benefits, and the relocation options.

The involvement of community leaders in the decision-making process has allowed the PROSAMIM to address all the communities' demands. Their involvement in the definition of the transparent criteria by which new houses are allocated has been essential in accommodating the beneficiaries' interests. Households attend workshops in which they select resettlement options in a transparent and participatory manner, using previously agreed-upon criteria. The community also participates in the selection of the public facilities built in the housing complexes. For example, if young residents want a skating rink, they can work hand in hand with the engineering team in the placement and design of the facility.

To validate the interventions, the PROSAMIM trained 30 community associations and established four new associations among the resettled population. Vigilance agents represented the residents of 49 housing blocks in the new complexes. The project used over 35 different types of instruments, including leaflets, information folders, manuals, and guidelines, to communicate with the community.

Some aspects of the project have been affected by unforeseen circumstances. Changes in the programming of the civil works have delayed construction of some of the new houses, which has postponed the relocation of some families. Some of the households that opted for the housing

Left picture

A significant portion of the land reclaimed in the implementation of the environmental improvement of the *igarapés* is used for recreational and urban facilities to prevent reoccupation by illegal settlers.
***Igarapé Manaus,*
Manaus, Brazil**

Right picture

Part of the population living on the banks of the *igarapés* is relocated to high-density neighbourhoods, but not in the form of apartment buildings. This avoids the problems of managing common property that contributes to the rapid deterioration of low-income apartment buildings.
Manaus, Brazil

Table 6.2 Resettlement Solutions by Igarapé by Mid-2008 (number of houses)

| Solution | Igarapé | | | | | |
	Quarenta	Cachoeirinha	Manaus	Bittencourt	Mestre Chico	Total
Compensation	661	409	518	162	367	2,117
Housing voucher	948	661	62	37	273	1,981
Housing complex	510	282	38	21	123	974
New house	0	0	196	114	257	567
Total	2,119	1,352	814	334	1,020	5,639

Source: Author's elaboration based on data from the PROSAMIM files.

voucher have also had a hard time buying homes due to price increases in the housing market and the fact that the vouchers were not indexed to inflation.

Many lessons have been learned from the design and implementation of the PROSAMIM, especially regarding the need for cooperation among institutions in the planning and implementation of joint activities. From the early stages of the design, the project identified all the partners required for the fluid implementation of activities to ensure their support and involvement. The dynamic relationships among the entities involved—which included the state government, the municipality, financing agencies, a university, and community associations—ensured the continuity and sustainability of the different programmes. The effective solutions found to the problems were made possible by a well-organised, educated, and aware community, with leaders who had wide support, were interested in the public good, and worked in partnership with an efficient government committed to social welfare. The proactive management of delays and the skilful execution of any necessary adjustments were also crucial for the successful completion of these complex projects. Delays in the execution of civil works are often justified, but they require careful management as they increase project cost and undermine the beneficiaries' confidence. To minimise the effect of delays, the PROSAMIM established a crisis management commission that included representatives from the community, the legal and social work teams of the project management unit, and the pertinent stakeholders. This commission helped guarantee coordinated action among various parties in dealing with unforeseen situations. The agreements reached between the entities implementing PROSAMIM and the community in the multiple and frequent meetings that they had were consigned in meeting minutes, which served as legally binding documents to guarantee their fulfilment.

7 THE FOUNDATIONS OF SUSTAINABILITY

EDUARDO ROJAS

The Management of Scarce Resources and the Scale of Interventions

Solving the problems of informal settlements is expensive. Providing sanitation, drainage, and access roads to one household in a settled neighbourhood may cost twice as much as providing these services in a new subdivision. There are several reasons for this. As is evident from the cases presented in this volume, the poor environmental condition of illegally occupied lands means that costly mitigation measures must be carried out before they can qualify for residential use. In addition, the distribution of lots in informal settlements is done with little regard for the orderly occupation of the land. As a result, some of the inhabitants often need to be resettled to create space for infrastructure, parks, access roads, and urban facilities—an expensive process, as it forces programme promoters to buy land and build new houses for the displaced households. Another cost stems from the illegal subdivisions' distance from and poor access to the urbanised areas of the city, requiring the construction of costly infrastructure to connect these neighbourhoods to the existing service networks (such as roads, potable water, electricity, sewerage, and drainage); although this infrastructure also tends to service the areas between the informal settlements and the consolidated city adding to the benefits of these investments.

Other factors increase the cost of settlement upgrading programmes. Promoters and beneficiaries have little incentive to economise when they do not pay for the goods and services provided by the projects' costs. The entities implementing these programmes often do not charge the beneficiaries, citing their low income and the goal of redistributing income to the poor. Indeed, according to the discussion in Chapter 6, beneficiaries do not have an incentive to limit the number of goods and services they request from the programmes. However, the higher the costs of individual solutions, the lesser the number of solutions can be provided by a fixed budget. Costs are also disregarded when the executing agency—usually the local government—receives financial transfers from the higher tiers of government (national or state); the local government has no incentive to limit the diversity and costs of the investments in the programmes.

Even when the executing agency forms part of the same tier of government financing programmes (for instance, the municipality), the incentive to spend less is absent. Settlement upgrading programmes compete for funds with other agencies and try to capture the largest possible budget to accomplish their objectives. Projecting higher costs per household, for example, serves this purpose.

The beneficial side of spending more resources per beneficiary—that is, implementing better solutions in the neighbourhood—can also be problematic. In some cases, the programmes provide the informal settlements with urban standards that are far above those of the surrounding formal neighbourhoods. Also, spending more per family reduces the programme's coverage to only a portion of the needy households, leaving the others (usually the majority) waiting a long time for solutions. To increase social equity in cities, the scale of the interventions must be expanded to cover all households, and the scarce resources available for settlement upgrades must be used more efficiently. This efficient use of resources—along with equitable management of land resources, improvement of housing markets, and urban economic development policies—is part of a multi-sector strategy to increase public interventions to prevent and solve the problems of the informal settlements and offer a better life for their inhabitants.

For the reasons discussed earlier, it is necessary to impose strict budget restrictions in the settlement upgrading programmes—that is, to set a maximum allowed expenditure per serviced house. The size of the expenditure depends on the objectives of the programme (including the desired standard of urbanisation) and local factors (such as complexity of the neighbourhoods, labour costs, and other input costs), but put simply, the cost of these solutions should not be higher than the benefits they bring to the society. Economic analysis has made a significant contribution to the design and evaluation of settlement upgrading programmes by establishing how much should be spent on each household and by assisting programmes to select the most beneficial combination of investments in the settlements. That is the central topic of this chapter. The chapter opens with a discussion of the key concepts of economic analysis applied to public investment and the different ways to analyse and measure the economic costs and benefits of the programmes. Later, the chapter shows the results of applying this type of analysis to the settlement upgrading programmes financed by the Inter-American Development Bank (IDB) in Ecuador and Colombia. The cases illustrate the conceptual and operational aspects of calculating costs and benefits and highlight the need for clear programme objectives to estimate these costs and benefits accurately. Such estimates are complicated due to the need to incorporate the multiple impacts—direct and indirect—of the investments in the city; they are also imperfect due to the difficulties in estimating the true economic costs to society of the investments. Nonetheless, assigning monetary values to the costs and benefits helps to maximise the impact of the invested resources, particularly if this analysis is done at the design phase of the programme. The economic analysis provides information that allows for a better distribution of the resources, enabling programme planners to estimate the maximum investment per household and providing criteria that justifies spending this amount in the face of multiple competing investments that can be made in a neighbourhood.

This type of analysis is complex and costly, so the programmes financed by the IDB undertake a detailed economic analysis of a sample of projects—representative of the universe of problems and the beneficiary neighbourhoods and cities—and use the results to define the parameters of the rest of the investments financed by the programme. These parameters are also used to monitor the programmes. Occasionally the promoters perform ex post analysis to measure the results of a programme and compare these results to ex ante analysis.

The chapter presents the IDB's experience in applying the methods of project economic analysis to settlement upgrading programmes and provides examples of its use in a variety of contexts and programmes. This discussion highlights the usefulness of economic analysis in spending scarce resources efficiently and improving programme design.

FERNANDO CUENIN — Economic Analysis for Settlement Upgrading Programmes

The central objective of economic analysis is to identify efficient and equitable uses for the available resources to maximise community welfare. This is a great challenge because resources are often scarce and the needs that they should satisfy are usually many. To confront this challenge, economic analysis relies on a variety of concepts and techniques to confront a complex and changing reality in a simplified way. The settlement upgrading programmes confront this very same problem, as decision makers and implementing agents must respond to growing urban shortages with severely restricted budgets.

As discussed in Chapter 5, the magnitude, variety, and interdependence of the problems in the informal settlements demand an integrated response that generates significant and sustainable changes in the quality of life of the inhabitants. Accordingly, the programmes have gradually become more complex. Whereas earlier programmes covered only basic infrastructure, mitigation of environmental risks, and security of tenure, many programmes now have components linked to the provision of social services (health, education, nurseries, community and recreation centres, and so on), the integration of the neighbourhoods into the formal urban structure, income-generation support (training and new productive activities), and the strengthening of community organisations and their involvement in the programmes (for example, by participating in the investment decisions and maintaining the facilities). The programmes' increased complexity demands an interdisciplinary approach to their design, implementation, and monitoring. Within this framework, economic analysis clarifies the objectives and strategy of the intervention in the settlements and identifies the best use of the available resources so that the investments generate benefits in excess of their costs. The analysis also helps to identify the key economic, social, and institutional aspects that need to be monitored during the execution of the investments to ensure that they produce the desired results.

The central objective of the present section is to show how this analysis helps in the design, monitoring, and evaluation of settlement upgrading programmes.[85] It should be especially useful for readers who are not familiar with the economic analysis of programmes; case studies following the discussion provide a more in-depth understanding of the concepts discussed. This section explains the contribution of economic analysis to the different phases of the project cycle, in particular the diagnosis of the problems, the definition of the objectives, and the selection of the solutions. The connection between economic analysis and the formulation of the logical framework of the project, as well as the midterm and final evaluations of its impact, are also discussed. Finally, the section presents general theoretical and technical concepts that facilitate the understanding of the case studies.

Economics and economic analysis in particular are grounded on the principle that the scarce resources available to society have an opportunity cost; for instance, a dollar allocated to health care is no longer available for education services. Economic analysis seeks to find the uses for the available resources that maximise society welfare. Such analysis requires a good understanding of the complex problems faced, an understanding that is obtained through models and analytical instruments developed with an interdisciplinary approach.

Economic analysis is helpful to the extent that it generates useful information for decision making. Its contribution is more significant if used in the initial phases of project preparation and in parallel with the rest of the technical studies. This ensures that the analysis contributes to screening alternatives and supports decisions that improve the effectiveness of the project. If performed at the final stage of project preparation and only to calculate a rate of return, the economic analysis may confront project administrators with the choice whether to continue a project or cancel it. But at this stage, high expectations make it very difficult to cancel a project, even if doing so is the best decision. Additionally, economic analysis at such a late stage of the project preparation process does not contribute to identifying ways of improving the project's impact. Figure 7.1 outlines the contributions of economic analysis to the different phases of the project cycle.

---

[85] The discussion that follows will use the world project to refer to the variety of government interventions used to solve a problem. The concepts and techniques of economic analysis discussed are equally applicable to policies and programmes.

Figure 7.1 Economic Analysis and the Project Cycle

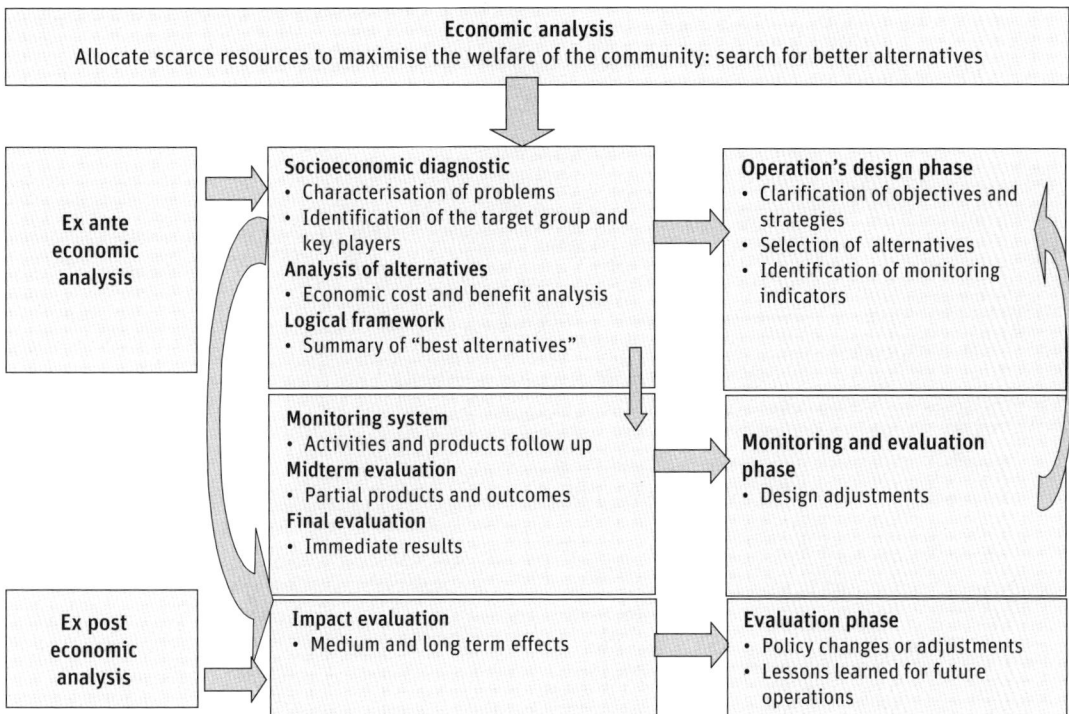

| Economic analysis |
| Allocate scarce resources to maximise the welfare of the community: search for better alternatives |

Ex ante economic analysis

Socioeconomic diagnostic
- Characterisation of problems
- Identification of the target group and key players

Analysis of alternatives
- Economic cost and benefit analysis

Logical framework
- Summary of "best alternatives"

Operation's design phase
- Clarification of objectives and strategies
- Selection of alternatives
- Identification of monitoring indicators

Monitoring system
- Activities and products follow up

Midterm evaluation
- Partial products and outcomes

Final evaluation
- Immediate results

Monitoring and evaluation phase
- Design adjustments

Ex post economic analysis

Impact evaluation
- Medium and long term effects

Evaluation phase
- Policy changes or adjustments
- Lessons learned for future operations

Source: Author's elaboration.

Ex Ante Analysis

In the initial stages of the programme design process, economic analysis contributes to clarifying the programme's objectives and strategies based on a diagnosis of the main economic and social problems to be solved, outlining efficient solutions to the root causes of the problems, and identifying the desired beneficiaries of the programme as well as the key actors in its implementation. During this stage, economic analysis reveals the possible ways of attaining an objective, selects the most efficient option, and demonstrates that its benefits outweigh its costs. The options analysed may consist of alternative policy measures; different quantities and types of goods and services to be provided; alternative implementation mechanisms; or, in the case of physical works, alternative locations, materials, or construction methods. There are four techniques available to the analyst to substantiate the choice among the available options: (i) minimum cost, (ii) cost effectiveness, (iii) weighted cost effectiveness, and (iv) cost-benefit analysis (see Box 7.1). The first three techniques allow for the identification of the most efficient option based on its cost, but they do not provide information on whether the benefits generated are larger than the

BOX 7.1 ECONOMIC ANALYSIS AND THE ASSESSMENT OF ALTERNATIVES

Cost-effectiveness analysis. This method is used when it is possible to measure in physical units the benefits or results of the alternatives under evaluation, basically comparing the median cost of the alternatives. For instance, the method can be used to determine which of the following three ways of reducing the incidence of diarrhoeic illnesses is cheapest: (i) provision of potable water and sewerage systems; (ii) provision of sanitary education; or (iii) provision of potable water, sewerage systems, and sanitary education.

Weighted cost-effectiveness analysis. This technique is used when the alternatives under evaluation generate more than one outcome or benefit, and do so in different quantities. Confronted with this situation, the analyst must assign relative weights to the different outcomes if some are more important than others. Following the previous example, this will be the case if the different alternatives can reduce not only the cases of diarrhoeic illness but also those of dengue fever.

Minimum cost analysis. This is a type of cost-effectiveness analysis used to compare alternatives that produce identical outcomes or benefits (qualitative and quantitative). In settlement upgrading programmes, this technique is commonly used to compare alternative materials or construction methods for the physical works.

Cost-benefit analysis. In contrast with the other methodologies, cost-benefit analysis evaluates the quantitative outcomes in monetary terms. Comparing each alternative's costs and benefits allows for the calculation of its economic rate of return. Following the case discussed previously, the monetary benefits of reducing the incidence of diarrhoea can be put in monetary terms based on labour productivity gains and reductions in medical expenses.

costs associated with its implementation. This is provided by the fourth technique, cost-benefit analysis, which involves the calculation of the economic returns of the proposed interventions.

To accurately determine the best way to spend scant resources, the programme's objectives must be clearly defined; this, in turn, requires a good social and economic diagnosis of the problem. This diagnosis is improved with the technical data required by the economic analysis. For instance, estimating the economic benefits of providing potable water requires an in-depth knowledge of the levels of consumption and the available sources of water, their quality, and their cost.

The diagnosis should consider the incentive systems under which the key actors operate, as these systems impact the programme results. There may be cases in which an option that is cost efficient and provides positive economic returns to society may not be feasible, as it is not aligned with the incentives under which the actors directly or indirectly impacted by its implementation operate. For instance, land titling may not succeed if the beneficiaries cannot or are not willing to shoulder the costs of formal land ownership (for instance, land taxes) or if access to subsidies to obtain a formal title means that they will be excluded from other, more attractive benefits (for instance, subsidies for acquiring a house).

The estimation of the costs and benefits of a given intervention is always made from the point of view of society as a whole rather than from the narrower perspective of the financiers or beneficiaries of the interventions. This approach also entails taking into consideration the positive and negative externalities that an intervention may generate. For example, if better access to potable water and sanitation reduces diarrhoeic illnesses, it not only improves the quality of life of a given population but leads to a reduction in public health expenditures for such ailments, thus releasing funds for other uses.

It is important to include in the analysis only the incremental costs and benefits linked to the interventions financed by the projects. In other words, "conditions with the project" should be compared with "conditions without the project" (the conditions if nothing were done) or a "counterfactual scenario". Conditions *with* and *without* the projects are often confused with conditions *before* and *after* the projects, but the two concepts are fundamentally different. "Before and after" involves a diachronic point of view that does not allow the identification of the outcomes exclusively attributable to the interventions financed by the projects. For instance, the morbidity rate of a neighbourhood may be decreasing not only as a result of improved access to potable water and sanitation supplied by a settlement upgrading programme, but also as a result of territorially targeted sanitation education programmes. Additionally, care must be taken not to include financial transactions that are transfers from one group to another in society—for instance, taxes and subsidies—among the economic costs and benefits. But it is important to study the distribution effects of these transfers—that is, who benefits and who loses—to implement compensatory measures and identify key supporters and detractors of the programme.

Costs

Several factors must be taken into account when identifying and valuing the economic costs of a programme. First, it is important to include all the incremental costs of construction, operation, and maintenance connected to obtaining the results expected from the programme, even for those interventions that are not financed by the programme (for instance, the cost of complementary works such as connecting water mains). The economic costs must also include the negative externalities with significant impacts on the welfare of a group. Sunken costs must be excluded—these are the investments that contribute to the attainment of the objectives of the project but have already been made and cannot be recovered. For example, suppose that two roads had been improved in a neighbourhood but never connected by a bridge due to a lack of funds and that the project under evaluation is to build the bridge to improve mobility in the neighbourhood. In this case, all the benefits associated with the increased mobility are included in the analysis, but only the incremental costs involved in building the bridge are included, not those associated with improving the roads.

Shadow prices (or market prices) must be used to value the resources used by the programme.[86] In general, accurate estimates of shadow prices for most economies in Latin America and the Caribbean (particularly the less developed ones) do not exist; therefore, they must be estimated whenever the selection of the right price has a significant impact on the conclusion of the analysis. This would be true for a programme that makes intensive use of an input whose market price is severely distorted.

Benefits

As with the costs, it is important to consider only incremental benefits attributable to the project in the analysis. Economic benefits must not be confused with financial benefits. For instance, the increased tax collection from land titling activities financed by the project—although positive from the point of view of municipal finances—is not an economic benefit but a transfer of resources from the private sector to the government. How, then, are the benefits of a project valued? This is a relatively simple problem when the goods and services provided by a project are privately consumed (for instance, the potable water supply). In such cases it is possible to esti-mate demand functions and calculate net consumer surplus generated by the proposed interventions.[87] But if the goods are public or semi-public—a common occurrence in settlement upgrading programmes that provide public lighting, roads, parks, and so on—then more complex valuation tech-niques are needed.[88] Generally speaking these techniques belong to two main groups: (i) objective valuations (for instance, estimation of avoided costs) and (ii) subjective valuations (for instance, hedonic prices/property valuation and contingent valuation/willingness to pay) (see Box 7.2).

Subjective valuation techniques are usually data intensive—they require the use of statistical and econometric tools, as well as well-designed and executed surveys. In practice, a variation of the hedonic prices technique is widely used in the evaluation of settlement upgrad-ing programmes. Instead of estimating econometrically a price function for the properties—that would allow planners to estimate their increase in value as a result of the improvement interventions—surveys of spe-

---

[86] When government- or market-based distortions such as monopolies, taxes, duties, subsidies, or fixed minimum or maximum prices exist, market prices do not reflect the true opportunity cost of the resources for society. However, shadow prices do reflect this cost.

[87] Consumer surplus is defined as the difference between what consumers are prepared to pay (valuation of the goods or services) and what they actually pay.

[88] These are goods and services for which it is not possible (or too costly) to exclude those that are not willing to pay for its consumption. The estimation of the demand curve is more complex for these goods and services.

BOX 7.2 VALUING ECONOMIC BENEFITS

Objective valuations. The benefits are estimated based on avoided costs. For instance, the benefits of reducing the incidence of an illness include decreased medical expenses and the avoided loss of production due to sick leave.

Subjective valuations. (i) Hedonic prices/property valuation: This valuation method assumes that real estate prices respond to changes in a property's surroundings—that is, that there is a functional relationship between real estate prices (the dependent variable) and attributes of the neighbourhoods (and individual properties) that impact these prices (parks, safety, and so on) (the independent variable). Thus, in cases where there is a reliable real estate market—one that produces information that is relevant and trustworthy—this methodology allows analysts to estimate changes in real estate prices due to changes in the attributes of the neighbourhoods or the houses built by the project. (ii) Contingent valuation: Through surveys, the analysts estimate the willingness of consumers to pay for a given good or service. The value of the payment is considered an economic benefit connected to the consumption of this good or service. The accuracy of results is highly dependent on the way the survey questions are phrased; for instance, households will not reveal their true willingness to pay if they perceive that they will ultimately receive benefits of the project regardless of their contribution.

cialised agents are conducted. In such surveys, these agents (i) are asked how much they expect the price to increase in view of the problems confronted by the neighbourhoods and the proposed government interventions ("informed judgment") and/or (ii) provide their estimates (or direct knowledge) of the median market values for the area to be intervened (situation without the programme) and a comparable area with a similar intervention (situation with the programme). The expected valuation is estimated as the difference between these two values.

Box 7.3 presents different ways of analysing real estate prices as a proxy to the economic benefits associated with settlement upgrading programmes. The analysis done in Mexico and Uruguay estimated the effect of each of the investments on the prices of the properties. This is useful when the package of investments varies from neighbourhood to neighbourhood or when there are doubts about the economic returns of some of the investments. Brazil incorporates in its calculations the increase in the built area of the houses after upgrading.

Good practices in economic project analysis indicate that the selection of a methodology must be fully justified on the basis of the information to be obtained by the analysis and the importance of this information for decision making. For instance, in the case of the provision of a basic need that would be socially and politically difficult to exclude from a settlement upgrading programme (such as access to potable water), it is better to focus the

BOX 7.3 THE USE OF REAL ESTATE PRICES TO ESTIMATE BENEFITS

Mexico: Habitat Programme. The Social Development Secretariat (SEDESOL) developed an interesting methodology to analyse the economic viability of the investments in basic infrastructure included in the settlement upgrading component of the Habitat Programme (potable water, public lighting, road shoulders and sidewalks, drainage or sewerage, electricity, and road paving). The benefits were estimated by comparing the average price of land in areas with similar income characteristics but different infrastructural qualities. In a departure from common practice, analysts attempted to isolate the individual contribution or economic benefit of each piece of infrastructure, a complex and costly procedure since the six types of investment could be combined into 64 packages. Despite conducting the analysis in 521 areas, it was possible to determine market prices for only 12 of the combinations. For the rest of the combinations, land prices were estimated on the basis of the cost of producing a parcel with access to the combination of services being analysed. The analysis of market prices and costs of producing a parcel was complemented with surveys to identify household preferences for the basic services offered by the programme. Based on the prices of each of the combinations of basic services, it was possible to calculate the betterment generated by each package of services. The valuation procedure was calibrated in three pilot areas in the municipality of Queretaro. The analysis was applied to 80 areas benefiting from the programme (60 cities) that were representative of the regional diversity of the country.

Uruguay: settlement upgrades. Since 1998, the IDB has supported the government of Uruguay in its efforts to improve the conditions in substandard neighbourhoods, first through the Regularisation of Informal Settlements Programme (PIAI I) and later with a new loan (PIAI II). PIAI II includes financing for (i) sanitation, potable water, rain drainage, roads, public lighting, and home sanitary units; (ii) land titling; (iii) social and human capital strengthening; (iv) resettlement of households; (v) infrastructure to connect the neighbourhood to the city; and (vi) social and community facilities. The economic benefits were calculated on the basis of the expected increase in the value of the properties that directly and indirectly benefited from the programme. The valorisation was estimated using hedonic price techniques with a survey of 882 cases distributed among the neighbourhoods that would benefit from the programme and others with similar characteristics that acted as the control group. The surveys gathered information on (i) the value of the properties (land and dwelling); (ii) characteristics of the land and the dwelling; (iii) availability of services; (iv) probability of floods; (v) distance to community centres and social services facilities; (vi) localisation and accessibility of the neighbourhood to the rest of the city; and (vii) socioeconomic characteristics of the households. Processing this information using econometric methods allowed the estimation of a hedonic price function to simulate the change in the market price of the property associated with each of the investments included in the programme. The full implementation of the package of works included in the programme translates into property-value increases of more than 150 percent, mostly as a result of the increased availability of potable water and sewerage systems, the elimination of the risk of floods, and adequate road access.

The betterment analysis was complemented by a study of the households' willingness to pay for the improvements. A survey of 629 randomly selected households estimated a global willingness to pay between US$1,600 and US$2,000 per household, a figure significantly less than the valorisation of the properties estimated by the hedonic price method (US$6,800 per dwelling). The results of the survey were not used, as there was evidence that the households either responded strategically or did not fully understand the questions. Finally, the economic returns of implementing the programme were estimated for two areas representative of the country: Pando Norte (representative of the interior of the country) and the northern area of Montevideo. The estimates were based on the valorisation study, the number of lots benefiting from the programme, and the investment and recurrent costs. In both cases the internal rate of return (IRR) was positive and above the

reference rate of 12 percent (28 percent and 25 percent, respectively).

Brazil: Favela Bairro II, Rio de Janeiro Urban Upgrading (PROAP II). This is another programme that invests in basic infrastructure to improve living conditions in the informal settlements (*favelas*) of Rio de Janeiro.[a] The economic benefits were estimated based on the expected change in the prices of the properties in the intervention area. The analysis calculated average prices for a sample of 143 real estate transactions in three areas targeted by PROAP I (situation with programme) and three areas included in PROAP II (situation without programme). Properties that benefited from PROAP I are worth almost twice as much as those that will benefit from PROAP II (+97 percent). The impact on the areas surrounding the informal settlements was also significant: the value of the land around the settlement benefiting from PROAP I increased by 20 percent and the dwellings by 170 percent. This analysis included the impact of settlement upgrading on home improvements and expansions, estimating that 30 percent of the households in the *favelas* increased the surface of their dwellings by 2.23 square metres on average. The cost-benefit analysis of the programme for each of the beneficiary informal settlements yielded rates of return that ranged from 13 to 71 percent (an average of 42 percent).

---

[a] See: http://www.iadb.org/projects/project.cfm?id=BR0250&lang=es

analysis on the identification of cost-efficient ways of providing the service rather than on making a detailed valuation of its costs and benefits.

Monitoring and Supervision

In addition to clarifying the objectives, alternatives, and viability of the programme, cost-benefit analysis identifies monitoring indicators to verify that the programme achieves its objectives and thus brings about the benefits estimated ex ante. These indicators are included in instruments such as the logical framework and are the basis for monitoring project progress and conducting the midterm and final evaluations (see Box 7.4).

The monitoring system provides constant feedback on progress made in achieving the key outcomes (identified in the logical framework for each component and activity) and facilitates the implementation of preventive or corrective actions. Independent of the frequency of the reporting (usually biannually), the monitoring system must have mechanisms that guarantee the continuous gathering of updated and reliable information.

Apart from the monitoring reports, the midterm and final evaluations measure the results by focusing on the outcome indicators included in the logical framework that formed the basis for the economic cost-benefit calculations. The midterm evaluation can also contribute to the timely identification of problems that may jeopardise attainment of a programme's development objectives. Therefore, the timing of this evaluation must be related more to landmarks in attaining the objectives of the programme than to progress in the execution of the resources assigned.

Ex Post Analysis

Impact evaluations seek to determine if the programme has had the expected effects on the individuals, households, and institutions it targeted, and if these effects can be attributed to the execution of the programme. The analysis focuses on the outcomes or impacts included in the ex ante cost-benefit analysis. The results of this analysis are important to support changes in policy or adjustments to subsequent phases of a programme. Box 7.5 summarises the principal characteristics and methodological options for the design of impact evaluations.

In settlement upgrading programmes—specifically those that address neighbourhoods one at a time—it is possible to analyse some of the impacts at the end of the programme based on the analysis of settlements that were attended to at the beginning.[89] It is not necessary to exclude

---

[89] In programmes financed by the IDB, the resources supplied by the loans are disbursed in a four-to-five-year time frame, and the improvement of a neighbourhood typically takes two years from the community participation exercise at the beginning of the implementation process to the delivery of the works. This provides two years from the interventions in the first settlements to the closing of the operation—sufficient time to detect some of the short-term and midterm impacts.

BOX 7.4 ECONOMIC ANALYSIS AND THE LOGICAL FRAMEWORK

The logical framework is a tool that allows analysts to monitor the expected results of a project in an economic and objective manner. It is composed of two main tools—the stakeholders' analysis and the problem tree—that produce alternative solutions to the problems. In simplified form, the logical framework presents a series of relationships among activities and products that lead to the attainment of one of more outcomes related to the objectives of the programme. But nothing in the tool registers if these products are generated in an efficient manner or if the costs of the components are less or more than the benefits. This is where economic analysis makes a contribution since it provides answers to these questions turning the logical framework into a summary of the best alternative to reach the expected outcomes (at least an alternative that is efficient in terms of costs). The indica-

tors used in the logical framework must be based on easily verifiable results and not on the estimated economic benefits. In the latter case, the logical framework loses its simplicity and thus its value as an economical instrument for monitoring projects. For instance, it is easier to verify that households increased their consumption of potable water than to estimate the economic benefits associated with increased consumption. When building a logical framework, it is important that (i) the indicators of output and outcomes reflect the objectives of the programme and can easily be verified without resorting to additional assumptions or complex valuation techniques and (ii) the alternatives identified are supported by the economic analysis so that if the expected results are attained, the project will contribute to the welfare of the community.

neighbourhoods from the programme to create a control group: neighbourhoods included in the second half of the implementation period are used as control groups for the evaluation. This method allows for an efficient use of the evaluation results and ensures that resources from the programme finance the evaluations.

The main aspects to be considered in the economic analysis of a settlement upgrading programme are discussed below. The economic analysis is of use if it generates information that is useful for decision making. To maximise the value added to the design and monitoring of the programmes, the economic analysis must be conducted at the initial phases of project preparation and in parallel with the technical analysis. It is also important to integrate the results of the economic analysis into the design of the monitoring mechanisms of the programmes.

The person in charge of the economic analysis must be actively involved in defining the indicators included in the logical framework and the midterm and final impact evaluations. This ensures proper monitoring of the critical factors that bring about the economic benefits forecasted in the ex ante evaluation and that justify the existence of the programme.

BOX 7.5 METHODOLOGICAL OPTIONS FOR IMPACT EVALUATION

The methodological precision of impact evaluation rests on the estimation of a counterfactual scenario, that is, the situation that would exist without the programme. Building such a scenario enables programme administrators to identify precisely which outcomes are a result of the implementation of the programme. Control or comparison groups (those not receiving the benefits of the programme) are compared to treatment groups (those receiving the benefits of the programme) to estimate the impacts. Both groups must be similar in everything but their participation in the programme. There are basically two methodologies to define a counterfactual scenario: (i) experimental designs and (ii) quasi-experimental designs.

The first method randomly selects the control and treatment groups from among those that are part of the target population of the programme—that is, both groups fulfil all the conditions to access the programme's benefits. This simple technique allows analysts to easily calculate the outcomes of the programme by observing the differences among average values observed in the two groups. Critics regularly argue that the methodology excludes the group not receiving benefits from the programme and that the method cannot be used when

the whole population benefits from the programme. But if budgetary restrictions prevent full coverage of the eligible population in the short term, a common situation on settlement upgrading programmes, this methodology can be useful.

The second method seeks to identify comparison groups that are similar to the treatment group in all its observable characteristics. Econometric techniques, some more sophisticated than others, are used, including (i) matching, in which comparison groups similar to the treatment groups are identified using econometric techniques and average values after the interventions are compared; (ii) double differences, which involve the calculation of the median differences among the treatment and control groups before and after the intervention; (iii) instrumental variables, which allow the identification of exogenous variations attributable to the programme; and (iv) reflexive comparisons, which compare the treatment group before and after the intervention. The main advantage of this type of design is that it can be used with existing information and thus yield quick and less costly results. But the results may not be as robust as those of other methods due to selection bias and cause-and-effect attribution problems.

The fact that estimating economic rates of return based on the monetary valuation of costs and benefits is not always feasible—often due to the lack of information—should not be a deterrent to analysing the economic feasibility of the alternative interventions proposed. The economic analysis must provide information to make sure that (i) the strategy and interventions included in the programme are coherent with the objectives, (ii) the effective beneficiaries are those intended by the promoters of the programme, (iii) the interventions are identified and dimensioned in accordance with the type and magnitude of the problems to be addressed,

(iv) the incentives for the stakeholders are operating in line with the programme's objectives, and (v) more efficient options to attain the stated objectives do not exist.

The scope and complexity of the economic analysis, as well as its cost, can be justified only if it is capable of producing information that is useful for reaching good decisions. This is a critical point to consider when evaluating settlement upgrading programmes, especially the components that supply basic services. Well into the twenty-first century, there is little doubt that all households, independently of their income, should have access to services such as potable water, sanitation, and protection against natural hazards. In these cases, the economic analysis adds little to the decision making if it is focused only on estimating the economic benefits of these services. But the analysis can make a significant contribution if it identifies the minimum cost of providing the services or more efficient options for doing so. It is important to be careful when making these arguments, as the actual quantitative valuation of benefits and costs may help to avoid spending too much, for instance, in surfacing secondary roads that have little traffic with costly materials designed for high traffic conditions or on the size and quantity of neighbourhood parks.

In practice, the economic analysis of settlement upgrading programmes usually focuses on (i) identifying the cost per household of the investment package and (ii) estimating the economic benefits gained by the land directly or indirectly impacted by the improvements to the neighbourhoods. To determine the amount to invest per household, it is customary to estimate a reference budget based on executed projects similar to those in the programme under analysis. In some cases this analysis is supplemented by an analysis of the technical options to execute the works (materials and construction methods). A full budget analysis is rarely made, except in cases where full prefeasibility studies are undertaken. Although it is widely used, the real estate valuation method frequently underestimates the benefits of the programmes, especially the externalities that are not revealed in the price of the real estate in the intervention area. But calculating the benefits of every infrastructural improvement (especially when the intervention packages differ from neighbourhood to neighbourhood) increases the complexity and cost of using this methodology significantly.

FERNANDO CUENIN   Economic Analysis in Guayaquil, Ecuador, and Colombia

This section presents two case studies: one in Guayaquil, Ecuador, and the other in Colombia. The Guayaquil case study is a good example of how economic analysis impacts the design, monitoring, and evaluation of a project through the preparation process—from the diagnosis of the socioeconomic conditions in the neighbourhood to the identification of key indicators to verify the attainment of the expected results. Here, the analysis is focused on the identification of the least-expensive option in the design and construction of infrastructure. Real estate valuation is used to estimate the economic benefits (as was also true in the cases of Mexico and Uruguay described in Box 7.3).

As with many national programmes, in the Colombian example the cost analysis must capture a diversity of regional situations not fully known at the time of designing the programme. The case also illustrates the contribution made by economic analysis to the evaluation of a variety of alternatives, such as finding the best procedures to implement a massive land-titling programme. Finally, this case shows that differentiating economic and financial costs and benefits leads to different conclusions concerning the alternatives that generate more benefits or cost the least.

Guayaquil: Cooperative Independence II (Trinitarian Island)

The Problem and the Interventions Financed by the Programme

The IDB supports the city of Guayaquil in financing urban rehabilitation and settlement upgrading programmes through an operation that has two components: (i) the urban rehabilitation of the Santa Ana and del Carmen hills located in the central area of the city (US$6.4 million investment) and (ii) the integrated upgrade of the neighbourhoods in the Cooperative Independence located on the periphery of the city (US$12.7 million investment). The second component is discussed in this section.

The Cooperative Independence II is located on the Trinitarian Island, an area of more than 40 hectares surrounded by marshes. In socioeconomic terms, this is one of the most problematic marginal settlements of the city of Guayaquil. Almost all of the approximately 7,500 persons living there have at least one unsatisfied basic need, and the majority face employment problems. Most of the houses are precariously built on the water or on garbage landfill, and a majority of the lots lack basic services and titles. The neighbourhood is affected by severe pollution (which impacts the health of the inhabitants); lacks adequate roads, recreation areas, and urban services; and faces significant security problems.

The settlement upgrading interventions contemplated in the programme include: (i) temporary relocation of households; (ii) landfills; (iii) provision of potable water, sewerage and drainage facilities, electricity, and vehicular and pedestrian access roads; (iv) land titling and registration; (v) provision of sanitary units inside the houses; (vi) sanitary education; (vii) community-driven recreational and social programmes; (viii) rehabilitation of the river-banks (pilot project); (ix) construction of a park with sports areas and paths; and (x) building of a multi-purpose centre (with space for microenterprises, non-governmental organisations [NGOs], a library, a technology centre, multi-purpose rooms, and a health-care centre for children and mothers).

The economic analysis helped to accomplish the following objectives: (i) to better understand the problems in the neighbourhoods; (ii) to rationalise the cost structure of the programme; (iii) to ensure that the interventions financed by the programme generate more benefits than their cost; (iv) to suggest design improvements to maximise the impact of some of the interventions; and (v) to identify indicators for monitoring and evaluation. Given the highly informal nature of the neighbourhood, the design team had very limited secondary information about the area to complete a diagnostic. This situation made it necessary to conduct extensive surveys, mainly among community leaders and priests (individuals widely respected in such conflict-ridden neighbourhoods). The main problems detected—which formed the basis of the calculation of benefits—included: (i) high incidence of diarrhoeic and respiratory illnesses associated with the environmental problems and lack of basic services; (ii) difficulties in accessing the neighbourhood from the city and in moving within the settlement; (iii) material losses due to the precarious conditions of the housing stock; (iv) lack of recreational space; and (v) high personal and financial costs to the community due to violence and crime.

Cost Analysis

The analysis was developed in two stages. First, the team estimated a reference budget based on cost information taken from 11 projects financed by the Integrated Neighbourhood Upgrading Programme (see Chapter 6). This provided a general idea about the average unitary costs and the relative weight of the components in the total cost structure of the programme. Second, the team completed a minimum cost analysis for the investments in infrastructure. This analysis centred on alternative materials and construction procedures and covered the most significant items of investment, representing at least 50 percent of the total cost of the project. The original budget (total and per household) was adjusted on the basis of the minimum cost option selected.

There are several examples of how the minimum cost analysis modifies the materials and construction techniques originally selected. Although filling the marsh areas with sand would have been less costly than hydraulic filling, it would have required a retention wall whose cost exceeded the savings in filling materials. The analysis also demonstrated that the savings in maintenance costs for roads did not justify the use of concrete or paving stones; thus, asphalt surfacing was selected.

Benefit Analysis

The economic benefits were evaluated in the following two ways: (i) by calculating the individual impact of each intervention through analysis of avoided expenses and increments in consumer surplus generated and (ii) by estimating the joint impact of the interventions in terms of changes in the price of the properties benefiting directly and indirectly from the project.

The first approach yielded limited results due to the difficulties in gathering reliable information at a reasonable cost. The results included estimates of net changes in consumer surplus caused by the increased consumption of potable water, the avoidance of septic tank cleaning expenses, and the lower incidence of houses sliding into the marshes.[90] It is worth noting that even though the lack of information prevented the monetary valuation of the benefits, their identification and description supplied valuable information for the design and monitoring of the project. For instance, to put a value on the benefits accrued from sewerage it was necessary to deepen the diagnostics focusing on the sections of the Trinitarian Island already with this service (an area with similar characteristics to the Cooperative Independence II). It was observed that many households did not connect to the sewerage network because it was costly. These households were not fully aware of the problems caused by the unsanitary disposal of wastewater, and they did not have resources to build bathrooms. Based on these observations, the following components were incorporated into the programme: (i) community education on good sanitary practices; (ii) financing for sanitary units in the houses; and (iii) public support for connecting the houses to the sewerage network. Additionally, the logical framework included indicators to effectively monitor the use of the services.

The second approach used as a basis for calculating the economic benefits was to observe the changes in real estate prices in the project area. In theory, the improvements in the neighbourhood should increase the market value of the properties in the direct and indirect area of influence of the project. But lack of reliable market prices in the area prevented the estimation of a hedonic price function (house transactions were scarce and informal). This led to the undertaking of a survey among real estate appraisers, builders, and community leaders. Among other questions, those interviewed were asked how much they believed house prices would rise due to the social and economic changes brought about by the project. The agents' answers were not very consistent, so the analysts estimated the betterment from the differences in house prices between the area of intervention (situation without the project) and the area in the Trinitarian Island that already had improvements similar to those financed by the project (situation with the project). The average price differential between the areas was very significant: undeveloped land was twice as expensive in the area with the project and houses were three times as expensive.

The expected valorisation was applied to the direct area of influence of the project (the whole area receiving investments) and the indirect area of influence (the built area within 150 metres of the project area). This yielded a total benefit of approximately 90 percent of the investment costs. It should be noted that this method of valuation underestimates the benefits that do not show in the real estate prices—for instance, the environmental

---

[90] Household water consumption is well below the recommended standards, a situation arising from the high prices paid to access alternative sources of potable water (tankers or water carriers).

externalities (pollution of the marshes by the dumping of wastewater), the benefits accrued by the users of the multi-purpose centre, and the avoided costs from the reduced incidence of illness and pests. Additionally, this approach does not allow for the separation and valuation of the benefits generated by each of the individual investments and project components.

Monitoring and Evaluation Indicators

Table 7.1 summarises some of the relationships that can be established between the benefits attributable to the project and the indicators and means of verification of the logical framework.

Colombia: Settlement Improvement and Land Titling

For years the IDB supported the government of Colombia in addressing the large housing deficit that affected mostly low-income groups. In 2008 the IDB approved an US$85 million loan to support a programme for the consolidation of the social housing system and a territorial development policy (IDB, 2008a). The programme included, among other things, two components that are discussed in this section: (i) a pilot programme for the integrated upgrade of the settlements (US$8.5 million) and (ii) public land titling for social housing (US$20.7 million). The first component finances the integrated improvement of at least six settlements made up of mostly low-income households. The average investment per household is US$3,700, which is devoted to basic infrastructure (roads, potable water, sewerage, public lighting), social development (interventions with priorities set by the communities), and land titling. The second component provides financial, technical, and legal support to provide legal titling to more than 320,000 public lots occupied by social housing.

The main objectives of the economic analysis are (i) to support the preparation of a reference budget to frame the investment per household in settlement upgrading and (ii) to analyse the available options for implementing the massive land titling programme and to evaluate the benefits (economic and financial) of land titling.

Cost Analysis of Settlement Upgrade

The analysis covers a sample of 11 projects that are representative of the regional diversity of the country (a necessity for a national programme). The estimates of the amount to be spent per household on basic services are based on observed values for investments including (i) unitary costs per type of infrastructure and type of construction materials and (ii) quantity of infrastructure per household. The national average investments per household defined by the programme took into consideration regional differences. These averages were to be reviewed during programme implementation with information supplied by the executed projects.

Table 7.1 Colombia: Monitoring Indicators Derived from the Economic Analysis

Economic benefits	Logical framework indicators	Means of verification
Avoided costs from the reduced incidence of diarrhoeic illness (associated to improved access to potable water, sewerage systems, and better sanitary practices)	*Incidence of diarrhoeic illnesses:* At the end of the project, the incidence of acute diarrhoeic illnesses was reduced by 15 percent (30 percent in the following two years). (Baseline 2006: incidence of 20 cases per 100 children.)	Final and impact evaluation
	Effective utilisation of basic services: At the end of the project (1) at least 80 percent of the households in the intervention area are connected to the sewerage network and are using it, and (2) consumption of potable water has increased from 5 cubic metres per month to 13 cubic metres per month.	Final evaluation
	Effective utilisation of basic services: Eighteen months after launching the project, at least 60 percent of the households have signed a contract to connect to the sewerage system.	Intermediate evaluation
	Service provision: Fifteen months after project launch, 9,800 metres of potable water mains, 10,200 metres of sewerage connections, and 1,504 domiciliary water and sewerage connections (and an equal number of sanitary units) and electricity connections have been built. Ten courses on sanitary education were delivered during project execution.	Monitoring system

Source: Author's elaboration.

Analysis of Alternatives for Land Titling

The first step evaluates the different phases of the land titling process, independent of the implementation mechanism to identify redundancies and unnecessary steps. The proposed steps are justified in legal and technical terms.[91] There are two options for implementing land titling: (i) legal validation of titles (current procedure) and (ii) free transfer of land (proposed by the programme). Under the first procedure, the municipalities undertake most of the work of hiring the required technical staff and the national government provides a direct subsidy to the beneficiaries. In the second option, the majority of the activities are executed by two national entities—the Agustín Codazzi Geographic Institute (IGAC) and the Super-

---

[91] There are five steps: (i) formalisation (call to municipalities, urban legalisation, concurrence by the municipal council, agreements with the municipalities, community awareness); (ii) identification (training, legal and technical analysis, inventory of plots); (iii) census (training, site visits, systematisation of information); (iv) cadastre (area recognizance, plot certification, land valuation); and (v) titling (list of beneficiaries, issuing of titles, notification, registration of resolutions, titling).

intendence of Notaries and Registration—eliminating the need for subsidies (as the execution is done under administrative agreements between the government entities). According to the financial analysis, the latter option reduces the costs by 14 percent; however, this type of analysis underestimates the full efficiency gains from the better use of economies of scale and the economic benefits of reduced processing times (from approximately two years to eight months). It is not possible to estimate the difference in economic costs, as the available information covers only the total amount of the agreements signed with the IGAC and the superintendence, and not the real costs confronted by these agencies while completing their duties (that is, the relevant benefits from the point of view of the society). This is a good example of how the financial and economic analyses can lead to different conclusions. Additionally, the elimination of the subsidy increases the acceptability of the process, as the households that receive titles face no impediments to opting for a subsidy for social housing (double government subsidies are not allowed under Colombian policy).

The expected valorisation of the land benefiting from titling (price differences observed between prices of properties similar to those benefiting from the programme with and without legal titles) was used to estimate the economic benefits. Data on rental rates were obtained from surveys undertaken by a related programme (*Programa Familas en Acción,* Families in Action Programme) that serves households similar to those benefiting from the titling. Results indicate that the value of a dwelling with a legal title is, on average, 37 percent above that of a house without one (approximately US$700 per dwelling), amply justifying the financial cost of the titling process (approximately US$80). Additionally, there are financial benefits for the state coming from increased land tax yield (US$11 per year per property) and the value added tax on notary services (US$4 per house sold in the market).

HEISDA DÁVILA and
FERNANDO CUENIN

The Integrated Settlement Upgrading Programme in Quito

This section discusses the launching of the Integrated Settlement Programme implemented by the Municipality of the Metropolitan District of Quito, Ecuador. The discussion covers the formulation of the economic analysis at the design stage, the implementation of specific projects in the beneficiary neighbourhoods, and the monitoring of indicators of the impacts of the programme included in the baseline for the evaluation.

The Problem and the Objectives

The settlement upgrading programme in Quito (IDB, 2006b) seeks to improve the quality of life of some of the poorest inhabitants of the city's informal settlements.[92] These neighbourhoods, which occupy agricultural lands surrounding the city, are the result of land occupation without municipal authorisation. Most are located in the northern and southern sections of the city: the northern settlements are situated in the highlands that encircle the city, whereas those in the south occupy flatlands (see Map 7.1).

The majority of the inhabitants of these settlements faced shortages of basic services. Most access roads and all internal roads were built with compressed earth, and there were no sidewalks or shoulders. The settlements did not have recreation areas nearby and faced several social problems, including lack of care for vulnerable groups and infants, low citizen security, and a high incidence of family violence. The settlements in the north were either surrounded or crossed by creeks that served as illegal garbage dumps and also the source of regular landslides. Most of their inhabitants came from the rural areas and preserved ancestral habits such as the *minga*.[93] The characteristics of the population were critical in the community involvement processes.

Components

The programme takes an integrated approach to the solution of the problems, including interventions in (i) basic infrastructure (road circuits, pedestrian circuits, sidewalks, shoulders, water and sewerage connections, street lighting); (ii) urban facilities (community and health centres, nurseries, small markets, and creek protection and rehabilitation); and (iii) social programmes (food banks, family violence prevention, citizen security, environmental education, garbage recycling, operation and maintenance of urban facilities). The inclusion of social programmes facilitates the engagement of the community, which is expected to have a positive effect on the sustainability of the investments.

The execution of the programme is supported by a multi-phase investment loan of US$67.8 million from the IDB. The first phase (US$37.8 million) is under way with two components. The first component, settlement upgrading (US$24.6 million), finances the provision of a basic package of services (including infrastructure, urban facilities, and social programmes) and benefits approximately 24,000 households. The second component finances the modernisation of the municipal government (US$13.2 million), strengthening fiscal and operational procedures and improving efficiency and transparency in the management of municipal affairs.[94]

---

[92] There are more than 280 informal settlements in and around Quito, 144 of which house between 50 and 80 percent of households that live in poverty.

[93] The *minga* is an ancient social practice in which the community joins hands to implement any community work or to assist one of their members.

[94] This component contributes to the financial viability of the settlement upgrading component, implementing a multi-purpose cadastre that—among other benefits—will

Map 7.1 Location of the Irregular Settlements in Quito, Ecuador

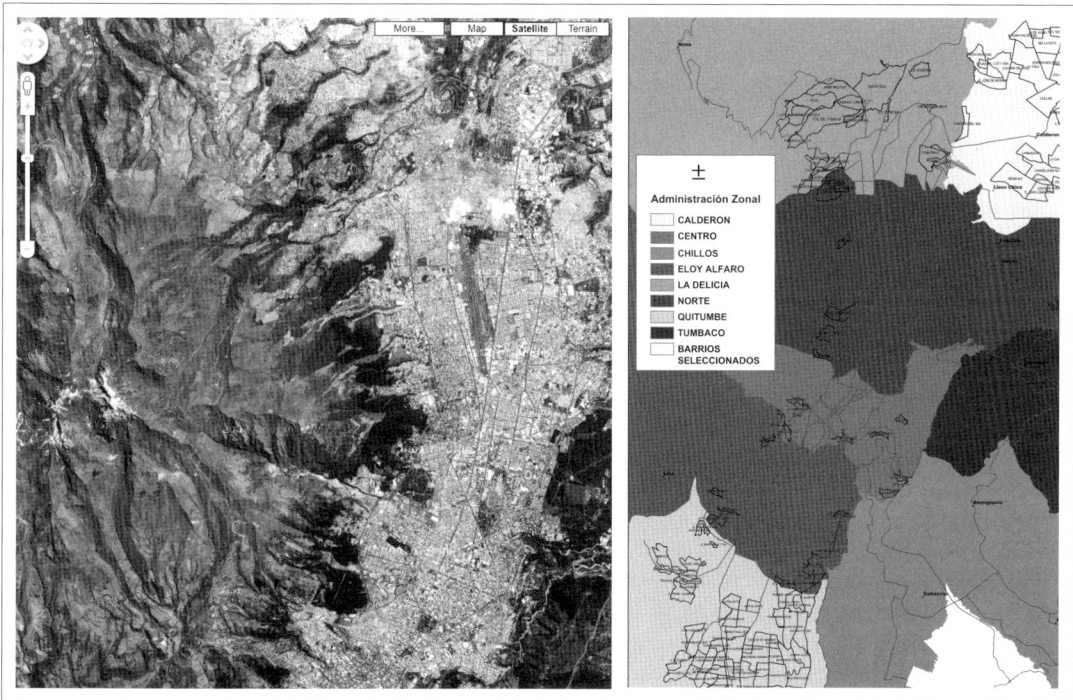

Source: Author's elaboration based on Google® Maps.

Project Design and Execution

The results of the technical and economic feasibility analyses guided the design of implementation strategy, which includes the following:

- A package of basic services that directly impacts the beneficiaries' quality of life and covers the maximum number of households. To tailor the interventions to the needs of each neighbourhood, the beneficiaries are allowed to choose from a list of eligible interventions.
- The maximum investment per household is US$1,000.
- Of the US$1,000 per household, up to 90 percent will be invested in infrastructure and community facilities and a minimum of 10 percent in social programmes.
- The involvement of the community is fundamental to the implementation of the programme's project cycle.

increase the yield of the land tax and provide information for land use planning and urban environmental management.

- Settlements to be included in the programme are selected from a list of eligible settlements through a point system that gives priority to variables such as a high percentage of occupied lots, a high percentage of households in poverty, and the existence of community organisations.[95]

During programme preparation, the technical team works with a sample of projects, and that includes neighbourhoods on hillsides and flatlands. This allows for the selection of different types of interventions and the estimation of cost parameters within the constraints specific to each neighbourhood. Detailed analyses were conducted in the Jaime Roldós and Pisulí settlements (hillsides) and Nueva Aurora (flatlands).[96]

The Quito settlement upgrading programme relies on the involvement of the community for its implementation. In addition to contributing to the operation and maintenance of certain investments, community involvement has other advantages: (i) the selection of the interventions financed by the programme is done through a democratic and participatory process, (ii) neighbourhood organisations are strengthened, and (iii) the social capital of the neighbourhoods is increased. The involvement of the community supports attainment of the equity objectives of the programme, which recognises the differences among beneficiaries living in the same neighbourhood. It creates equal opportunities to participate in the selection of the projects and emphasises the gender perspective, which increases the involvement of women in neighbourhood organisations and promotes equity among genders, increasing consciousness, leadership, and self-esteem among women.[97]

The results of community involvement in the identification and selection of the basic services package are the basis for the project that is designed by the multidisciplinary technical team from the zone administrations of the municipality of Quito. The project is discussed with representatives from the neighbourhood organisations, community leaders, and the beneficiary population. The community presents the neighbourhood project to the programme's executing unit along with the application for funding supported by the signatures of at least 70 percent of the heads of households of the neighbourhood.

Project Evaluation

The objective of the economic analysis is to support the design and monitoring of the programme through the diagnosis of the main problems that

---

[95] Seventy-three neighbourhoods were selected, 34 on hillsides and 39 on flatlands. On average, 60 percent of the population had incomes under the poverty line.

[96] The Roldós and Pisulí neighbourhoods are contiguous and share an area at the foot of the mountains that surround Quito.

[97] The programme also promoted joint actions among different dependencies of the Municipality of Quito.

the neighbourhoods must confront, the definition of cost-effective alternatives, the identification of the economic benefits that justify the investments, the provision of information for dimensioning the interventions, and the selection of the indicators to monitor and evaluate the programme. The analysis focuses on the interventions proposed for the three neighbourhoods included in the sample. A representative survey undertaken in these neighbourhoods provides information on (i) the general characteristics of the neighbourhoods, (ii) the characteristics of the households, (iii) the characteristics of the dwellings, (iv) access to basic services, (v) education services, (vi) public transportation, (vii) recreation facilities, (viii) community involvement, and (ix) training needs. This information is used to calculate the economic benefits and dimensions of some of the interventions.

The cost analysis for the investments considers at least two comparable alternatives in terms of impacts and useful life. The analysis includes the most significant investment items jointly representing more than 60 percent of the total investment. The identification of minimum cost alternatives generates savings ranging from 5 to 60 percent. The final budget calculation is based on these alternatives. The cost-effectiveness analysis estimates the total present value of the programme, the present value of the investments, and the total operation and maintenance costs. A cost-benefit analysis is completed for the technical alternatives that have the minimum costs.

The valuation of the benefits is based on the avoided costs method and made possible due to the richness of information that the surveys provide. Specifically, benefits were estimated for the following items:

- *Roads and sidewalks*. Improving roads and sidewalks would reduce the operation and maintenance costs of vehicles, the circulation time of vehicles (increased average speed) and pedestrian comfort, and the expenses associated to respiratory illness (less dust in the air, though this benefit could not be estimated).
- *Neighbourhood parks*. Savings in transportation cost and time would result from the reduction of the distance that the beneficiaries must travel to access a park, and also a reduction in pest control in the abandoned community areas.
- *Potable water and sewerage*. The larger consumption of water would increase the consumer surplus, and the costs of maintaining latrines and controlling plagues would be avoided.
- *Preventing family violence*. The reduced incidence of violence would reduce the cost of medical treatment and policing resulting from such acts.
- *Training for child care (general training)*. The difference in the salary of childcare workers with and without training was used as an indicator of the productivity gains from training.

Cost-benefit analysis allows the estimation of the economic returns for each of the main interventions of the programme. Programme designers can thus identify actions that do not contribute much to improving the quality of life of the population—actions that would not be detected in an aggregated analysis. Additionally, the economic analysis helps to dimension some of the investments, such as the inner road circuits and the parks. In the first case, the low volume of vehicular traffic in the neighbourhoods made it uneconomical to improve all the inner roads (the costs were higher than the benefits); instead, only the roads on a designated circuit were improved, facilitating waste collection and access to public transportation throughout the neighbourhood. In the second case, the benefits were not enough to justify the construction of separate parks for contiguous neighbourhoods; instead common parks were proposed that, in addition to reducing cost, promoted the social integration of the inhabitants.

Contributions of the Economic Evaluation to the Design of the Programme

The design of the package of basic services was bound by the investment limit of US$1,000 per household, a minimum of 10 percent of which was devoted to social programmes. The remaining US$900 per household was allocated in such a way as to maximise the benefit to the community. Streets, public stairs, pedestrian paths, public lighting, walkways, and shoulders were improved; garbage containers, bus stops, and other forms of street furniture were provided or improved; connections to the water and sewerage systems were made or improved; parks, community recreational areas, lineal parks in the creeks were created; and community centres, health clinics, and nurseries were built or rehabilitated. The economic evaluation helped to optimise the use of the resources available and to create the solutions on the proper scale. The main contributions of this analysis are discussed next.

The Use of Mobility Circuits

Considering the limited resources available and the low volume of vehicles circulating through the neighbourhoods, the decision was made to create movement circuits that allowed vehicular and pedestrian access to the urban facilities, brought public transportation closer to the houses, and facilitated garbage collection from a larger number of waste assembly places. Improvement of the streets on the circuits required less capital investment and fewer resources for operation and maintenance and was expected to generate more economic benefits.

The first run of the economic evaluation included only the benefits accruing to the residents who lived on the improved streets (approximately 20 percent of the households), as they were the direct beneficiaries of the investment. But the benefits did not outweigh the costs. Using economic analysis, engineers selected to improve streets according to their strategic role in the neighbourhood to expand their area of influence. The road circuits of the neighbourhoods in the sample were redesigned so that a majority of inhabitants benefited from the improvements yielding positive economic returns that assured the profitability of the investment.

Parks to Satisfy the Needs of All Inhabitants

The informal settlements of Quito—which lack urban planning—have very limited open land for community and recreational facilities. As a scarce resource, unused community land has a high opportunity cost, which increases the costs of the projects.

The analysis of the economic viability of the parks included in the sample projects clearly indicates the necessity of concentrating all the parks and recreational facilities in one area for land use optimisation. This shared park includes spaces for passive recreation (walking paths, benches, family pergolas), active recreation (playing fields, bicycle paths), and children's recreation (playgrounds, active learning areas).[98]

Rehabilitation of Past Investments

Cost-benefit analysis of the rehabilitation of existing community facilities indicates that while these investments did not increase the supply of services to the community, they improved the quality of the services provided at relatively low cost. The interventions included maintenance of the buildings—roofs, walls, flooring, doors, windows, and ceilings—and rehabilitation of the electrical wiring.

Projects in Association: The Curiquingue Park

The contiguous Roldós and Pisulí neighbourhoods are located in a hilly area and home to approximately 6,000 households. The Roldós neighbourhood is older and more consolidated, although both are the result of invasions. The communities have had land disputes in the past, leading them to request separate parks, which were included in the initial design.

The economic evaluation made it clear that the separate parks would not generate positive returns as they duplicated facilities in close proximity.[99] With the results of the economic evaluation in hand, the design team decided to recommend the building of one park for both neighbourhoods in an easily accessible area to all inhabitants. The resulting lineal park, Curiquingue Park, took the name of one of the old creeks in the area and comprised 21 hectares. By making optimal use of the investment

[98] According to the users, this solution—sharing one integrated recreation space—strengthened family and community ties.
[99] The economic rate of return of the neighbourhood park in Roldós was negative (–11 percent), while the rate of return on the Pisulí neighbourhood park was close to the opportunity cost of the capital (13 percent).

resources, it has had a rate of return of 14 percent and is used not only by the inhabitants of the Roldós and Pisulí neighbourhoods, but also by people from nearby areas, making it a zone park.

Synergies among Investments and Social Programmes

During the project preparation stage, the technical team worked with the community to identify the needs that the social programmes could satisfy. As part of the economic analysis, a qualitative validation of the potential benefits of these programmes was performed, showing that many of these benefits coincided with the positive impacts of the infrastructural improvements and the basic package of services, specifically with regard to health and the environment. This concurrence of benefits prompted the design team to link the social programmes with the investments in infrastructure so the former could contribute to the maintenance of the latter, ensuring their timely upkeep and a sustained flow of economic benefits.

Identification of Monitoring and Evaluation Indicators

This design of the settlement upgrading programme in Quito allows for the accurate measurement of short-term and midterm outcomes because of the sequential improvement of the neighbourhoods: the interventions in the first group of settlements end more than two years before the last projects in the programme are executed. This gap enables programme administrators to evaluate the treatment and control groups starting from the baseline drawn during the design phase of the programme (see Box 7.5). The settlements benefiting from the investments in the second half of the programme act as control groups for the settlements upgraded in the first half. Using the matching method, a sample of 28 neighbourhoods was evaluated, including 14 treated settlements and 14 control settlements; in both cases, there were 7 neighbourhoods on hillsides and 7 on flatlands.

The evaluation focused mostly on the behaviours and outcomes that were key for the materialisation of the economic benefits of the investments: (i) physical, social, and environmental conditions of the neighbourhoods (actual and perceived); (ii) pedestrian and vehicular mobility, and access times for using public transportation; (iii) changes in behaviours concerning waste disposal and use of public transportation and rehabilitated public spaces; (iv) changes in the prices of land and houses; (v) households' investments in their dwellings; (vi) environmental conditions in the neighbourhood (elimination of illegal waste dumping in the creeks); (vi) improved safety of the neighbourhoods (actual and perceived); (vii) health conditions of the households and improved economic opportunities; (viii) participation in training activities; and (ix) community involvement and impacts on the social life of the neighbourhoods. This evaluation showed whether the observed outcomes corresponded to the

Table 7.2 Quito: Examples of Monitoring Indicators Derived from the Economic Analysis

Economic benefits	Logical framework indicators	Means of verification
Reduced costs of accessing recreation areas and reduced expenses in pest control in community areas (linked to the creation of neighbourhood parks)	*Change in behaviour:* Two years after the completion of the interventions, 80 percent of the population agrees that the parks are a good place for recreation and make regular use of them. (Baseline 2005: 100 percent of the population found the parks unsuitable for recreation.) The park areas are no longer used as waste dumps.	Final and impact evaluations studies and reports
	Acceptance of the service: After completion of the parks, at least 80 percent of the population finds that the parks are a good recreation option.	Intermediate evaluation
	Provision of the service or good: Fifteen months after the intervention began, at least one multi-purpose park (passive, active, and infant recreation) had been built. During the execution of the programme, at least one sanitary and environmental education course had been provided to each of the beneficiary neighbourhoods.	Monitoring system

Source: Author's elaboration.

expected outcomes; if not, adjustments could be made in subsequent phases of the programme. Table 7.2 summarises the main relationships between the benefits identified and measured in the economic analysis and the corresponding indicators included in the logical framework.

REFERENCES

Abramo, P. 2003. "A teoria econômica da favela: quatro notas sobre a localização residencial dos pobres e o mercado imobiliário informal". In P. Abramo, ed., *A cidade da informalidade: O desafio das cidades latino-americanas*. Rio de Janeiro: Livraria Sete Letras/FAPERJ.

Acosta, P. 2007. "Identificación de buenas prácticas en recuperación de barrios y viviendas sociales. Lecciones para América Latina de la experiencia de la política de vivienda pública y rehabilitación de conjuntos en los Estados Unidos". Washington, DC: IDB. Unpublished.

Alfonsin, B. 2004. "Para além da regularização fundiária: Porto Alegre e o urbanizador social". In B. Alfonsin and E. Fernandes, eds., *Direito à moradia e segurança da posse no Estatuto da Cidade: Diretrizes, instrumentos e processos de gestão*. Belo Horizonte: Fórum.

Arriagada, C. 2000. "Pobreza en América Latina: Nuevos escenarios y desafíos de políticas para el hábitat urbano". *Serie Medio Ambiente y Desarrollo* 27, United Nations, Santiago, Chile.

Baltrusis, N. 2007. "Las Áreas Especiales de Interés Social (AEIS) en Diadema. Haciendo viable el acceso a la tierra urbana". In A. Larangeira, ed., *Regularización de asentamientos informales en América Latina*. Cambridge, MA: Lincoln Institute of Land Policy.

Basualdo, J. L. 2007. "El barrio Unión de Cooperativas: una experiencia de articulación de políticas públicas". In *Regularización de asentamientos informales en América Latina*, ed. A. Larangeira. Cambridge, MA: Lincoln Institute of Land Policy.

Beato, C. 2006. "Medo e criminalidades nos centros urbanos brasileiros". Latin American Programme Special Reports, Woodrow Wilson International Center for Scholars, Washington, DC.

Beltrán, B. 2008. *Características relevantes de la pobreza urbana. Estimaciones con base en la Encuesta Nacional de Ingreso y Gasto de los Hogares 2006 del Instituto Nacional de Economía, Geografía e Informática*. México, D.F.: Unidad de Programas de Atención de la Pobreza Urbana, SEDESOL.

Bentes, D. 2003. "Plano Diretor, Regularização Fundiária e Destinação das Áreas Especiais de Interesse Social: A construção de caminhos para a efetivação do Direito à Moradia. Versão Preliminar". Grupo Temático Plano Diretor, Regularização Fundiária e Destinação de Áreas para a Habitação de Interesse Social. V Conferência das Cidades, Brasília, December 2–4. Unpublished.

Bobbio, N. 1986. *El futuro de la democracia*. México, D.F.: Fondo de Cultura Económica.

Brakarz, J., M. Greene, and E. Rojas. 2002. *Cities for All. Recent Experiences with Neighbourhood Upgrading Programmes*. Washington, DC: IDB.

Brueckner, J. K., and H. Selod. 2008. "A Theory of Urban Squatting and Land-Tenure Formalization in Developing Countries". Working Paper Series 2328, Centre for Economic Studies and Ifo Institute for Economic Research, Munich.

Buvinic, M., A. Morrison, and M. B. Orlando. 2005. "Violencia, crimen y desarrollo social en América Latina y el Caribe". Article in *Desarrollo Social en América Latina: Temas y Desafíos para las Políticas Públicas*. Washington: World Bank and Flacso-Sede Costa Rica, 2002. Available at: http://www.flacso.org/biblioteca/violencia.doc

Calderón, J. 2007. "Política de formalización de la propiedad en el Perú urbano (1996–2004)". In *Regularización de asentamientos informales en América Latina*, ed. A. Larangeira. Cambridge, MA: Lincoln Institute of Land Policy.

CIDEU (Centro Iberoamericano de Desarrollo Estratégico Urbano). 2008. *Diez años de planeación estratégica en Iberoamérica*. Barcelona: CIDEU.

CONEVAL (Consejo Nacional de Evaluación de la Política de Desarrollo Social [National Board for Social Development Policy Assessment]). 2007. *Informe ejecutivo de pobreza México 2007*. México D.F.: CONEVAL.

CG Consulting Group. 2007. "Evaluación técnica y operativa del Promib". Quito: CG Consulting Group Unpublished report.

Damásio, C. 2007. "Urbanizador social. Alternativa para la democratización del acceso a la tierra urbanizada en Porto Alegre". In A. Larangeira, ed., *Regularización de asentamientos informales en América Latina*. Cambridge, MA: Lincoln Institute of Land Policy.

Dammert, L., E. Alda, and F. Ruz. 2008. "Desafíos de la seguridad ciudadana en Iberoamérica". Document presented in the *II Foro Iberoamericano sobre Seguridad Ciudadana Violencia y Políticas Públicas en al ámbito local*, Flasco, Santiago, Chile.

De Soto, H. 2000. *The Mystery of Capital: Why Capitalism Triumphs in the West and Fails Everywhere Else*. New York: Basic Books.

Dirección General de Estadísticas y Censos. 2008. *VI censo de población y V de vivienda 2007*. San Salvador: Ministerio de Economía de El Salvador.

Durand-Lasserve, A. 1996. "Regularization and Integration of Irregular Settlements: Lessons from Experience". Working Paper No. 6, Urban Management Programme, UND/UNCHS/World Bank, Kenya (May).

ECLAC (Economic Commission for Latin America and the Caribbean). 2000. Consensos urbanos. Aportes del Plan de Acción Regional de América Latina y el Caribe sobre Asentamientos Humanos. Santiago de Chile: ECLAC.

————. 2004. *The Millennium Development Goals: A Latin American and Caribbean Perspective.* Santiago, Chile: ECLAC.

————. 2007. *Social Panorama of Latin America 2007.* Santiago de Chile: ECLAC.

Fay, M. ed. 2005. *The Urban Poor in Latin America.* Washington, DC: World Bank.

Fernandes, E. 2004. "Política nacional de regularização fundiária". *Boletim Eletrônico do Instituto de Registro Imobiliario do Brasil IRIB/ANOREG-SP* No. 974 (09/01/2004) São Paulo.

Filgueira, F. 2004. "Tendencias, coyuntura y estructura: la crisis social en Uruguay". Montevideo: Henciclopedia. Available at: http://www.henciclopedia.org.uy/autores/Filgueira/CrisisUruguay.htm

Flores, A. R. 2007. "Política habitacional en el Paraguay desde 1989 hasta nuestros días". In A. Larangeira, ed., *Regularización de asentamientos informales en América Latina.* Cambridge, MA: Lincoln Institute of Land Policy.

García, J. C. 2009. "Experiencias de gestión urbana recientes en Medellín: Iniciativas públicas". In Patricia Torres, ed., *Las ciudades del mañana: Gestión de suelo urbano en Colombia.* Washington, DC: IDB.

Graham, J. 2007. "Casos internacionales de mejoramiento de barrios y viviendas sociales". Washington, DC: IDB. Unpublished.

Greene, M., and E. Rojas. 2007. "Incremental Construction: A Strategy to Facilitate Access to Housing". *Environment & Urbanisation* 20(1): 89–108.

Habermas, J. 1988. *The Theory of Communicative Action: Reason and the Rationalization of Society.* Boston: Beacon Press.

————. 1995. *Between Facts and Norms.* Cambridge: MIT Press.

Held, D. 1996. *Models of Democracy Fully Reused.* London: Polity.

IBGE (Instituto Brasilero de Geografía y Estadísticas [Brazilian Institute of Geography and Statistics]). 2000. "Censo de Población y Vivienda 2000". Brazil: IBGE. Available at: http://www.ibge.gov.br/censo

————. 2001. Diretoria de pesquisas, coordenação de população e indicadores sociais. Pesquisa de Informações Básicas Municipais. Available at: http://www.ibge.gov.br/english(estatistica/economia/perfilmunic/default.shtm

IDB (Inter-American Development Bank). 2004. "Estrategia para promover la participación ciudadana en las actividades del Banco". IDB Strategy Document. Washington, DC: IDB.

————. 2005. "Assessment of Participatory Budgeting in Brazil." Sustainable Development Department. Washington, DC: IDB. Available at: http://www.iadb.org/publications/search.cfm?query=Assessment+of+Participatory+Budgeting+in+Brazil&context=Title&lang=en

————. 2006a. "Sharpening the Bank Capacity to Support the Housing Sector in Latin America and the Caribbean". Document SOC 142, Sustainable Development Department. Washington, DC: IDB.

—————. 2006b. "Análisis económico del programa 'Mejoramiento integral de barrios de Quito: primera fase' (EC-L1017)". Internal document, available in the technical archives of the programme. Washington, DC: IDB.

—————. 2008a. "Marco de referencia del Banco en seguridad y convivencia ciudadana". Internal document, Institutional Capacity and State Division. Washington, DC: IDB.

—————. 2008b. *Beyond Facts. Understanding Quality of Life. Development in the Americas.* Washington, DC: IDB.

IMF (International Monetary Fund). 2009. *World Economic Outlook (WEO). Sustaining the Recovery.* Washington, DC: IMF.

IMM (Intendencia Municipal de Montevideo). 1998. *Plan de Ordenamiento Territorial 1998–2006, Plan Montevideo III. Memoria Normativa de Gestión y Seguimiento.* Montevideo: IMM.

IMM and PIAI (Progama de Integración de Asentamientos Irregulares). 2008. "Proyecto de intervención en área 'Cuenca baja del arroyo Pantanoso'". IMM and PIAI, Montevideo. Unpublished.

INDEC (Instituto Nacional de Estadísticas y Censos [National Institute of Statistics and Census]). 2001. "Censo de Población y Vivienda 2000". Buenos Aires: INDEC.

INE (Instituto Nacional de Estadística). 2006. *Relevamiento de Asentamientos Irregulares 2005–2006.* Montevideo: Convenio INE-PIAI.

INEGI (Instituto Nacional de Estadística y Geografía [Nationa Institute of Statistics and Geography]). 2005. "Conteo de Población y Vivienda 2005". Mexico, D.F. Available at: http://www.inegi.org.mx/inegi/default.aspx?c=10215&s=est

Interconsult. 2005. "Políticas de Desarrollo Urbano. Algunas reflexiones preliminares." Investigación realizada en el marco de una consultoría licitada por el PIAI (Préstamo del BID N° 1186/ OC–UR). Montevideo: PIAI–IBD.

Jesús, A. R. L. de, A. A. Veríssimo, and S. M. da S. Pereira. 2007. "Núcleo de regularización y programa *Morar Legal*: Un relato de la experiencia en regularización de loteos de la ciudad de Rio de Janeiro". In A. Larangeira, ed., *Regularización de asentamientos informales en América Latina.* Cambridge, MA: Lincoln Institute of Land Policy.

Katzman, R., ed. 1999. *Activos y estructuras de oportunidades: Estudios sobre las raíces de la vulnerabilidad social en Uruguay.* Montevideo: PNUD-CEPAL.

Kessides, C. 1997. "World Bank Experience with the Provision of Infrastructure Services for the Urban Poor: Preliminary Identification and Review of Best Practices". General Operational Review, Report TWU-ORS. Washington, DC: World Bank.

—————. 2004. "Mejores prácticas de política social". International conference, SEDESOL–World Bank, México, D.F. Unpublished.

Larangeira, A., ed. 2002. *Estudo de Avaliação da Experiência Brasileira sobre Urbanização de Favelas e Regularização Fundiária. Relatório Final* (3 vol.). Rio de Janeiro: IBAM/Cites Alliance.

Magalhâes, F., and E. Rojas. 2007. "Facing the Challenges of Informal Set-
    tlements in Urban Centres: The Re-urbanisation of Manaus, Brazil".
    Washington, DC: IDB. Available at: http://www/iadb.org/publicatiolns/
    search.cfm?query=Facing+the+Challenges+of+Informal+Settlements
    &context=Title&lang=en
Maldonado, M. 2007. "¿Es posible anticiparse a la urbanización infor-
    mal? Reflexiones a partir de la Operación Urbanística Nuevo Usme,
    Bogotá, y del Macroproyecto Ciudadela Gonzalo Vallejo Restrepo,
    Pereira (Colombia)". In A. Larangeira, ed., *Regularización de asenta-
    mientos informales en América Latina*. Cambridge, MA: Lincoln Insti-
    tute of Land Policy.
Maricato, E. 1996. *Metrópole na periferia do capitalismo: Ilegalidade,
    desigualdade e violência*. São Paulo: Hucitec.
Miller, S., and M. Cohen. 2007. "Cities without Jobs?" Document prepared
    for the Employment Policy Department of the International Labour
    Organisation (OIT) (by a team including Anushay Anjum, Pamela Her-
    shey, Erin Hopkins, and Sara Rowbottom), the New School, New York.
Ministério das Cidades. 2005. Secretaria Nacional de Programas Urbanos.
    "Decisão pioneira em usucapião coletivo beneficia 376 famílias em
    Olinda/PE". Electronic report, October, Brazil.
MINVU (*Ministerio de Vivienda y Urbanismo* [Ministry of Housing and
    Urban Planning]). 2004. *Chile, un siglo de políticas en vivienda y
    barrio*. Santiago de Chile: MINVU.
Muncipality of Porto Alegre. 2000. "Lomba do Pinheiro, Porto Alegre".
    Serie Memoria de los Barrios, Secretaría Municipal da Cultura, Porto
    Alegre.
————. 2004. "Construindo a Lomba do Futuro. Bases para o Plano de
    desenvolvimiento Local" (vol. 1). Secretaria Municipal da Cultura,
    Porto Alegre.
Musona, D. T., and D. M. Mbozi. 1998. "CARE Peri-Urban Lusaka Small
    Enterprise (PULSE) Project, Case Study of a Microfinance Scheme".
    Studies in Rural and Microfinance No. 4, African Region. Washington,
    DC: World Bank.
Petrella, L., and F. Vanderschueren. 2003. *Ciudad y violencia*. Santiago
    de Chile: Economic Commission for Latin America and the Caribbean
    (ECLAC).
Ponce Solé, J. 2007. *Segregación escolar e inmigración. Contra los güetos
    escolares: derecho y políticas públicas urbanas*. Madrid: CEPC.
Programa Hábitat. 2007. *Reglas de operación del Programa Hábitat para
    el ejercicio fiscal 2008,* publicadas en el Diario Oficial de la Federación
    el 31 de diciembre de 2007. México, D.F.: Programa Hábitat.
Prud'homme, R., and C. W. Lee. 1999. "Size, Sprawl, Speed and the Effi-
    ciency of Cities". *Urban Studies* 36(11): 1848–58.
Rojas, E. 2001. "The Long Road to Housing Sector Reform: Lessons from
    the Chilean Housing Experience". *Housing Studies* 16(4): 461–83.
————. 2004b. *Volver al centro.* Washington, DC: IDB.

Rau, M. 2007. "Prevención situacional en América Latina y el Caribe". In Eric Alda y Gustavo Beliz, eds., *¿Cuál es la salida?* Washington, DC: IDB.

Rees, W. 1988. "A Role for Environmental Assessment in Achieving Sustainable Development". *Environmental Impact Assessment Review* 8: 273–91.

Sabatini, F. 2005. "The Social Spatial Segregation in the Cities of Latin America". Washington, DC: IDB.

Smolka, M. O. 2003. "Regularização da ocupação do solo urbano: a solução que é parte do problema, o problema que é parte da solução". In Pedro Abramo, ed., *A cidade da informalidade. O desafio das cidades latino-americanas*. Rio de Janeiro: Livraria Sete Letras/ FAPERJ.

―――. 2005. "El funcionamiento de los mercados de suelo en América Latina. Conceptos, antecedentes históricos y nexos críticos". In J. L. Basualdo, ed., *Manejo de suelo urbano. Posibilidades y desafíos en el desarrollo de la ciudad de Corrientes*. Cambridge, MA, and Corrientes, Argentina: Lincoln Institute of Land Policy and Instituto de Vivienda de Corrientes.

Smolka, M. O., and C. P. Damásio. 2005. "The Social Urbaniser: Porto Alegre's Land Policy Experiment". *Land Lines Newsletter* (April). Cambridge, MA: Lincoln Institute of Land Policy.

Smolka, M. O., and C. DeCesare. 2006. "Property Taxation and Informality: Challenges for Latin America". *Land Lines Newsletter* (July). Cambridge, MA: Lincoln Institute of Land Policy.

Souza, M. T. 2009. "The Effect of Land Use Regulations on Housing Price and Informality: A Model Applied to Curitiba, Brazil". Working Paper. Cambridge, MA: Lincoln Institute of Land Policy.

Tedeschi, S. E. 2007. "El caso de Villa la Cava (Gran Buenos Aires, Argentina). Estudio sobre el Programa de Renovación Urbana del Barrio La Cava y el Programa Arraigo (1984–1999)". In A. Larangeira, ed., *Regularización de asentamientos informales en América Latina*. Cambridge, MA: Lincoln Institute of Land Policy.

UN-HABITAT (United Nations Human Settlements Programme). 2003a. *Slums of the World: The Face of Urban Poverty in the New Millennium?* Nairobi: UN-HABITAT.

―――. 2003b. *The Challenge of Slums: Global Report on Human Settlements 2003*. Sterling (VA) and London: Earthscan Publications Ltd.

―――. 2007a. *Global Report on Human Settlements. The Face of Urban Poverty in the New Millenium?* Nairobi: UN-HABITAT.

―――. 2007b. *Enhancing Urban Safety and Security: Global Report on Human Settlements 2007*. London: Earthscan Publications Ltd.

Vanderschueren, F. 2007. *Documento de referencia de prevención de la criminalidad*. London: UN-Hábitat.

Velásquez, F. 1986. *Crisis municipal y participación ciudadana en Colombia*. Bogotá: Editorial Foro.

————. 2003. "La participación ciudadana en Bogotá: mirando el presente, pensando el futuro". Alcaldía Mayor de Bogota, Bogota. Unpublished.

Viloria-Williams, J. 2006. Urban Community Upgrading: Lessons from the Past Prospects for the Future. Washington, DC: World Bank Institute.

Vittrup, E. 2004. "Programa Hábitat de Naciones Unidas. Mejores prácticas de política Social". International conference, SEDESOL–World Bank, México, D.F. Unpublished.

VMVDU (Viceministerio de Vivienda y Desarrollo Urbano [Vice Ministry of Housing and Urban Development]). 2008. Sistema de Información de Lotificaciones de El Salvador. San Salvador: Ministerio de Obras Públicas y Transporte, y de Vivienda y Desarrollo Urbano.

Weber, M. 1968. *Economy and Society*. New York: Bedminster Press.

World Bank. 1991. *Housing Policy and Economic Development. An Agenda for the 1990s*. Washington, DC: World Bank.

————. 2002. *Upgrading Low Income Urban Settlements. Country Assessment Report, Ghana*. Washington, DC: World Bank AFTU 1 & 2.

————. 2004. *La pobreza en México: una evaluación de las tendencias y la estrategia del gobierno*. México, D.F.: World Bank.

————. 2009. *World Development Report 2009: Reshaping Economic Geography*. Washington, DC: World Bank Publications.

WEF (World Economic Forum). 2008. *Global Competitiveness Report*. Davos, Switzerland: WEF. Available at: http://www.weforum.org/en/media/publications/CompetitivenessReports/Index.htm

ABOUT THE AUTHORS

Beatriz Abizanda is an independent consultant specialising in topics related to the modernisation of the state, including citizen security, public management by results, and foreign trade. She holds a degree in economics from the *Universidad de Valencia* (Spain) and has a diploma in international management from the Business School of Marseille (France). She obtained an MBA from Georgetown University through a scholarship from the *Caixa de Barcelona* (Barcelona Savings Bank) of Spain.

Nathalie Alvarado has worked for the Inter-American Development Bank since 2000 as a specialist in modernisation of the state, with a focus on citizen security and coexistence. She works in the design and appraisal of Bank operations and led the drafting of a frame of reference for the Bank's programme in these sectors. She is a lawyer and holds a master's degree in economic law from the *Université Libre de Bruxelles* (Belgium).

Barbara Araújo dos Santos works in the implementation unit of the Social and Environmental Programme of the Igarpés of Manaus where she coordinates social projects. She has worked in the *Legião Brasileira de Assitência Social* (Brazilian League for Social Work) where she coordinated the decentralised implementation of the social assistance law. A social worker, she graduated from the *Universidade Federal do Amazonas*, specialising in the planning and management of social programmes.

José Brakarz is a senior urban development specialist at the Inter-American Development Bank, where he has worked since 1993 in the design and appraisal of urban, social, and municipal development projects. Prior to entering the Bank, Mr. Brakarz worked with the federal government of Brazil and at the *Instituto Brasileiro de Administração Municipal* (Brazilian Institute of Municipal Management). He has worked on housing and settlement upgrading programmes in several countries of Latin America and the Caribbean. He holds a PhD from the University of California at Berkeley.

Ramiro Martín Burgos is the manager of the *Barrio de Verdad* Programme implemented by the municipality of La Paz, Bolivia. He holds a master's degree in development projects from the *Universidad Andina Simón Bolivar* and has done postgraduate studies in governance, public management, and informal settlements at the *Universidad Católica San Pablo* and *Universidad Del Valle*, both in Bolivia.

Michael Cohen is professor of international relations and director of the graduate programme in international affairs at the New School University in New York, a programme he founded in 2001. From 1972 to 1999 he worked on urban development policy at the World Bank. He has published several books on urban development and impact evaluation of development assistance. He has advised governments, NGOs, UN-HABITAT, and academic institutions around the world. He was president of the International Institute for the Environment and Development. He earned a PhD in political economy from the University of Chicago in 1971.

Jack Couriel is the vice minister of the *Ministerio de Vivienda, Ordenamiento Territorial y Medio Ambiente* (Ministry of Housing, Territorial Planning, and Environment) of Uruguay. He has been adjunct professor at the Faculty of Architecture of the *Universidad de la República de Uruguay*, where he conducted research on urban management and housing. He holds a degree in architecture and a master's degree in territorial planning and urban development from the *Universidad de la República*. He also completed postgraduate studies at the Latin American and Caribbean Institute for Economic and Social Planning.

Fernando Cuenin is project economist at the Inter-American Development Bank. Prior to joining the Bank, he worked as an economist for the province of Buenos Aires and as assistant professor of microeconomics and spatial economics at the *Universidad Nacional de La Plata* in Argentina. He holds bachelor's and master's degrees in economics from the *Universidad Nacional de La Plata* and an executive certificate in project evaluation and risk analysis from Duke University.

Aderbal José Curvelo worked for 20 years at the municipality of Rio de Janeiro, where he managed the *Fundo Municipal do Desenvolvimento Social* (Municipal Social Development Fund) and worked in development projects in low-income areas. One of those projects was the *Favela Bairro* Programme, where he was coordinator and executive secretary. He joined the Inter-American Development Bank in 2004 as an urban development specialist. He holds a degree in civil engineering from the *Universidade do Estado de Rio de Janeiro*.

Heisda Dávila Armas is a manager at the *Banco del Estado* (State Bank) of Ecuador. She coordinated the implementation unit of the Integrated Settlement Upgrading Programme of Quito and was the technical manager for the Municipal Development Programme at the *Banco del Estado* in Ecuador, which was financed with loans from the Inter-American Development Bank and the World Bank. She holds a degree in economics from the *Universidad Católica de Ecuador* and diplomas in project design and evaluation and project management from the *Universidad de los Andes* (Colombia) and the *Universidad de Monterrey* (Mexico).

Sonia Fadiño is a specialist in the management of community participation processes and social development planning (health, education, and housing). She also specialises in urban and regional planning, with an emphasis on participatory management. She holds a degree in social work from the *Universidad Mayor de Cundinamarca* and a master's degree in social policy from the *Unversidad Externado* in Colombia.

Elisabete França has been the low-income housing manager at the *Secretaría de Habitaçăo* (Housing Secretariat) of the municipality of São Paulo since 2005, where she is responsible for coordinating social housing programmes, including settlement upgrading projects. Between 2001 and 2004 she coordinated projects financed with funds from multilateral donors (UN-HABITAT, World Bank, and Inter-American Development Bank) and bilateral funds in countries of Latin America and the Caribbean, Africa, and Asia. She has published several books and technical articles on settlement upgrading and development. An architect and town planner, she holds a master's degree in urban environmental structures from the *Universidade Federal de São Paulo*.

Vicente Fretes Cibils heads the Fiscal and Municipal Management Division of the Inter-American Development Bank. Prior to joining the Bank, he worked for 20 years at the World Bank. He has taught at the *Universidad Nacional del Nordeste* (Argentina) and the University of North Carolina and is the author of publications on applied econometrics, public finance, international economics, and economic development. He studied at the *Universidad Nacional del Nordeste* in Argentina and the University of Pennsylvania. He obtained an MBA and a PhD in economics from the University of North Carolina.

Maria Eugenia González Alcocer is the head of the urban poverty programmes unit at the *Secretaría de Desarrollo Social* (Social Development Secretariat) of Mexico. She has worked as a researcher on social and education issues and on social and organisational communication processes at public and private institutions. She is a docent at the *Instituto Politécnico Nacional* and *Unversidad Femenina* in Mexico. She holds a bachelor degree in teaching from the *Universidad Autónoma* of Mexico and a master's degree in social communications from the *Universidad Iberoamericana* of Mexico.

Pamela J. Hershey is teaching assistant and coordinator of the legal counsel office and administrative secretary of the treasury office at the New School University of New York. Her research experience is centred on infrastructure development. She has worked as an international consultant with the New School University, for the UN's International Labour Office (ILO), and as a Peace Corps volunteer in Benin. After graduating from the University of Southern California, she earned a master's degree in international affairs from the New School University.

Adriana de Arauho Larangeira is a member of the team in charge of the social housing plan of the municipality of Rio de Janeiro, Brazil, and lecturer at the Lincoln Institute of Land Policy in Cambridge, Massachusetts. She was project supervisor in the *Favela Bairro* Programme. She holds a degree in architecture from the *Universidade Santa Úrsula, Rio de Janeiro* (Brazil) and a master's degree in territorial planning and a PhD in engineering from the *Universidad de Cantabria*, Spain.

Clara López Obregón is the *Secretaria de Gobernación* (Government Secretary) of the municipality of Bogotá. She has been general auditor of the Republic of Colombia, comptroller and council member of the municipality of Bogotá, and an advisor to various institutions, including the *Asamblea Nacional* (National Assembly) of Venezuela, two ministries of the government of Colombia (mining and energy; economic development), the Colombian *Asamblea Nacional Constituyente* (National Constitutional Assembly), and the *Secretaría Económica* (Economic Secretariat) of the office of the president of the Republic of Colombia. She holds degrees in economics from Harvard University and law from the *Universidad de Los Andes* (Colombia) and is a PhD candidate at the *Universidad de Salamanca* (Spain).

María de la Luz Nieto Ríos works at the *Ministerio de Vivienda y Urbanismo* (Ministry of Housing and Urban Development) of Chile as housing policy advisor and head of the housing and urban studies unit. She is consultant to the UN Development Programme and the Inter-American Development Bank. She holds a degree in economics from the *Universidad de Chile*.

Cléia Beatriz H. de Oliveira has worked since 1979 at the *Secretaria do Planejamento* (Planning Secretariat) of the municipality of Porto Alegre (Brazil) in the design and implementation of the master plan. Currently, she is the manager of the *Porto do Futuro* (Port of the Future) programme. She holds a degree in architecture from the *Universidade Federal do Rio Grande do Sul* (Brazil), with a specialisation in urban and regional planning and sustainable development.

Patricia Palenque has been the coordinator of the Settlement Upgrading Programme of Argentina (PROMEBA) since 2006. Previously she was responsible for the legal area of the programme. She has worked with the judiciary in Argentina and as advisor to human rights organisations. With the *Centro de Estudios Legales y Sociales* (Centre for Legal and Social Studies) she developed alternative mechanisms for conflict resolution in the slums of Buenos Aires. She holds a law degree from the *Universidad de Buenos Aires* (Argentina) and completed other postgraduate studies in the same university.

Denise Bonat Pegoraro has worked at the *Secretaria do Planejamento* (Planning Secretariat) of the municipality of Porto Alegre (Brazil) since 1997. Currently she coordinates the Integrated Project of Lomba do Pinheiro and the preparation of legislation for the Consortium of the Lomba do Pinheiro Urban Project. She teaches at the school of architecture at the *Universidade Federal do Rio Grande do Sul*. She holds a degree in architecture from the *Universidade Federal do Pelotas*, Brazil.

Carlos Pisoni is the general manager of the *Instituto Provincial de Vivienda* (Provincial Housing Institute) of the government of the province of Buenos Aires. He is the director of the graduate programme on habitat and urban poverty at the school of architecture of the *Universidad de Buenos Aires* and a member of the board of the Güemes Thermoelectric Company. He is a former under-secretary for planning and urban development for the city of Buenos Aires. He holds a degree in architecture from the *Universidad de Buenos Aires* and in construction from the *Escuela Industrial Otto Krausse*. He also holds a master's degree in political science and in habitat and housing from the *Universidad de Buenos Aires*.

Juli Ponce Solé is the director of the *Escuela de Administración Pública* (School of Public Administration) of Catalonia and professor of administrative law at the *Universidad de Barcelona*. He has published several books and articles on public law and urban development issues. He holds a PhD in public law from the *Universidad de Barcelona* and is a member of the European Network for Housing Research and the European Group of Public Law.

Eduardo Rojas is the principal urban development specialist at the Inter-American Development Bank, where he has worked since 1989. Prior to joining the Bank, he worked at the Regional Development Department of the Organization of American States and as adjunct professor of urban planning in the centre for urban studies of the *Universidad Católica de Chile*. He holds a degree in architecture from the *Universidad Católica de Chile*, an MPhil in urban and regional planning from the University of Edinburgh (UK), an MBA with a concentration in finance from Johns Hopkins University, and a certificate in environmental management from the *Centre d'Études Industrielles* in Geneva.

Margarita Romo is a consultant to the Inter-American Development Bank for the sanitation programme of the municipality of Quito and the Housing Sector Support Programmes I and II implemented by the *Ministerio de Vivienda y Urbanismo* (Housing and Urban Development Ministry) of Ecuador. She has been the urban development director and national planning director for the ministry and the *Junta de la Vivienda* (Housing Council) and the head of external cooperation programmes. She holds a degree in architecture, with a concentration in urban planning, and a master's degree in economics, with a concentration in decentralisation and local economic development, from the *Universidad de las Américas*. She also has diplomas in integrated project evaluation and advanced management from the *Instituto Centroamericano de Administración de Empresas* (INCAE). She did postgraduate studies on housing policies with the Japan International Cooperation Agency (JICA).

Verónica Ruiz is as a housing specialist for the *Banco Centroamericano de Integración* (Central American Integration Bank) in Honduras. She is a consultant to the Inter-American Development Bank in the area of land regularisation and incremental housing. She has been advisor on strategic planning to the *Ministerio de Gobernación* (Ministry of Government) of El Salvador and lecturer at the *Facultad de Economía y Negocios* (School of Economics and Business Administration) of the *Universidad del Desarrollo* (Chile). She holds a master's degree in financial economics and an MBA from the *Universidad Católica de Chile*.

Martim O. Smolka is senior fellow, director of the Latin American Programme, and co-president of the International Department of the Lincoln Institute of Land Policy in Cambridge, Massachusetts. He is cofounder and former president of the *Asociación Nacional de Postgrado e Investigación en Planificación Urbana y Regional* (National Association of Post Graduate Studies and Research in Urban and Regional Planning) of Brazil. He holds a master's degree and a PhD in economics from the University of Pennsylvania.

INDEX